Human-tech

Human-tech

Ethical and Scientific Foundations

KIM J. VICENTE
Edited and with commentary by Alex Kirlik

OXFORD
UNIVERSITY PRESS

2011

OXFORD
UNIVERSITY PRESS

Oxford University Press, Inc., publishes works that further
Oxford University's objective of excellence
in research, scholarship, and education.

Oxford New York
Auckland Cape Town Dar es Salaam Hong Kong Karachi
Kuala Lumpur Madrid Melbourne Mexico City Nairobi
New Delhi Shanghai Taipei Toronto

With offices in
Argentina Austria Brazil Chile Czech Republic France Greece
Guatemala Hungary Italy Japan Poland Portugal Singapore
South Korea Switzerland Thailand Turkey Ukraine Vietnam

Copyright © 2011 Oxford University Press

Published by Oxford University Press, Inc.
198 Madison Avenue, New York, New York 10016
www.oup.com

Oxford is a registered trademark of Oxford University Press

Library of Congress Cataloging-in-Publication Data
CIP data on file

ISBN 978-0-19-976514-0

9 8 7 6 5 4 3 2 1
Printed in the United States of America
on acid-free paper

The widening gap between technology and human needs can only be filled by ethics.

Freeman Dyson, *The Scientist as Rebel*

Acknowledgments

Kim J. Vicente would like to thank all of his co-authors who contributed to the articles collected here. This work would literally not be possible without their essential contributions. Thank you also to Catharine Carlin of OUP for finding an enthusiastic home for this collection. Finally, countless thanks to Alex Kirlik for being so receptive to this project, and for working so hard on the commentaries.

Alex Kirlik thanks his editor, Catharine Carlin, for her sage advice in guiding this work through to completion; Anna Cianciolo, for her patience and support; and Heather Ash, for her insight. On technical matters, thanks go to Frank Ritter, John Lee, Mike Byrne, John Flach, Peter Hancock, and David E. Goldberg, who provided valuable feedback along the way.

Preface

When I was approached in 1999 about writing a book about my area for a popular audience, I divided my deliberations into two phases. First, I wondered whether such a book was needed, irrespective of the author. After all, Don Norman's *Design of Everyday Things* had already been a bestseller, so what could anyone possibly add to that? I realized that, as influential as it was, Don's book dealt primarily with comparatively simple systems, mainly consumer products. I concluded there was a need for a book that dealt with complex sociotechnical systems, such as nuclear power and aviation.

Second, I wondered, if such a book needs to be written, am I the person to do it? I had started writing a few draft chapters, and I enjoyed turning my knowledge about my discipline into more accessible prose (although I still had a lot to learn about writing for a mass audience). I also looked around me and saw that nobody else was taking up this task, so I concluded that I would go ahead and make the strong commitment to writing a book about human factors engineering for a general audience.

It took three years to write that book—*The Human Factor: Revolutionizing the Way People Live with Technology*. I wrote it according to various layers of human–technology interaction, namely: physical, psychological, team, organizational, and political. Human factors engineers deal almost exclusively with the first two of these layers, so I was going into largely uncharted territory. The basic idea was—at each level—to identify a human or societal need, and then to tailor the technology to what we know about human nature at that level. Indeed, I wound up coining a new term—Human-tech—to represent this broader systems approach.

To set an example, I created the term "Human-tech" using a Human-tech approach. It's easy to remember because it consciously mimics the conceptual structure of the idea it refers to—what you see is what you get. First, it's a compound word made up of two parts to remind us that people and technology are both important aspects of one system. Second, the hyphen connecting the two parts highlights the importance of the *relationship* and *encounter* between people and technology. Third, "Human" comes first to remind us that we should start by identifying our human and societal needs, not by glorifying some fancy widget in isolation. Fourth, "Human" is capitalized, and thus more salient, to remind us that designs should be compatible with human nature; "tech" is in lower case because technical details, like the laws of physics, obviously have to be heeded.

On the Readings Collected in this Book

When it came to writing many of my journal articles—some of which are included here—I found a similar pattern. My students and I started off with a pressing practical problem, but it often turned out that the requisite fundamental research had not been conducted, so we had to go into uncharted territory to solve it.

On Chapter Three

This pattern began when I first got hired as a research assistant in 1984. I was preoccupying myself with the minutiae of a project on mental workload, but I also started noticing that there were some very fundamental questions that had rarely been asked in my discipline. What is the relationship between applied problems and basic research? It seemed that people in industry and those in academe were constantly at odds. Academics were criticized for doing research that was completely irrelevant to applied concerns, and those in industry were criticized for doing work that was neither rigorous nor generalizable. These ideas bounced around in my head for 16 years, and the end result is a research article that attempts to reconcile basic and applied concerns and methods. As it turns out, this was not a new idea, but the specific framework that I laid out was novel.

On Chapter Four

In 1999, I wrote a book about cognitive work analysis (CWA)—a way of analyzing how people can do their jobs, providing insights into how to design computer-based systems to help them do their work in a way that it is safe, productive, and healthy. The CWA framework consists of various layers, with the first (work domain analysis) equivalent to providing workers with a map that they can use to navigate their job landscape, and the second (task analysis) equivalent to providing workers with a rote set of directions that they can use for the same purpose, but in a radically different way.

In my head, there existed a relationship between work domain analysis and task analysis, but in retrospect, I learned that this relationship: (a) was not fully explained in my book, and (b) consisted of several conceptual transformations, not just one. John Hajdukiewicz, a student of mine, happened to be doing his doctoral dissertation in a way that brought this lacuna to light. He and I wrote an article showing the relationship between these two forms of analysis, both in generic terms that other people could instantiate for their own context, and in concrete terms for the work system that John had investigated in his dissertation. The generic form provided generalizability and the concrete form provided pedagogical insights. Both were important steps forward from the incomplete treatment provided in Vicente (1999).

On Chapter Five

Two researchers were at a conference. One said, "What area do you do research on?" The other replied, "I conduct research on human reaction time."

"I've never met anyone who conducts research on a dependent variable before."

This anecdote highlights the unsophisticated nature of many human performance measures. We can measure reaction time, we can measure percent correct, and we can inundate people with subjective measures like those found in questionnaires. All of these methods have significant limitations. Sometimes, the measures don't reveal differences between people in experiments, thus defeating their purpose.

The need for more objective and meaningful performance measurement drove the research conducted by Xinyao Yu, Elfreda Lau, me, and Michael Carter. These measures are all quantitative, derived from data that are automatically collected by a computer while a human participant is performing a task. The derivation is based on mathematical equations, and most important of all, the performance measures revealed important differences between people—differences that many other measures, failed to uncover. Using more traditional measures, people looked the same, but using these novel measures we saw—for the first time—that these individuals were actually performing the same task in completely different ways. On top of all that, these new ways of analyzing human performance data were derived from a conceptual framework, which means that other researchers using other tasks could derive analogous measures for their own context.

On Chapter Six

I've taken courses on statistics three times in my career. The first time, I was given a voodoo-like ritual akin to painting by numbers. I had no idea what any of the steps meant and what they were for, partially because I had never conducted an experiment. The second time, I had a new insight: if $p < 0.05$, then something good had happened. And finally— after having conducted several experiments of my own, I had a relatively solid understanding of statistical inference. What I didn't realize was that my knowledge was focused almost exclusively on one kind of statistics, namely analysis of variance (ANOVA).

Later, I realized that there is a thriving debate in psychology about the strong limitations of ANOVA, and the merits of alternative methods of statistical inference, such as confidence intervals, power analyses, and so on. Gerard Torenvliet and I wrote a paper describing these alternative methods, and the important insights that they provide compared to ANOVA. This debate had not taken place in our home discipline, so we thought that we were presenting something of value, particularly to grad students who had yet to be inculcated in the older, traditional methods.

On Chapter Seven

When I was finishing up my PhD, I actually didn't want an academic job. Given the approach of my mentor, Jens Rasmussen, to conduct problem-driven research, I thought I should gain some industry experience before going to a university as a tenure-track professor. For various idiosyncratic reasons, it turns out that I didn't find a suitable applied job, so I took up a university position at Georgia Tech. I was disappointed by this turn of events because I thought, "How can I teach students about something with which I have no direct experience?" So, the need to do research in the field—any field—stayed on the back burner. One day, I would gain this practical experience, and it would fuel my teaching and laboratory research.

As luck would have it, a few years later, the Atomic Energy Control Board (AECB)—the Canadian government regulator of the nuclear industry—was interested in funding research to investigate how nuclear power plant operators monitor the plant. Because of the increasing visibility of our process control research, the AECB came to us, eventually funding a series of field studies. Although the initial focus was on the task of monitoring, the research quickly expanded to include almost all of an operator's job. Even more important, we were able to conduct our research at three different plants, spending dozens of hours of field observations at each. Moreover, each plant had different control room designs but similar reactor designs, creating a naturalistic experiment isolating the contribution of control room design on operator monitoring writ large. This research was conducted with two researchers from Westinghouse, Randy Mumaw and Emilie Roth, and culminated in an article integrating the results from each of the three field studies into a conceptual whole.

On Chapter Eight

In 1997, Jens Rasmussen wrote a very important scientific article, showing how complex sociotechnical systems could be analyzed to great effect by encompassing several layers: work, staff, management, company, regulators/associations, and government (Rasmussen, 1997). In addition to the knowledge brought to bear by each individual level, the relationships across levels are also very important. If the levels are coordinated, with each rowing to the same safe beat, then safety is enhanced. In contrast, if the levels are misaligned, with each rowing to the beat of a different unsafe drummer, then safety can be threatened. Thus, it is important to determine the degree to which these systems are coherent or incoherent across these multiple levels.

I thought this paper was very important, but to be honest, I didn't really know what to do with it. A tragedy changed all that. In May 2000, the water supply system in Walkerton, Ontario, became contaminated with deadly *E. coli* bacteria. In a town of 4,800 residents, seven people died and an estimated 2,300 became sick. Some people, especially children, are expected to experience lasting health effects. The total economic cost of the tragedy was estimated to be over $64.5 million CAD.

As I followed the details of this situation in the media, I started making connections between Rasmussen's framework and the events at Walkerton. I brought in Klaus Christoffersen, a former master's degree student of mine, to analyze what had happened at Walkerton through the lens of Rasmussen's framework. We used Part 1 of the Walkerton report, which focuses on the events surrounding the accident, as the source document for our analysis. The results, reprinted here, provided a seamless fit. This holistic framework did indeed provide life-and-death insights into real world tragedies.

On Chapter Nine

Since 1983, when I took my first human factors engineering course, human factors researchers and practitioners are still complaining that we are not having the practical impact that we deserve. A quarter of a century is a long time. Like many others, I became very frustrated by this state of affairs, so I started reading well outside of my discipline but within the broader Human-tech approach, namely in the management and political science literatures. My rationale was that companies and governments change all the time, and that researchers in these disciplines have spent their entire adult lives studying these events. Surely, they have learned things that can help foster societal change systematically, if chaotically.

My bet paid off (Vicente, 2008; reprinted in Chapter 8). I found several bodies of work in these macro social science disciplines that have a direct bearing on not just this discipline, but on any discipline consumed by societal change. More important, these works can be used to develop "design implications" to tilt the playing field in the name of activist aims. It's possible to change society in a principled way.

Kim J. Vicente

Contents

Human-tech

I

Introduction

Alex Kirlik

In *The Human Factor: Revolutionizing the Way People Live with Technology* (2003), Kim Vicente coined the term "Human-tech" to describe a more encompassing and ambitious approach to the study of human–technology interaction (HTI) than is now evident in any of its participating disciplines, such as human factors, human–computer interaction, cognitive science, industrial or cognitive engineering, ergonomics, informatics or applied psychology. Researchers and practitioners in these HTI disciplines are increasingly involved, or at least hope to be involved, in designing the world in which many of us live and work, ideally, for the better. Observing that the way forward is "not by widgets alone," instead, Vicente advocated a Human-tech approach that addresses every level—physical, psychological, team, organizational, and political—at which technology impacts quality of life, identifies a human or societal need, and then tailors technology to what we know about human nature at that level.

This Human-tech approach contrasts sharply with many currently prevalent approaches to the design of interactive technologies, or technologies that structure the activities of other people (mainly, human work). Many researchers working from primarily engineering or computer science perspectives often focus on what can possibly be engineered or designed, and only later (if ever) address questions about the impact of their inventions on people or society. And many other researchers, working largely from psychological or cognitive science perspectives, often claim that their research will somehow be relevant to applications improving the human condition. But, upon close examination, all too often one sees that the prime motivation for much of this research is actually a desire to contribute to the scientific literature, rather than to solve a socially relevant problem (Klatzky, 2009).

Clearly, many HTI researchers *do* work in the problem- and need-driven manner that Vicente recommends. Yet, his *The Human Factor*, and the Human-tech approach he created and presented there, has made two notable contributions. First, as evidenced by various awards and breadth of market (Canadian National Business Book Award and the Science in Society General Audience Book Award), his book has had success in popularizing these ideas to those who might otherwise be unaware of them. Second, the Human-tech approach structures and articulates what a research agenda should, in his view, look like, if one desires to pursue HTI research that is truly focused on understanding how technology should be marshaled to best suit human needs.

Vicente approached me with the idea of compiling the HTI research articles collected here, in part, for the reader's convenience, with my commentary on each. His notion was that because I am at greater remove, I might be better at making explicit the tacit themes uniting these pieces and possibly identifying insights that might be available only to one at a distance.

After studying the articles, I noticed that they provided much of the technical material behind the work that had been presented in a more mass-market form in the *The Human Factor*. That nontechnical presentation makes sense, as Vicente originated the Human-tech approach in his struggle to make a significant body of research understandable to a lay audience. However, there is no book that integrates the underlying theoretical and methodological work for the audience of HTI students and researchers.

As I worked to find a vantage point from which to relate and comment upon Vicente's work, I observed that a recurring theme across these articles was a desire to not merely inform, but to reform. Anyone who knows Vicente or his work will understand immediately what I mean. His career has been marked by a series of contributions with an occasionally subtle, and often not so subtle, reformist tone. One can read the pieces collected here simultaneously as an extended complaint and, more importantly, a set of recommendations—or at least object lessons—for how HTI research ought to broaden both its perspective and its practical, even moral, aspirations. At least, this is my reading of the motivation behind the Human-tech approach.

Vicente's complaint is that rapid advances in both the complexity and ubiquity of technology have, in his view, rendered much of recent and modern practice in HTI research inadequate to meet society's current needs and insufficiently ambitious to address its emerging challenges. In the final article reprinted here, he goes so far as to recommend that, to be ultimately effective, HTI researchers need to adopt an activist stance, even in the face of significant risk. There, he also alludes to efforts (by him and a colleague) that resulted in a positive change in how a "Big Pharma" corporation does its business. Unfortunately, details on this case could not be provided.

In pondering the undercurrent of reform running throughout these articles, I was reminded of a thought-provoking article by noted physicist Freeman Dyson on the all-too-frequent mismatch between society's needs and the products of both basic and applied scientific research, published a number of years ago in the *New York Review of Books*. I was delighted to find that Dyson had collected and updated this piece, *The Scientist as Rebel*, along with a variety of his articles on related themes, in a recent book of the same name (Dyson, 2006). Since I first encountered it, I have been strongly swayed by Dyson's analysis of the relationship between basic and applied science, of their different goals, their different motivations, and most importantly, of the fact that neither, unchecked by ethical decisions by scientists or engineers themselves, provides any built-in guarantee for improving the human condition. Dyson is perfectly positioned to provide this sort of analysis. He not only made fundamental contributions to theoretical physics, he also joined a company to successfully invent, produce, and sell inherently safe and modestly priced nuclear reactors to hospitals to make isotopes used for medical purposes.

I will not belabor Dyson's treatment here (I draw on it, as well as the work of others, opportunistically throughout this book). Suffice it to say that it provided a fruitful and hopefully informative perspective from which to relate and comment upon Vicente's work. And, almost immediately after I realized this, I understood why. Anyone who has ever read Edwin Abbott's scientific classic *Flatland* (1884) will appreciate the impossibility of organizing a reality spanning N dimensions using only N dimensions to do so. One requires at least one additional dimension. Vicente has described his Human-tech approach as addressing *every* level—physical, psychological, team, organizational, and political—at which technology impacts quality of life. This book, as is the case with *The Human Factor*, is generally laid out in terms of these five successive levels or dimensions, from the physical all the way through to the political (the final Vicente article).

But I do not believe Vicente could have conceived an approach spanning these five dimensions without a sixth from which to organize his thoughts. This sixth dimension, the ethical dimension, is only implicit in Vicente's Human-tech approach. But I have come to believe that it provided the motivation for the whole thing. I thought that, if I could make this sixth dimension explicit, I could use it to create a perspective from which to organize these articles, and a vantage point of sufficient altitude to comment on them.

Because I enjoy no privileged perspective on ethical matters or on the relations between basic and applied science, as Dyson does, I have chosen to co-opt his analysis in the perspective I have chosen to take in my contributions to this book. In a sense, by doing so, I am suggesting that it will be useful to view ethics as the missing sixth dimension in a Human-tech approach aiming to address *every* level at which technology impacts quality of life.

To briefly foreshadow the discussion in Chapter 2, I should also say right up front that, of course, Vicente is hardly the first scientist-engineer to have been motivated to consider the ethical consequences of technology. Founding cyberneticist Norbert Wiener devoted *The Human Use of Human Beings* (1950) to this issue, and Sheridan and Ferrell were explicit in calling attention to the dangers of mistaking scientific and engineering abstractions of human work for human workers themselves in their classic *Man-Machine Systems* (1974). Human factors pioneer Peter Hancock (1994) has also written eloquently about the importance of ethics, and technology alienation was a core theme in Pirsig's enormously popular *Zen and the Art of Motorcycle Maintenance*.

But the concrete ways in which ethical matters get fleshed out in the design and use of technology change just as quickly as technology itself. For this reason, to give ethical considerations added currency and renewed visibility, I have chosen to frame my comments on the papers reprinted in this book, where appropriate, not only from a scientific perspective, but from an ethical perspective as well.

My work on this book has reinforced my belief that engineering and ethics are becoming intertwined in an even more fundamental and intimate way, owing to the ever-increasing ubiquity of technology in human life. There is a grain of truth in philosopher Karl Jaspers' observation that many people tend to become "their situations personified." If our "situations" are increasingly designed for purposes counter to those bringing forth our better nature, against the grain of those promoting health, happiness, and peace, then engineering has indeed become fundamental and even central to ethics. Back in the father of scientific management Frederick Taylor's day, the engineer's idea of the "one best way" to get things done could be promoted only softly, by training and incentives. Today, what was once soft inducement has become, through technology, hard constraint: we either do it the engineer's way, or we don't do it all. Taylor would probably be thrilled.

Winston Churchill once said, "We need a lot of engineers in the modern world, but we do not want a world of modern engineers." We may not (yet) be living in a "world of modern engineers," but we are increasingly living in a world of their creations. The difference may wind up being no difference at all.

2

The Origins of Human-tech

Alex Kirlik

> *Science flourishes best when it uses freely all the tools at hand, unconstrained by preconceived notions of what science ought to be. Every time we introduce a new tool, it always leads to new and unexpected discoveries, because Nature's imagination is richer than ours.*
>
> Freeman Dyson, *The Scientist as Rebel*

Kim Vicente began his research career in the discipline of human factors engineering in the mid 1980s. This was an era of increasing disillusionment, especially among those with design orientations, with the received view that dominated the prevailing culture of his field: that human factors was both largely and essentially a branch of experimental psychology, one known as engineering psychology. The assumption behind the received view was that experimental design, statistical analysis, and information processing theory provided a nearly sufficient basis for human factors researchers and practitioners to inform the design of technology, artifacts, and products, which today, comprise the near total Western human ecology.

In one form of this model, the idea was that design engineers or computer scientists would act responsibly in calling in the human factors experts prior to delivering or fielding their creations. Then, these experts would run experiments to ensure that the resulting technologies achieved their aims, whether in the realm of productivity, safety, reliability, and so forth. A second form of this model was that engineering psychology could get ahead of the design curve, albeit in a limited way. The notion here was that a large body of engineering psychology experiments would result in a collection of findings that a designer would consult for some reason or another, or that these findings could be integrated into a set of design principles or guidelines.

Significant advances have indeed been made from this perspective, and these advances should not be overlooked or underappreciated, even if advances may still be needed in additional directions. For example, perhaps the very best of what we now have along these lines is reflected in human factors textbooks: Wickens, Lee, Liu, and Gordon-Becker (2003) is a notable example. This text is a particularly valuable resource for providing guidance on optimizing the efficiency and effectiveness of the relationship between a person and the information and actions made immediately, or proximally, available from a system interface, such as an automobile cockpit, cell phone, or website (e.g. stimulus–response compatibility is a prime example). Many of the products and devices we use every day, unfortunately, still do not benefit by the tremendous amount of knowledge and guidance texts such as these provide. Only rarely is a human factors course considered to be an essential aspect of engineering education (see Pew and Mavor, 2007 for related observations). Although the handling qualities of my car benefit from state-of-the-art technology, its cockpit design nearly completely ignores some 60 years of accumulated human factors research and wisdom. When I put on my polarized sunglasses, the electronic cockpit displays disappear. (I bought the car in a dark winter.) Did the design engineers never imagine that people might want to wear sunglasses and drive at the same time? (Perhaps it was also designed and tested in one.)

Despite the important advances made by the engineering psychology approach, back in the mid 1980s, it was becoming increasingly apparent that the (high) technologies then requiring creation were becoming so incredibly complex (some going by the name "sociotechnical systems"— nuclear power plants, health care delivery, military command and control, to name a few) that the limitations of the received view were increasingly being felt in quite tangible ways, and from many different quarters. Systems such as these have so many degrees of design freedom that it was becoming increasingly implausible to argue that every design decision having a human or social dimension could be decided empirically, via experimentation and analysis of variance (ANOVA), or that these systems would be amenable to analysis and design in terms of the types of context-free design principles available in traditional human factors textbooks. Research sponsors were more frequently expressing dissatisfaction with what human factors had to offer. Human factors researchers were themselves becoming ever more frustrated with the inadequacy of their training, their methods, and their techniques for effectively engaging research problems in their full complexity.

A variety of human factors researchers wrote scholarly, often searching, pieces offering their own diagnoses of the situation, and sketching possible remedies and alternative futures. Jens Rasmussen, who, along with Donald Norman championed the use of the term "cognitive engineering" in an attempt to define a new discipline transcending solely the engineering psychology approach, offered a particularly cogent diagnosis of the situation, and an especially influential way ahead. Rasmussen observed a variety of mismatches between both the theoretical and methodological tools available in the human factors marketplace and the pressing needs of cognitive engineering researchers and practitioners.

First, Rasmussen, a control engineer working to ensure the safety of nuclear power plants and operations, observed that, in the crucially important area of interface design, semantics had overtaken syntax as the chief barrier to effective plant control and problem diagnosis. It was not that operators had great difficulty perceiving or attending to their displays, but rather in understanding what they meant.

Adopting a largely extensional semantics as a theory of meaning, Rasmussen cashed out meaning in terms of external reference. The operator's actual task is to control, diagnose, and manage a plant, not to observe and manipulate an interface. In other words, an interface must be functionally considered not as the (proximal) target of human interaction, but instead as a window to a (distal) plant or other environment comprising the true target of work. Just as Jerome Bruner had characterized cognition as "going beyond the information given," Rasmussen described an operator's cognitive task in terms of exactly the same sort of going beyond, but in this case, going beyond the interface given.

This description simultaneously describes the challenge and opportunity for interface design. It has a direct parallel in the challenge and opportunity I am now facing in trying to make myself understood to you. Presumably, the publisher's production technology is not to blame if I am not making myself clear, as I expect that a legible and possibly even visually appealing page (or display) of text lies before you. No, if I am failing to meet my challenge, and missing out on the opportunities editing this book affords, it is likely to be a semantic, rather than syntactic failure on my part. Rasmussen realized that the demands of good interface design had, in terms of the reading metaphor, moved beyond font legibility to the need to write well.

But the methods of experimental psychology—dealing as they typically do with a human participant presented with a proximal display and a proximal control, and asked to do one task or another—focus almost exclusively on proximal interaction, with legibility rather than comprehension. Instead, from an empirical perspective, what seemed to be needed, according to Rasmussen, were studies having not merely high levels of fidelity with respect to the proximal "stimulus," but also those faithfully representing the often complex, and possibly even uncertain, relations between proximal information sources and the state of the true target of human interaction, the distal plant, system, or work environment. Rasmussen's insights and research contributions had a profound impact on Vicente. As a graduate student, he traveled to Denmark for a year to study under Rasmussen's mentorship.

A second, perhaps less direct but nevertheless highly influential influence on Vicente were James J. Gibson's (1979) theories of direct perception and affordances. The intuition behind Gibson's affordance concept is that much fluent, perceptually guided behavior involves the "pickup" of information that directly specifies the existence of the action opportunities made available by the environment or "the ecology" (those aspects of the environment with behavioral and psychological relevance). Unlike today, the University of Illinois, where Vicente was doing his graduate study, at the time had a critical mass of faculty members with a Gibsonian bent, across campus units such as aviation, psychology, mechanical & industrial engineering, kinesiology, and others. Vicente did his PhD research in what was then a hotbed of Gibsonian collaboration.

Strongly inspired by both Rasmussen and Gibson, in his PhD dissertation Vicente had seemingly found a way to leverage the resources of both these theorists, resulting in an interface design framework called *ecological interface design* or EID. Research questions surrounding EID dominated Vicente's research agenda, not only during his dissertation, but also during perhaps the first half of his career as an engineering faculty member. Research associated in one way or another with EID has resulted in numerous publications by Vicente and others (e.g. Burns and Hajdukiewicz, 2004; Vicente, 2002), and has been influential in the design of industrial interfaces at an international level. This book is devoted largely to his research activities post-EID, but a few comments on the approach are necessary to better convey the ideas that follow.

Rasmussen's *abstraction hierarchy* (AH) lies at the heart of EID. When Rasmussen sought to understand how the operators he observed monitored and diagnosed a plant, he noticed that their cognitive encounter with the plant bounced among multiple levels of abstraction: physical, functional, and teleological, with the latter indicating the purpose that motivated the plant's design (e.g. to generate power). Rasmussen had done due diligence in reviewing the cognitive science literature at the time on problem solving and found it lacking, exactly because of this multilevel type of plant representation that appeared to be necessary to understand operator cognition. For example, Rasmussen reviewed the influential problem-solving research of Newell and Simon (1972), and noted that the representation that they had chosen to describe the task environment, the "problem space," had two properties that limited its relevance to power plant troubleshooting and diagnosis.

First, all of the Newell and Simon (1972) research had been conducted in closed worlds of puzzles and games, where the state space can be defined once and for all. In contrast, a power plant is an open system. The state of the plant itself can be influenced by external, environmental factors: the operator cannot be certain that the state of the plant is one that had been observed previously or had even been anticipated. Second, with regard to the multilevel representation of the plant necessary to understand operator cognition as represented in the AH—physical form: how it looks, feels, sounds, and smells; how it functions; and purpose, or why it was designed in the first place—Rasmussen noted that, instead, Newell and Simon had assumed a "flat" or single-level problem space. Their problem spaces were essentially nodes (states) connected by possible state transitions that would result by taking actions (e.g. moving a disk from one peg to another in the Tower of Hanoi puzzle).

Vicente's notion underlying the creation of EID was to marry the multilevel, AH representation with Gibsonian direct perception, to make visible the invisible in interface design. Classical single-sensor, single-indicator (SSSI) plant interfaces create proximal–distal barriers for operators, Vicente hypothesized, because they provide information solely at the level of physical function (e.g. pressures, temperatures, flow rates).

If the operator wants (or needs) higher-level functional information (e.g. information relating to the physics governing the plant's operation), then he or she has to overcome a cognitive barrier in going beyond the SSSI interface given.

Ecological interface design also includes a framework for classifying these barriers. Here, Vicente leveraged the *skills, rules, and knowledge* (SRK) framework, also a product of Jens Rasmussen's research (Rasmussen, 1985). The idea behind SRK is that operators work in three possible modes, and their activity shifts among these modes as necessary:

- *Mode 1:* When the operators are continuously responding to continuously displayed signals (e.g. in target tracking or manual piloting or driving), they are said to be exhibiting skill-based behavior.
- *Mode 2:* When they are treating displayed information as discrete signs that trigger practiced actions based on a storehouse of prior experience, they are said to be exhibiting rule-based behavior.
- *Mode 3:* When displayed information is inconsistent with their prior experience (e.g. when diagnosing a novel fault), they treat this information symbolically, mentally integrate it with their understanding of system operation, and are said to be exhibiting problem-solving or knowledge-based behavior.

A core idea behind EID is to allow the operator to work at the lowest possible level in the SRK hierarchy. That is, do not design an interface display that forces an operator to work at any level higher than he or she otherwise could.

Ecological interface design is obviously a highly original contribution. But with the benefit of hindsight, I can see now how the collection of articles reprinted here are also original, yet in a different and perhaps more expansive sense. Vicente notes in his Preface, "When my students and I started off with a pressing practical problem, it turned out that the requisite fundamental research had not been conducted." These articles, from the post–EID phase of Vicente's research career, reflect research done in a context where a problem had been presented for which available theory and method were not ready at hand. It is no coincidence, then, that the articles he proposed to be reprinted here originally appeared in perhaps the most theoretically oriented journal in the HTI discipline: *Theoretical Issues in Ergonomics Science.* They reflect his primary theoretical contributions, to complement his original, design-oriented contributions in EID.

The fruits of this research agenda gave rise to Vicente's *The Human Factor,* and the Human-tech approach. As suggested by the framing and organization of this book, these fruits may provide a point of departure for all HTI students, researchers, educators, and practitioners who would like to improve the way we live with technology. What the reader will see in the articles reprinted here, in contrast to the earlier, EID phase of Vicente's career, is the signature of a researcher who has refused to put the cart of tools and methods ready at hand in front of the horse of a socially relevant problem or opportunity. The privilege of helping to design the future world of human experience and the playing field of human behavior requires an opportunistic attitude toward scientific and engineering research, one in which all the tools at hand are used freely and wisely.

It is sometimes said that some areas of the social and behavioral sciences suffer from "physics envy." Although I do not know how widely this view is shared, or if it provides a fair characterization of contemporary research practice, there is one aspect of physics that is too rarely seen in these sciences, in my opinion: when we speak of using freely "all the tools at hand," we include application and invention among these tools. Consider the following illustration, from Dyson (2006: 206). What were the origins of the theory of relativity?

> Einstein grew up in a family of electrical engineers. His father and uncle ran a business in Munich, manufacturing and selling electrical measuring equipment. One of his uncle Jakob's parents dealt with equipment for electrical control of clocks. Einstein's early familiarity with electrical machinery helped him to get his job at the Swiss patent office, and helped him to do the job well. As soon as he started work, he was confronted with numerous applications for patents concerned with electric clocks and with their coordination by distribution of electric time signals. In the year 1904, when the theory of relativity was in process of gestation, fourteen such patents were approved by the Bern office. The number of applications that were disapproved is not recorded.

At that time, Switzerland was becoming a world leader in the manufacture of precision clocks, and applications for Swiss patents were pouring in from hopeful inventors all over the world. For Einstein, analyzing and understanding these inventions was not just a convenient way to pay the rent. He enjoyed the work at the patent office and found it intellectually challenging. Later in his life, he remarked that the formulation of technological patents had been an important stimulus to his thinking about physics.

I understand that the view of basic versus applied science held by most scientists (and even some engineers) is that, once the basic science is done, the applied scientists or engineers begin looking at how this new knowledge can be put to practical use. Cases of this clearly do occur. However, scholarship on this issue convincingly demonstrates that this unidirectional flow of information is highly oversimplified and actually surprisingly rare. Two of the best critiques of the naïve, unidirectional model of the relation between basic and applied science are the works of Walter Vicenti (1993) and Donald Stokes (1997). Both authors convincingly demonstrate that the belief that practically relevant applications arise solely from pure or basic science is both surprisingly recent and also at odds with the historical facts.

Vicenti (1993) bases his analysis on the history of research in aeronautics. Surely, all of us learned that the Wright brothers, Orville and Wilbur, invented the airplane, right? Well, it turns out that the answer is not so simple. As Vicenti convincingly shows, what the Wright brothers actually invented was human flight (also see Bernstein, 1996). Clearly, part of what the Wright brothers did was design and assemble a vehicle that would come to be known as an airplane. Crucially, though, that vehicle would only attain this distinction if it could be successfully piloted for a significant duration by a human. Both Vicenti and Bernstein clearly demonstrate that the major barrier that the Wright brothers had to overcome was creating a flyable vehicle, that is, to overcome the aerodynamic stability and control problems that had vexed other would-be inventors of human flight. It would take a half a century or so until a mathematical theory of feedback control systems and, more generally, the field of cybernetics, would be founded by Weiner (1948) and others such that it became capable of understanding and describing the Wright brothers' accomplishment in scientific terms.

Furthermore, as demonstrated by Stokes (1997), the accomplishment of Louis Pasteur was nothing short of the Wrights and Weiner rolled up into one. Pasteur is famous not only for inventing procedures and vaccines that have saved countless lives, but also as one of the founders of the science of microbiology and the germ theory of disease. To fully understand Pasteur's accomplishment, Stokes found that he had to abandon the naïve notion of a unidirectional flow of information from basic to applied science. Instead, Stokes charted a map of research in two dimensions, with basic and applied axes at 90 degrees. Pure science, that is, research focused solely on basic (or so-called, "fundamental") questions Stokes' characterized with the model of the great physicist Niels Bohr. Purely applied research, in contrast, Stokes' characterized with the model of Edison. However, in the upper right quadrant of his map, he placed the work of Pasteur, as it contributed—simultaneously and in a mutually reinforcing way—to both basic and applied research. As such, the name Stokes gave to research conducted in this, Pasteurs' quadrant, is *use-inspired basic research*.

To me at least, Vicente's Human-tech approach, one that "identifies a human or societal need, and then tailors technology to what we know about human nature" seems perfectly aligned with Stokes' concept of use-inspired basic research. However, and as noted in Chapter 1, a great deal of research claimed to be relevant to HTI remains occupied in either Bohr's quadrant (much of psychology and cognitive science research) or Edison's quadrant (much of engineering and computer science research)—that is, the discoverers and the inventors. Vicente asks those us of involved in HTI research to become discoverers-inventors, or perhaps inventor-discoverers, followers in the intellectual footsteps of Pasteur, rather than of Bohr or Edison. Or, perhaps more realistically, he asks those of us involved in HTI research to work together in collaborations of inventors and discoverers in conducting our research.

Will this be possible on a scale urged by Vicente? One of the most accomplished scholars in overcoming the clash of worldviews between inventors and discoverers was cybernetics pioneer Heinz von Foerster, who worked with colleagues such as Norbert Wiener, John von Neumann, and Warren McCullough in the creation of cybernetics. He was also was director of the Biological Computer Laboratory (discoverers-inventors) at the University of Illinois at Urbana-Champaign from 1958 until 1975. Here is how von Foerster described the situation, in an invited address given in Paris in 1990:

> Here is the decisive pair of questions:
> "Am I apart from the universe?"
> That is, whenever I look I am looking as through a peephole upon an unfolding universe.
> Or, "Am I a part of the universe?
> That is, whenever I act, I am changing myself and the universe as well.
> Whenever I reflect upon these two alternatives, I am surprised again and again at the depth of the abyss that separates the two fundamentally different worlds that can be created by such choices.
> Either to see myself as a citizen of an independent universe, whose regularities, rules, and customs I may eventually discover, or to see myself as a participant of a conspiracy, whose customs, rules, and regulations we are now inventing.
> Whenever I speak to those who have made their decision to be either discoverers or inventors, I am impressed again and again by the fact that neither of them realizes that they have ever made that decision.
> I was once asked the question of how the inhabitants of the different worlds as I have sketched them, the inhabitants of the world they discover, and the inhabitants of the world they invent, how can they ever live together? There is no problem to answer that … as long as the discoverers discover the inventors, and the inventors invent discoverers.
> I have a dear friend who grew up in Marrakech. The house of his family stood on the street that divides the Jewish and Arabic quarters. As a boy, he played with all the others, listened to what they thought and said, and learned of their fundamentally different views.

When I asked him once, "Who was right?" he said, "They are both right."

"But this cannot be," I argued from an Aristotelian platform, "Only one of them can have the truth!"

"The problem is not truth," he answered, "The problem is trust."

3

A Human-tech Research Agenda and Approach

Alex Kirlik

> *If we can agree with Thomas Jefferson that these truths are self-evident, that all men are created equal, that they are endowed with certain inalienable rights, that among these are life, liberty, and the pursuit of happiness, then it should also be evident that the abandonment of millions of people in modern societies to unemployment and destitution is a worse defilement of the earth than nuclear power stations. If the ethical force of the environmental movement can defeat the manufacturers of nuclear power stations, the same force should also be able to foster the growth of technology that supplies the needs of impoverished humans at a price they can afford. This is the great task for technology in the coming century.*
>
> Freeman Dyson, *The Scientist as Rebel*

In the article reprinted in this chapter, Vicente presents and advocates a Human-tech research approach and agenda grounded in the tenets of Jeffersonian, representative democracy. Jefferson, along with others such as James Madison and Nathaniel Bacon, argued that such a democratic form is required to prevent tyranny by the majority (i.e. in a modern research context, "tyranny" cashes out as methodological fetishism or imperialism, or any crisply formulated—thus necessarily false—distinction between "basic" and "applied" research). As noted by Koch and Peden (1993), Jefferson was an advocate of the notion that research should strive to achieve, and could attain, at the same time both a richer understanding of nature and practical relevance (e.g. to a farmer). Jefferson was clearly an advocate of use-inspired basic research.

Vicente's key message in this piece is that a Human-tech research approach necessarily requires a broad, catholic perspective on viewing and selecting one's research methods and techniques ("working freely with all the tools at hand, unconstrained by preconceived notions"; Dyson, 2006). The use of these methods and techniques must be driven by the nature and phase of the problem-solving process in which a researcher is engaged. Doing otherwise gets the cart before the horse. Field studies, tightly controlled laboratory experiments, quantitative models, qualitative models, analysis of variance (ANOVA), computational models, and design and prototyping skills each have their place. And, just as important, they each have their limitations and boundary conditions. Vicente challenges us to avoid methodological dogmatism or imperialism, much in the spirit of Danzinger's (1994) classic critique of psychology methodology in *Constructing the Subject*.

In this article, Vicente, like Stokes before him, puts forth his own map of the research space, and like Stokes, uses two dimensions or continua, although not, like Stokes, simultaneously. The first dimension, depicted in Figure 3, ranges from traditional laboratory experiments, which Vicente labels as "controlled, but unrepresentative," to field studies, which Vicente labels "representative, but uncontrolled." Representativeness (Brunswik, 1956) refers the degree to which a research situation faithfully represents the psychologically relevant aspects of the target domain to which the generalization of research findings is intended. Mid levels of representativeness in Vicente's continuum are given to "microworld" research (think video-game style simulation) and "full-scope simulator" (think Delta Airlines flight simulators used for training and research).

In this context, Vicente marshals Kenneth Hammond's (1989) "Law of the Laboratory," that "rigor is inversely related to the representation of [environmental] complexity" (in empirical research). Vicente relies on this notion to interpret his continuum as implying that the human–technology interaction (HTI) researcher faces a necessary zero-sum trade-off between rigor (perhaps the detection of cause-effect relations) and the degree to which these findings will also be relevant to the target context of generalization.

I believe that it is important to note, however, that Hammond presented his "Law of the Laboratory" as a *false* dichotomy: he believes it to be *descriptive* of how most psychologists tend to view the matter, but hardly necessary, and largely an artifact of the confusion that ensued when psychology took Fisherian statistics (ANOVA, etc.) as *the* gold standard for experimental methodology—one instance of the methodological fetishism alluded to previously. However, I will not go into great detail on this issue here, but instead point the reader to the fact that these concepts are dealt with in much greater depth in Chapter 6: Statistics for Human-tech Research. For the purpose of the current chapter, it is sufficient merely to indicate that the demands for both experimental control and the representation of task complexity need not necessarily be seen as creating a zero-sum game for the HTI researcher.

Simulation technologies (both actual and virtual) and even "living laboratories" (e.g. a hospital ICU in which health care providers volunteer an afternoon a week to participate in—nearly—in situ, yet highly monitored and controlled research) are increasingly sapping much of the zero-sum nature between control and representativeness to which Vicente points. Yet, although this zero-sum game is not logically necessary, getting around it often comes with a high price. So, the gist of Vicente's observations along these lines have merit. I merely want to stress that what is in play here is a question of resources, and not necessarily a law of HTI research, one that cannot be broken with enough cash and access to relevant research participants (e.g. experts or people knowledgeable about various tasks).

The second of Vicente's continua that I wish to question, or perhaps complicate, is presented in Figure 4, ranging from "knowledge-oriented" (e.g. basic research) to "market-oriented" (e.g. system development). My first reason for differing with Vicente's perspective as displayed here is that, as discussed in Chapter 1, I prefer Stokes' two-dimensional map of the research space, which places basic and applied research at 90-degree angles, to Vicente's one-dimensional continuum. This is based on my own analysis and understanding of the Human-tech approach, which seems to me to be much in the spirit of use-inspired basic research, for which I see no comfortable home in Vicente's Figure 4.

My second comment on this issue is that, particularly in the realm of information and communication technologies, we are now seeing an even more sweeping democratization in effect, more sweeping in that it transcends the academic or even corporate research environment. A college student able to foster a revolution in how peers communicate or interact has, without collecting a data point or writing a research article, already had more societal impact than many HTI researchers may ever hope to achieve. The quality of that impact is still unknown (as compared to research enhancing, say, aviation or health care safety). But it is impact nonetheless.

In accordance with the Human-tech approach that Vicente advocates, we need also to recognize that the design questions in play are not solely restricted to "high" technology. Enrique Penalosa, the former mayor of Bogota, Columbia, was recently (June 6, 2008) quoted in *The New York Times* as saying "when you construct a good sidewalk, you are constructing a democracy." Penalosa now works as a consultant for those officials in Asia and the developing world intent on building the world-class cities of the future.

In sum, while I mainly support Vicente's central thesis in the reprint, I would suggest it should be bootstrapped to further push the envelope to recognize the full range of opportunities to shape our technology, as well as the risks or harm that come with doing so. Those participating in Human-tech advances, when they are made, include not only academic researchers publishing articles, but also inventors, and others at many different levels (e.g. public policy makers, funding agencies, corporate executives), who are currently pushing levers that have a direct and often profound impact on the design of our world.

Toward Jeffersonian Research Programmes in Ergonomics Science

Kim J. Vicente

Abstract

Thomas Jefferson believed that scientific research could lead to a fuller understanding of nature, while simultaneously addressing a persistent social problem of national or global interest. The two-fold ideals of this "Jeffersonian research programme" fit well with the inherently practical aims of ergonomics science. However, in the past, basic and applied concerns have not always been well integrated in the discipline. This article makes a contribution, by proposing a novel metascientific framework consisting of a two-dimensional research space that addresses this problem. One dimension is methodological, representing the trade-off between experimental control and representativeness, while the other dimension is intentional, representing the trade-off between knowledge- and market-oriented purposes. The framework helps explain why it has frequently been difficult to integrate basic and applied concerns, and, at the same time, it shows that a Jeffersonian research programme for ergonomics science can be achieved by opening up degrees of freedom for research that have been comparatively unexplored. The importance of demonstrating contributions to fundamental understanding and to applied practice within the same research programme may be essential for survival and success in a climate of restricted research funding.

1. Introduction

Ergonomics science is different from some other disciplines, because it is inherently practical. One of its ultimate goals is to design sociotechnical systems that lead to improved safety, productivity, and worker health. Thus, generalizability to industry-scale problems is a central consideration. At the same time, however, ergonomics science should also be concerned with fundamental research questions. Otherwise, cumulative and unified knowledge—the hallmarks of scientific progress—will be hard to come by. Considerations of practical use and the quest for fundamental understanding have traditionally been referred to as "applied" and "basic" research, respectively. Using these terms, one can state that both applied and basic research have important contributions to offer the ergonomics science community.

Unfortunately, it has proven to be very difficult to solve practical problems and contribute to fundamental understanding at the same time (Rouse, 1985; Meister, 1989). Although the boundary between practice and theory is admittedly a fuzzy one, there seems to be an inherent tension between applied and basic concerns. The motivation for this article is that this tension has yet to be resolved in a productive manner by the ergonomics science community. Somehow, one must be able to develop research programmes that respect the unique benefits of applied and basic research without letting one dominate the other. The purpose of this article is to propose a novel metascientific framework that can foster research that contributes to the enhancement of fundamental understanding as well as the resolution of practical problems in ergonomics science. Following the noted historian of science, Holton (1993), I will refer to this type of research as the "Jeffersonian research programme" in honour of Thomas Jefferson's appreciation for research that led to a fuller understanding of nature, while also addressing a persistent social problem of national or global interest (Koch and Peden 1993).

How can ergonomics science achieve the two-fold aims of a Jeffersonian research programme? The framework proposed in this article shows that there are alternative ways of conducting research that have been relatively unexplored, and that, by exploring these alternatives within a single research programme, it is possible to contribute simultaneously to both basic and applied concerns. That there is a need for such a framework can be illustrated with a simple case study from research on translucent human–computer interfaces.

1.1. A case study: Translucent human–computer interface design

Because of the prevalence of graphical user interfaces (GUIs), computer users have to interact with many different objects, such as text menus, tool palettes, and overlapping windows. As a result, it is not at all uncommon to find that these interface objects can obscure underlying images or text that are also of interest to users. For example, Figure 1 shows a tool palette obscuring a substantial portion of an underlying wire-frame image. Users may be interested in viewing the obscured portion of the image while the interface object is still on the screen. In such cases, users wind up spending a great deal of time managing these interface objects (e.g. moving palettes back and forth, resizing windows, opening and closing menus). These activities are overhead tasks, in the sense that they do not directly accomplish productive work (e.g. creating a 3-D model of an object). Therefore, one unintended side-effect of a GUI-style interface is that users are not as productive as they otherwise might be if they were able to spend more time on the central domain task of interest.

Harrison and colleagues (Harrison et al. 1994, 1995a,b; Harrison and Vicente 1996a,b) addressed this problem by designing translucent human–computer interfaces. An example is shown in Figure 2, where a translucent text menu is superimposed on a solid object. With this type of design, it is possible for users to divide their attention between the foreground (i.e. the text menu) and the background (i.e. the solid object)

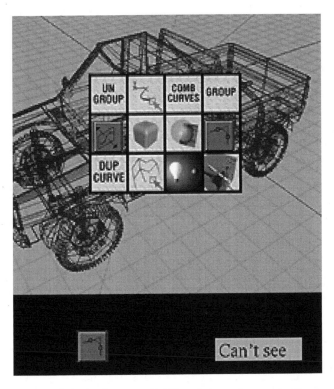

FIGURE 1   A sample image from a study of interface translucency by Harrison
et al. (1995b). An opaque tool palette obscures an underlying wire frame object.
Reprinted from Harrison *et al.* (1995b),© 1995 ACM, Inc. Reprinted by permission.

at will, without having to engage in wasteful overhead activities. However, to optimize the design, it was necessary to determine an appropriate
level of translucency. If the foreground object were too opaque, it would
not be possible to see the background object to accomplish domain tasks
because the object would be covered up. Conversely, if the foreground
object were too translucent, it would not be possible to see it to accomplish domain tasks because it would not be legible. The optimal translu-
cence point represents a trade-off between these two factors, allowing
users to focus effectively on either foreground or background, as needed.

Harrison and Vicente (1996a) conducted an empirical study to
determine this optimal translucency point for text menus like that shown
in Figure 2. The menus consisted of 12 commands (e.g. Revolve X,

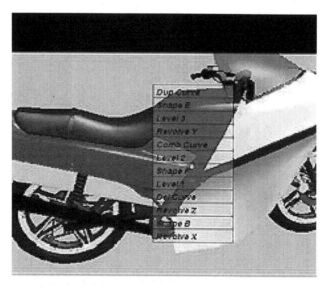

FIGURE 2   A sample image from a study of interface translucency by Harrison and Vicente (1996a). A translucent menu can be seen over an underlying solid object. Reprinted from Harrison and Vicente (1996a), © 1996 ACM, Inc. Reprinted by permission.

Revolve Y, Revolve Z, Dup Curve, Comb Curve, Del Curve). In designing their experiment, Harrison and Vicente were faced with the question of whether to keep the position (and, thus, the order) of the commands in the menu constant across trials, or whether to vary the position of the commands randomly across trials. Computer menus in commercial software have a fixed order, which suggests that the first option is more appropriate because it is representative of the conditions that users would encounter outside of the laboratory. After all, results with randomly varying menu items could not be expected to generalize to the normal case of fixed order. Perhaps surprisingly, Harrison and Vicente decided to vary the position of the commands randomly across trials, despite the fact that this situation is not representative. Why would they make such a counterintuitive choice?

The purpose of Harrison and Vicente's (1996a) experiment was to investigate the impact of translucency on the legibility of the text in the foreground layer (see Figure 2). To obtain a sufficient number of data points for statistical analysis, participants were given many trials of practice at the task. Therefore, if the position of the commands on the menu was kept constant across trials, then it is possible that participants might memorize the position of each command with practice. Under these circumstances, participants would be able to perform the task accurately without even reading the text on the menu. For example, if Revolve X was always the top item on the menu, then participants might be able to select this item merely by clicking on the top of the menu, even if the text was illegible due to a high level of translucency. This possibility was inconsistent with the experimental goal of assessing the impact of translucency on text legibility. Thus, Harrison and Vicente (1996a) adopted the counterintuitive choice of randomizing the position of the commands in the menu across trials because it better served the objectives of their experiment.

This simple example shows that the conflict between experimental control (to obtain a fundamental understanding of phenomena) and representativeness (to solve practical problems) can be subtle, even in the seemingly most straightforward of cases. Furthermore, recognizing this subtlety can lead to research decisions that are, perhaps, counterintuitive from other perspectives. Thus, it is important to try to understand better the complex relationship between basic and applied concerns.

1.2. Outline

The remainder of this article is organized as follows. First, a methodological continuum of research with experimental control on one end and representativeness on the other will be described. The concept of representativeness was originally defined by Brunswik (1952: 30) as follows:

> The study of functional organism–environment relationships would seem to require that . . . situational circumstances should be made to represent . . . conditions under which the organism has to function. This leads to what the writer has suggested to call the "representative design of experiments". . . . Any generalized statement of relationship requires specification of a "reference class" or "universe" from which the material is drawn.

This definition implies that representativeness is always relative because research must explicitly be representative of some reference class. In the case of ergonomics science, the reference class is usually the set of work situations to which one wants to generalize research results. Note also that representativeness has several dimensions (e.g. work domain, scenarios, tasks, social-organizational structure, participants). A study that is representative along one dimension may not be on another. Nevertheless, for the purposes of this article, it is sufficient to discuss representativeness as if it were a unidimensional construct. Secondly, an intentional continuum of research with a knowledge-oriented purpose on one end and a market-oriented purpose on the other end will be described. Thirdly, these two continua will be used to create a novel metascientific framework consisting of a two-dimensional research space. This framework will show that ergonomics science has tended to focus on certain areas of the space and has relatively ignored other areas. Finally, the implications of this framework will be discussed, showing that it is possible to attain the two-fold benefits of a Jeffersonian research programme by conducting research in the unexplored areas of the aforementioned research space and by adopting a methodologically diverse research programme.

2. A methodological continuum of research

Part of the tension between basic and applied research concerns is well captured by Hammond's (1989) Law of the Laboratory, which states that "rigour is inversely related to representation of complexity" (p. 2; see also Cook and Campbell, 1979). This fundamental trade-off in empirical research can be used to create a continuum of research types with highly controlled, but unrepresentative investigations on one end and highly representative, but uncontrolled investigations on the other end (Vicente, 1997). Figure 3 illustrates this continuum along with four prototypical research types. In ergonomics science, as well as psychology, much more emphasis has been given to the controlled but unrepresentative end of this continuum. This historical trend can be noted by briefly describing the four categories in Figure 3. Note that both the continuum and the four types are not intended to be exhaustive or unique. There are many other ways to categorize research. Nevertheless, these distinctions are useful for the purposes of this article.

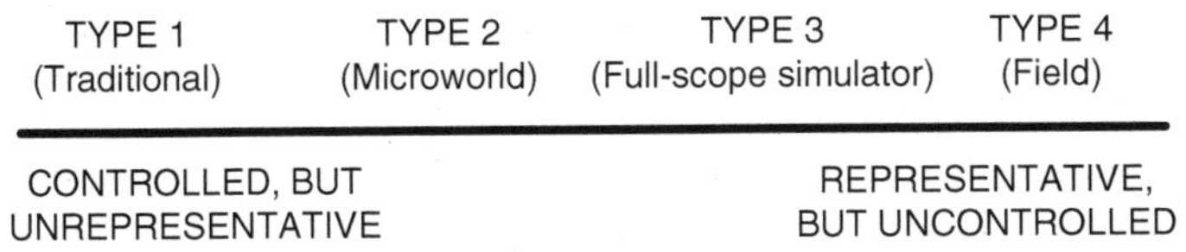

| TYPE 1 | TYPE 2 | TYPE 3 | TYPE 4 |
| (Traditional) | (Microworld) | (Full-scope simulator) | (Field) |

CONTROLLED, BUT
UNREPRESENTATIVE

REPRESENTATIVE,
BUT UNCONTROLLED

FIGURE 3   A methodological continuum of research showing the trade-off between experimental control and representativeness (adapted from Vicente 1997).

2.1. Types of research

2.1.1. Type 1—Highly Controlled Laboratory Experiments

These studies use simplified tasks and either hold constant, or independently manipulate, each factor that may be relevant to the phenomenon under study to obtain an unconfounded understanding of the effect of each independent variable.

An outstanding example is the work of Gould et al. (1987). These ergonomics scientists sought to isolate a single-variable explanation for why people read more slowly from CRT displays than from paper. To achieve this goal, they conducted 10 experiments, each of which tried to isolate the impact of a single independent variable. The conclusion obtained from this sequence of 10 studies was that the reading speed difference between CRT displays and paper is likely due to a combination of variables, probably centred on image quality. The fact that this highly controlled, reductionistic research was awarded the Jerome H. Ely Award for the outstanding paper published in volume 29 of *Human Factors* shows that this type of work was highly valued by the ergonomics science community.

2.1.2. Type 2—Less-controlled but more complex laboratory experiments

These studies do not explicitly try to control for every factor, but instead present participants with more complex tasks than Type 1 research. Most microworld research belongs in this category, the idea being to have some experimental control and some representativeness as well, thereby improving the chances of generalizability to operational settings.

A particularly representative example is the 6-month-long, longitudinal study of ecological interface design conducted in a process control microworld by Christoffersen et al. (1996, 1997, 1998). Participants were only told what the task goals were, not how they should achieve them, so that the impact of interface design on participants' strategies could be assessed. As a result, participants sometimes controlled the microworld in qualitatively different ways, even within interface groups. In addition, equipment failures were modelled in the simulation to mimic the risk present in industrial processes, albeit on a much smaller scale. Thus, an inappropriate action by a participant would cause a component to "blow up," prematurely ending a trial. Because different participants experienced a different number of such "blow ups," the number of trials they completed and the amount of time they spent controlling the microworld differed. Furthermore, single and multiple component failures were unexpectedly introduced into the simulation at pre-defined times to investigate participants' ability to manage disturbances. However, the participants did not have the microworld in the same state or configuration at the times when faults were introduced, so the impact of any one fault could differ substantially across participants. In the extreme case, if the participant was not using the failed component, there would be no disturbance for them to detect, diagnose, or compensate. For these and other similar reasons, this experiment was much more representative of industrial process control than a typical laboratory experiment, thereby enhancing the generalizability of results. However, a price was paid in terms of a concomitant decrease in experimental control. Because of all of the uncontrolled variability, it was not possible to develop a rigorous, causal explanation for the results that were obtained over the course of the study. Despite these limitations, many novel hypotheses were generated and some of these have since been investigated in more controlled laboratory studies (e.g. Hajdukiewicz and Vicente, 2000).

2.1.3. Type 3—Evaluations conducted in high-fidelity simulators

These studies try to increase representativeness further with the hope of increasing generalizability to operational settings, but give up a great deal of experimental control as a result.

A good example is the investigation of safety parameter display systems (SPDSs) conducted by Woods et al. (1982). They investigated the impact of two different SPDSs on the performance of professional, licensed operators in a full-scope nuclear power plant simulator-a very representative, albeit simulated, setting. Data were collected for 16 complex accident events, representing the types of disturbances that can be experienced in a commercial nuclear power plant. Because of the strong representation of realism, many variables were not controlled for and there was a great deal of variability in the data. As a result, "the study was not able to provide quantitative results in answer to the question of how much of an impact the SPDS will have on operator performance" (Woods et al. 1982: S-10). Nevertheless, qualitative data analyses of the decisions made by the operators revealed important insights into the impact of the SPDSs on operator strategies. The fact that this study is still cited as a notable example of how to conduct a full-scope simulator study illustrates the impact that it has had on the literature.

2.1.4. Type 4—Descriptive field studies

These studies are concerned with observing and documenting highly representative behaviour in the field, to obtain a better descriptive understanding of naturalistic phenomena. Usually, there are no independent variables because it may not be possible to manipulate any factors in a systematic fashion during actual work conditions. Consequently, there is no experimental control at all.

An influential example is the field study of maritime navigation conducted onboard a U.S. Navy ship by Hutchins (1995). Because of the naturalistic nature of the investigation, Hutchins was not able to manipulate any variables in a systematic fashion. He had to be content to study the idiosyncratic events that the sailors happened to be faced with during his observation periods. Thus, there was no experimental control whatsoever, meaning that it was not possible to conduct any rigorous tests of competing hypotheses. This did not stop Hutchins from making a scientific contribution. On the contrary, his descriptive field study methodology allowed him to make novel, creative observations about the nature of cognition in the wild. These insights are quite different from those that had been obtained by cognitive scientists who had studied cognition in

the laboratory. Even more importantly, Hutchins' work has had a tremendous impact on several disciplines, leading to more controlled studies in cognitive science (e.g. Zhang and Norman 1994) and analogous
field studies in ergonomics science (e.g. Vicente and Burns 1996). These
studies have deepened our understanding of distributed cognition.

2.2. The traditional view

How have these types of research been traditionally viewed in the ergonomics science community? It is always difficult to characterize people's
attitudes to very broad issues without being accused of presenting a straw
man position. To side-step this criticism, this study will deliberately present a caricature of what is perceived to be the traditional view.

2.2.1. Type 1—Highly controlled laboratory experiments

In the traditional view, this is "real" science. It is purported to be the only
reliable way to discover fundamental principles that are pure in the sense
that they are not tied to any particular context. In the words of Banaji
and Crowder (1991: 79), "If you wish to do research that is useful
(i.e. practical, functional) the *optimal* path is controlled experimentation"
(see also Shiffrin 1996).

2.2.2. Type 2—Less-controlled but more complex laboratory experiments

These are poorly designed experiments. Because some factors are not
meticulously controlled for, the results are confounded. Doherty (1993:
362) frankly described the traditional aversion to this type of research:
"I still have the deep intellectual and emotional attachment of the
experimental psychologist to the simple, single variable experiment."

2.2.3. Type 3—Evaluations conducted in high-fidelity simulators

In the traditional view, this research will not lead to the discovery of
scientific laws because the study is not conducted in a "pure" manner.
In the words of Kelso (1995: 32): "most naturalistic behaviour is too
complicated to yield fundamental principles."

2.2.4. Type 4—Descriptive field studies

This research is not considered to be scientific, because usually no factors are manipulated by the experimenter (orthogonally or otherwise). Thus, it is not possible to isolate the causal factors that are responsible for the phenomenon of interest. Furthermore, there is usually a great deal of variability in the data, so even in the rare cases where it is possible to conduct statistical tests, they rarely yield significant findings (Baker and Marshall 1988). Therefore, in the traditional view, findings from this type of research are considered to be highly subjective and completely speculative.

2.3. Alternative views

Critiques of this comparatively narrow view of science are hardly new (e.g. Brunswik, 1956; Chapanis, 1967; Gibson, 1967/1982; Lorenz, 1973; Neisser, 1976; Sheridan and Hennessy 1984; Meister, 1989). In fact, the limitations of the traditional view have been recognized by an increasing number of ergonomics scientists in recent years, probably because research emphasizing experimental control to the detriment of representativeness has not had much success in technology transfer to industry-scale problems (Rouse, 1985; Meister, 1989). As a result, there has been a counter movement to study human behaviour under more naturalistic conditions (Klein et al., 1993; Zsambok and Klein, 1997). The rationale behind much of this work is that Type 1 research, as defined above, and in Figure 3, does not generalize to experienced workers performing representative tasks under naturalistic work conditions. Thus, the naturalistic movement has increased the emphasis given to representativeness. Frequently, it has been concerned with Type 3 or Type 4 research. The hope is that research results will be more generalizable and that technology transfer to industry-scale problems will be more successful than in the past.

As shown in Figure 3, microworld research can be viewed as a compromise between traditional, controlled research and naturalistic, representative research (Brehmer and Dörner, 1993). It tries to capture some of the features of work settings (albeit in simplified ways), thereby enhancing the possibility for generalizability to operational settings, and, thus, technology transfer. At the same time, microworld research tries to include some experimental control (although less than traditional controlled

experiments), thereby avoiding some of the threats to validity that usually plague simulator and field studies (Baker and Marshall, 1988).

The author believes that too much emphasis has been placed on
highly controlled experimentation in ergonomics science, and that both
naturalistic and microworld research have something important to offer.
Having said that, there is a danger that these alternatives can be thought of
as replacements for traditional research (Kirlik, in press). Hammond's (1989)
Law of the Laboratory reminds one that there is a fundamental trade-off
between experimental control and representativeness within any individual study. Therefore, any single point along the continuum in Figure 3
represents a compromise with some advantages over other points, but,
unavoidably, some disadvantages as well. As Kirlik (in press) has pointed
out, this point is not always recognized by researchers who advocate
naturalistic and microworld research. Thus, there is a danger that these
alternative forms of research will replace traditional highly controlled
experimentation, resulting in a new set of limitations that are complementary to those of traditional research. As a step towards avoiding this risk, a
second continuum of research is presented in the next section.

3. An intentional continuum of research

Scientific research is a very complex human activity, and so it can be
classified in many different ways. The continuum in Figure 3 is based on
methodological considerations. Some readers may have interpreted the
left (controlled) pole of the continuum as corresponding to basic research
and the right (representative) pole of the continuum as corresponding to
applied research. Note, however, that the terms "basic" and "applied"
were never used in the previous section to describe Figure 3. Thus, if
some readers have interpreted the figure in this way, it is because they
believe that the distinction between basic and applied research is a
methodological one. The author believes that this view is unproductive
because it leads to an overly restrictive view of research that fails to integrate basic and applied concerns (Vicente, 1994). To see why this is so, it
is necessary to classify research in a different way from that in Figure 3.

Figure 4 illustrates a continuum of research that is based on intentional considerations (i.e. the main purpose that researchers had in mind
at the time that they conducted the work). It was borrowed from the

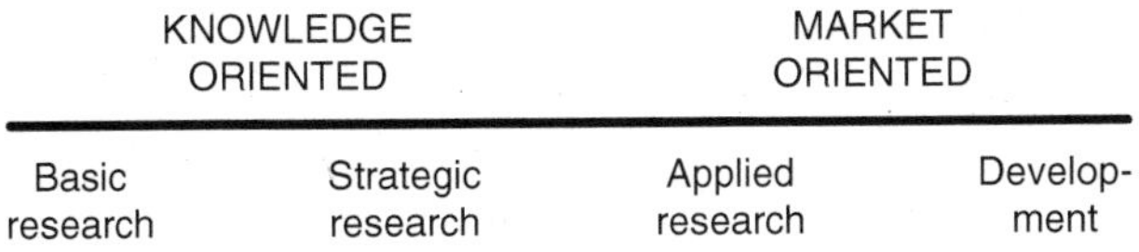

KNOWLEDGE ORIENTED		MARKET ORIENTED	
Basic research	Strategic research	Applied research	Develop-ment

FIGURE 4   An intentional continuum of research showing the trade-off between knowledge-and market-oriented purposes (adapted from Vicente 1994).

mission statement, circa 1994, of Risø National Laboratory in Roskilde, Denmark. Risø is a government research laboratory that is involved in multidisciplinary research, a small subset of which has been very influential in the ergonomics science community (Vicente, in press). Around 1994, Risø's stated objective was to further technological development in energy, environment, and materials. The results of Risø's research have been widely applied in agriculture, industry, and public services. The most relevant part of the mission statement dealt with the research profile of the laboratory. There, it stated that the emphasis was on "long-term and strategic research providing a solid scientific foundation for the technological development of society." Figure 4 is an adaptation of a figure that was used by Risø to graphically illustrate the emphasis of its research profile.

On the left end of the continuum, the primary purpose of the research is *knowledge-oriented*. The goal here is to answer questions of broad theoretical significance in a manner that leads to a principled understanding of the phenomenon being investigated. On the right end of the continuum, the primary purpose of the research is *market-oriented*. The goal here is to answer questions of very specific practical interest in a manner that leads to the resolution of an industry-relevant problem being investigated. Note that no direction of flow is specified, because either type of research can inform and influence the other, a point that will be explored in more detail later. Risø identified four areas along Figure 4 corresponding to different research types.

3.1. Types of research

3.1.1. Basic research

Basic research falls on the knowledge-oriented part of the continuum. In this case, the exclusive purpose motivating a study is to contribute to theoretical understanding. Note that such research may eventually have practical applications and lead to technology transfer to industry, but these pragmatic considerations are not the original motivation behind the research. In fact, in many cases, the practical implications of this type of knowledge-oriented research are unforeseeable.

3.1.2. Strategic research

Strategic research is still aimed at contributing to theoretical understanding, but it is also usually constrained by some market-oriented considerations. For example, in the case of the Natural Sciences and Engineering Council of Canada (www.nserc.ca), several scientific areas have been identified as being particularly important to the Canadian economy (e.g. biotechnology, energy-efficient technology, environmental technology, information technology, manufacturing and processing technology, and materials technology). Accordingly, targetted funding has been provided for strategic research that is aimed at these areas. Nevertheless, researchers are still expected to contribute to theoretical knowledge and publish their results in peer-reviewed publications in the scientific community.

3.1.3. Applied research

Applied research falls on the market-oriented part of the continuum. Here, more attention is paid to industry-relevant considerations. While some of this research can still be conducted in a university, it is explicitly targetted at technology transfer to industry rather than contributions to scientific theory. Accordingly, applied research is usually primarily evaluated, not based on journal publications, but on patents, spin-off companies, impact on commercially available products or services, and other such market-oriented criteria. Interestingly, however, this category is not the pole of the market-oriented part of Figure 4.

3.1.4. Development

Development serves as the pole of market-oriented activities. Here, the goal is pragmatic to the point that the activities being conducted may no longer be classified by many as research. The goal of development is to design and build a product that is satisfying a market need. Frequently, this type of work cannot be published in scientific journals, either because the research is proprietary or because the insights gained are *ad hoc* and idiosyncratic, rather than principled and generalizable. In many cases, this type of work is (justifiably) conducted in industry rather than in academe.

3.2. Conclusion

The intentional continuum in Figure 4 has a clean correspondence with the ideals embedded in the Jeffersonian research programme. To satisfy the two-fold purposes that were so valued by Jefferson, a research programme must be both knowledge-oriented (thereby contributing to the principled understanding of nature) and market-oriented (thereby contributing to the resolution of a persistent social problem of national or global interest). But, how is this possible? How can research be at two points along a single continuum at the same time?

A resolution to this conundrum can be obtained in two moves. First, one must change one's level of analysis. So far, a comparatively detailed level of resolution has primarily been adopted, focusing on an individual study as the fundamental unit of analysis. However, it is possible to adopt a more coarse level of resolution, focusing on a research programme comprising multiple studies as the fundamental unit of analysis. By making this change, one can obtain new insights. For example, one can see that Hammond's Law is only true for a single study. In that case, there is a fundamental trade-off because one experiment cannot be designed to maximize both experimental control and representativeness. However, if the level of analysis is moved to that of a research programme, this trade-off may be overcome. Similarly, it can be seen that the apparent conflict between knowledge-oriented and market-oriented aims only exists at the level of a single study. If the level of analysis is moved to that of a research programme, this trade-off can be overcome as well.

Secondly, one must clearly distinguish between the methodological and intentional dimensions represented in Figures 3 and 4, respectively. Despite the fact that the two figures represent different dimensions, it may seem like there is a great deal of correspondence between the four categories of research in Figure 3 and the four categories in Figure 4. The reason for this apparent similarity is that researchers have not explored the full range of possibilities that are available to them. The rationale behind this claim will be explained next by adopting a morphological approach (Zwicky, 1967), thereby showing that the continua in these two figures are actually orthogonal to each other.

4. A two-dimensional research space

One of the contributions of this article is to show that ergonomics scientists have tended to conflate the methodological dimension of research, represented in Figure 3, with the intentional dimension, represented in Figure 4. Figure 5 disambiguates these dimensions by presenting them as orthogonal to each other. The result is a two-dimensional metascientific space, with different areas corresponding to different types of research. A single study is represented as a point in this space because it adopts one particular methodology and was conducted with one primary purpose in mind. Accordingly, a research programme consisting of a sequence of studies is represented as a trajectory connecting together a number of points in the space. Figure 5 provides several important insights.

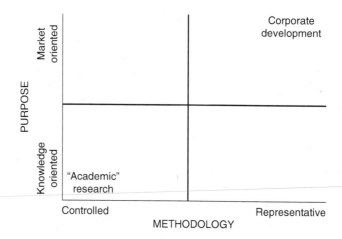

FIGURE 5   A novel framework consisting of a two-dimensional research space that is constructed using the two continua in figures 3 and 4.

First, it can be seen why there has traditionally been a gap between so-called basic and applied research. In the behavioural sciences, at least, most academic research and corporate development have been conducted at diametrically opposite corners of the space. Thus, these activities have differed both methodologically and intentionally. Traditional academic research has been knowledge-oriented and highly controlled, but unrepresentative. Corporate development has been market-oriented and highly representative, but uncontrolled. No wonder the former has had a limited impact on the latter in terms of technology transfer.

Secondly, one can also see that there are certain areas of the space that have been comparatively unexplored, at least in the ergonomics science community. For instance, the upper left corner of Figure 5 represents research that is market-oriented and controlled, but unrepresentative. An example would be marketing research (e.g. a focus group) that is aimed at discovering what features potential customers might want to have in a consumer product. The benefit of this type of research is perhaps more obvious to the interests of industry (e.g. to determine what features should be eliminated from an overly complex design). However, as will be discussed below, this area of the space can also benefit academe. The lower right corner has also been comparatively unexplored, although recent research in naturalistic decision making is helping to fill this gap (Klein et al., 1993; Zsambok and Klein, 1997). The interesting feature of this area of the space is that it explicitly shows that knowledge-oriented research can be conducted in the field, not just in the laboratory (Lorenz, 1973; Woods, 1993; Hutchins, 1995). This fact contradicts the more traditional view that research that is conducted under representative conditions is inherently applied, a view that probably arises from a failure to distinguish between research methodology and research purpose. Figure 5 shows the limitations of such a view by showing that these two dimensions are actually orthogonal to each other.

Thirdly, and perhaps most importantly of all, the space in Figure 5 also shows that research programmes can benefit from visiting different areas of the research space *in particular orders*. Several prototypical examples are shown as trajectories in Figure 6. Beginning in the upper left corner, *market-driven* research can be initiated by a market need that has been identified by interviewing customers (e.g. identifying what types of information companies would like to have in their control rooms) and

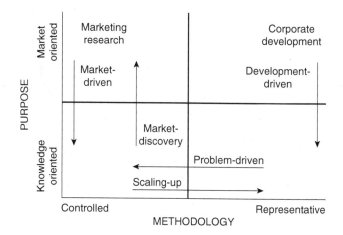

FIGURE 6   Types of research programmes that have been comparatively unexplored in human factors, mapped as trajectories in the space in figure 5.

then subsequently using that need as a focus for conducting knowledge-oriented controlled experiments (e.g. on the technical properties of new sensors that could provide the desired information; cf. Reising and Sanderson, 1996). Conversely, *market-discovery* research can be initiated by first conducting controlled experiments to contribute to understanding and then subsequently canvassing people in industry to determine if the knowledge or technology that has been generated can satisfy an existing or future market need.

Moving to the bottom of Figure 6, *problem-driven* research can be conducted by first observing and describing phenomena under naturalistic conditions to identify a research problem that is worth solving, and then subsequently conducting controlled experiments to understand the factors contributing to that problem in a rigorous manner. Conversely, *scaling-up* research can be conducted by taking the theories and results obtained from controlled experimentation and using them to design more representative but less controlled studies, to see if those theories and results generalize to situations that are typical of those encountered in the field.

Moving to the upper right corner of Figure 6, *development-driven* research can be conducted by using corporate design activities as an opportunity to understand the fundamental principles that govern the interaction between people, technology, and work in the field (Woods et al., 1996). Although design activities are usually highly opportunistic and idiosyncratic, they do have the benefit of usually being highly representative. Thus, if the requisite time and resources are available, it may be possible to examine successive design iterations from a theoretical perspective to extract lessons learned that may be generalized to other contexts. Such principles would represent a contribution to knowledge because they would provide a theoretical basis for making predictions, for instance, about the impact of particular technological interventions on human performance *in situ*.

Figure 5 could probably also be used to map other types of research programmes, conceivably even for other areas of science and engineering. However, the prototypical examples traced in Figure 6 should suffice to make the point. Ergonomics scientists have not yet made full use of the research opportunities that are available to them. This may help explain why an integration between basic and applied concerns has been hard to come by.

5. Implications

The key implication arising from Figures 5 and 6 is that, by exploring several areas of the research space within the same research programme, it is possible to conduct research that contributes to a fundamental understanding, while also contributing to the solution of practical problems of social significance. In short, a Jeffersonian research programme for ergonomics science is a viable pursuit. To achieve this ideal, however, certain conditions must be met.

5.1. Pre-conditions for a Jeffersonian research programme

First, it is necessary to explore areas of the space in Figure 5 that have typically been under-represented in ergonomics science. Several examples were given in Figure 6 to show that these types of research can be put to good use. If one sticks to the traditional, diametrically opposed corners of traditional academic research and corporate development, then one is likely to keep getting what has been had in the past—an unfortunate gap between fundamental research and practical problems of social significance. For an inherently applied discipline like ergonomics science, this is an unacceptable state of affairs (Meister, 1989). Opening up the degrees of freedom in research programmes can be of tremendous benefit by providing a tighter coupling between basic and applied concerns.

Secondly, there must also be methodological diversity within the same research programme. Ergonomics scientists have tended to stick to a consistent methodology within a research programme (e.g. a sequence of highly controlled experiments, or a sequence of naturalistic field studies). In doing so, they do not escape the limitations of that methodology, or conversely, they do not enjoy the complementary benefits of other methodologies. Through methodological diversity, we can overcome these problems and cut through Hammond's Law.

For instance, one model for a research programme that exploits the benefits of methodological diversity has been described by Sheridan and Hennessy (1984). Field studies can be used to observe behavior *in situ* to identify phenomena that are worthwhile studying under more controlled conditions. Laboratory studies can then be conducted under more controlled conditions to try and develop causal explanations for the observed phenomena. The generalizability of these causal explanations can then be tested under more representative conditions by conducting experiments that are complex in nature, say with microworlds. Finally, a theory or design intervention can be evaluated in high-fidelity simulators or in the field, in the presence of a wide range of factors that had been controlled for or eliminated in the laboratory, to see if the same results are still obtained.

5.2. An example of a Jeffersonian research programme

The research programme on translucent human–computer interfaces mentioned earlier is an example of the application of this model (Harrison et al., 1994, 1995a,b; Harrison and Vicente, 1996a,b). Figure 7 shows the trajectory representing the sequence of studies that was conducted as a part of this Jeffersonian research programme.

The first (unpublished) phase was to observe users interacting with a commercially available 3-D modelling and paint application *in situ,* to identify a practical problem that could serve as a worthwhile subject for

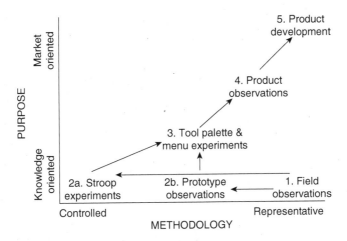

FIGURE 7   The trajectory approximately describing the process followed by Harrison and colleagues in their research programme investigating translucency in human–computer interface design.

knowledge-oriented research (point #1 in the space). Harrison and colleagues found that users spent a great deal of time managing interface objects rather than accomplishing productive work. This finding provided a focus for all subsequent research. The idea of using translucency to address this practical problem was generated, and two paths were followed in parallel to explore this option (Harrison et al., 1994, 1995a). On the highly controlled end, the impact of translucency on the Stroop (1935) effect was investigated experimentally (point #2a in the space). The Stroop effect is a well-known phenomenon that has been extensively studied in experimental psychology. In a traditional Stroop task, a series of words is presented in randomly chosen colours (e.g. red, green, blue, yellow). Participants must name the ink colour while ignoring the word. Some words are neutral (e.g. uncle, shoe, cute, nail), whereas other words are the names of conflicting colours (e.g. yellow, blue, green, red). Consistent, significant performance degradation occurs when conflicting colour words are used and participants attempt to name the colour of the ink (e.g. the word "red" appears in green ink; the correct response is "green"). In later studies, a consistent and significant Stroop effect was found even when the word was printed in black ink, presented adjacent to a colour bar. It is virtually impossible for participants to consciously block or prevent the Stroop effect in selective looking tasks. The idea was that this would provide a worst case estimate of the translucency level representing a balance between foreground and background legibility. If one could eliminate interference in the notoriously interference-prone Stroop task, then one would have a conservative estimate of the lower bound of translucency level that would be appropriate for more representative stimuli. Interestingly, this experiment made a novel contribution to fundamental understanding because the effect of transparency on the Stroop effect had never been investigated before, despite the fact that over 700 studies had been conducted using this paradigm (see MacLeod, 1991, for a review)! At the same time, more representative interface prototypes were created to observe the effects of translucency with real images and foregrounds (point #2b in the space). These observations were conducted informally, thereby giving up experimental control. Nevertheless, they provided some useful fundamental insights into the impact of translucency on human performance in divided and focused attention tasks.

As shown in Figure 7, the insights obtained from these activities fed into a third stage of research. The results from the Stroop and prototyping studies were used to design less-controlled experiments using more representative stimuli (point #3 in the space). One set of experiments was conducted to evaluate the impact of translucency level with typical tool palettes like that shown in Figure 1 (Harrison et al., 1995b). Another set of experiments was conducted to evaluate the impact of translucency level with text menus like that shown in Figure 2 (Harrison and Vicente, 1996a). These studies were conducted, in part, to further understanding of the impact of translucency on human performance (a knowledge-oriented purpose), and, in part, to further understanding of how translucency should be implemented in commercial software products (a market-oriented purpose).

The results from these studies were used to modify an existing 3-D modelling and paint application so that it would incorporate translucency (Harrison and Vicente, 1996b). A representative set of users was then asked to work with the product for a few weeks, and their reactions and experiences were recorded (point #4 in the space). A great deal of experimental control was given up, but the situation investigated was much more representative of work conditions. The primary purpose was to determine how translucency should be implemented in a commercial product, given the stringent limitations of the existing technology (a market-oriented purpose). At the same time, however, more was also learned about the impact of translucency on human performance under representative conditions (a knowledge-oriented purpose). Finally, the insights obtained from these observations guided a product development phase of work (point #5 in the space). Translucency was implemented in a new version of a commercially available 3-D modelling and paint application, thereby successfully completing the technology transfer cycle.

This type of two-fold contribution to fundamental understanding and to the design of a commercially available product is relatively rare in the ergonomics science literature. Although it is difficult to prove it, the author believes that this atypical success can be attributed, in large part, to the unique advantages of the Jeffersonian research programme that was adopted as a basis for this work.

5.3. A pluralistic wrinkle

The case study just described is only one model for achieving a tighter integration of theory and practice. Ergonomics science can only benefit from a pluralistic approach. Thus, to avoid any misunderstandings, it is important to point out explicitly that the Jeffersonian programme is intended to be broadly inclusive. For example, the integration of "basic" and "applied" concerns that have been focused on in this article need not occur within the work of a single individual. It could very well occur across the work of various individuals, some who are solely concerned with market development and others who are solely concerned with fundamental knowledge, for instance. In other words, not all ergonomics scientists need to be concerned with both market- and knowledge-oriented purposes. There is no reason why, in some cases, different individuals can not focus on particular areas of Figure 5 where their unique skill sets can be put to greatest use. Having said that, at some point, someone has to take on the responsibility of bringing together the isolated contributions of such individual specialists for a particular area of research. Otherwise, Jeffersonian integration will not be achieved, and it will continue to be difficult to satisfy the two-fold objectives of ergonomics science.

6. Conclusions

This article has sought to clarify the distinction between basic and applied research in ergonomics science. A novel metascientific framework consisting of a two-dimensional research space has been proposed by explicitly separating research methodology from research purpose. The framework helps explain why there has not been a tight coupling between basic and applied concerns. More importantly, the resulting space also opens up degrees of freedom for research that have been comparatively unexplored. By making full use of various research methodologies within a single research programme, it is possible to realize a Jeffersonian research programme that contributes to fundamental understanding and practical problems at the same time. A case study on translucency in human-computer interface design provides a concrete example, showing that this type of work can lead to achievements that have been difficult to obtain using more traditional approaches to ergonomics science.

In closing, the author would like to emphasize a broader positive feature of the Jeffersonian research programme that goes well beyond ergonomics science. In times of scarce research funding, it will be increasingly important to demonstrate to the public and to government that scientists in every discipline can contribute to fundamental understanding and address considerations of use in the same research programme. As Stokes (1997: 81) put it:

> Freed from the false, "either–or" logic of the traditional basic/applied distinction, individual scientists would more generally see that applied goals are not inherently at war with scientific creativity and rigour, and their overseers and funders would more generally see that the thrust toward basic understanding is not inherently at war with considerations of use.

Therefore, the Jeffersonian programme may be just what ergonomics science and other branches of science and engineering need to survive and succeed in the face of the stringent economic constraints that are sometimes imposed by science policy.

7. Postscript

Although the metascientific framework in Figure 5 is novel, the general philosophy of a Jeffersonian research programme is not entirely new to ergonomics science. As a reviewer of this article pointed out, some of the best work in the discipline has already followed this general approach. A balanced attention to fundamental understanding and practical problems can be found in the research of several founding fathers of ergonomics science, including Broadbent, Christensen, and Fitts, to mention just a few. However, somewhere along the way, the value of this type of research seems to have been overlooked. Most contemporary research programmes in ergonomics science would not qualify as Jeffersonian. For this reason, it seems worthwhile to revisit the insights of one's founding fathers by providing an explicit metascientific framework that can help one obtain a fuller understanding of nature while simultaneously addressing a persistent social problem of national or global interest.

Acknowledgements

This article is based on a keynote address presented at the Scaled Worlds '99 conference held at the University of Georgia in Athens, GA on 24–27 June 1999. I would like to thank Rob Mahan for giving me the opportunity to make that presentation. This research was sponsored in part by a research grant from the Natural Sciences and Engineering Research Council of Canada. I would like to thank reviewers, Renée Chow, John Hajdukiewicz, and Greg Jamieson for their helpful and thorough comments.

References

Baker, S. and Marshall, E. 1988, Evaluating the man-machine interface–the search for data, in J. Patrick and K. D. Duncan (eds.), *Training, human decision making and control* (Amsterdam: Elsevier), 79–92.

Banaji, M. R. and Crowder, R. G. 1991, Some everyday thoughts on ecologically valid methods, *American Psychologist*, 46, 78–79.

Brehmer, B. and Dörner, D. 1993, Experiments with computer-simulated microworlds: Escaping both the narrow straits of the laboratory and the deep blue sea of the field study, *Computers in Human Behaviour*, 9, 171–184.

Brunswik, E. 1952, *The conceptual framework of psychology* (Chicago, IL: University of Chicago Press).

Brunswik, E. 1956, *Perception and the representative design of psychological experiments*, 2nd edn. (Berkeley, CA: University of California Press).

Chapanis, A. 1967, The relevance of laboratory studies to practical situations, *Ergonomics*, 10, 557–577.

Christoffersen, K., Hunter, C. N. and Vicente, K. J. 1996, A longitudinal study of the effects of ecological interface design on skill acquisition, *Human Factors*, 38, 523–541.

Christoffersen, K., Hunter, C. N. and Vicente, K. J. 1997, A longitudinal study of the effects of ecological interface design on fault management performance, *International Journal of Cognitive Ergonomics*, 1, 1–24.

Christoffersen, K., Hunter, C. N. and Vicente, K. J. 1998, A longitudinal study of the effects of ecological interface design on deep knowledge, *International Journal of Human-Computer Studies*, 48, 729–762.

Cook, T. D. and Campbell, D. T. 1979, *Quasi-experimentation: Design and analysis issues for field settings* (Boston: Houghton-Mifflin).

Doherty, M. E. 1993, A laboratory scientist's view of naturalistic decision making, in G. A. Klein, J. Qrasanu, R. Calderwood and C. Zsambok (eds.), *Decision making in action: Models and methods* (Norwood, NJ: Ablex), 362–388.

Gibson, J. J. 1967/1982, James J. Gibson autobiography, in E. Reed and R. Jones (eds.), *Reasons for realism: Selected essays of James J. Gibson* (Hillsdale, NJ: Erlbaum), 7–22.

Gould, J. D., Alfaro, L., Barnes, V., Finn, R., Grischkowsky, N. and Minuto, A. 1987, Reading is slower from CRT displays than from paper: Attempts to isolate a single-variable explanation, *Human Factors*, 29, 269–299.

Hajdukiewicz, J. R. and Vicente, K. J., 2000, Ecological interface design: Adaptation to dynamic perturbations, in *Proceedings of the Fifth Annual Conference on Human Interaction with Complex Systems* (Urbana, IL: University of Illinois, Beckman Institute), 69–73.

Hammond, K. R. 1989, What is naturalism? Why do we need it? How will we get it? *Paper presented at Workshop on Naturalistic Decision,* Yellow Springs, OH, 25–27 September.

Harrison, B. L. and Vicente, K. J. 1996a, An experimental evaluation of transparent menu usage, in *Human Factors in Computing Systems: CHI '96 Conference Proceedings* (New York: ACM), 391–398.

Harrison, B. L. and Vicente, K. J. 1996b, A case study of transparent user interfaces in a commercial 3-d modeling and paint application, in *Proceedings of the Human Factors and Ergonomics Society 40th Annual Meeting* (Santa Monica, CA: HFES), 375–379.

Harrison, B.L., Ishii, H., Vicente, K. J. and Buxton, W. A. S. 1995a, Transparent layered user interfaces: An evaluation of a display design to enhance focused and divided attention, in *Human Factors in Computing Systems: CHI '95 Conference Proceedings* (New York: ACM), 317–324.

Harrison, B. L., Kurtenbach, G. and Vicente, K. J. 1995b, An experimental evaluation of transparent user interface tools and information content, in *Proceedings of the ACM Symposium on User Interface Software and Technology* (New York: ACM), 81–90.

Harrison, B. L., Zhai, S., Vicente, K. J. and Buxton, B. 1994, *Designing and evaluating semi-transparent 'silk' user interface objects: Supporting focused and divided attention* (CEL 94-08) (Toronto: University of Toronto, Cognitive Engineering Laboratory).

Holton, G. 1993, *Science and anti-science* (Cambridge, MA: Harvard University Press).

Hutchins, E. 1995, *Cognition in the wild* (Cambridge, MA: MIT Press).

Kelso, J. A. S. 1995, *Dynamic patterns: The self-organization of brain and behavior* (Cambridge, MA: MIT Press).

Kirlik, A., 2000, Conducting generalizable research in the age of the field study, in *Proceedings of the Human Factors and Ergonomics Society 44th Annual Meeting* (Santa Monica, CA: HFES), in press.

Klein, G. A., Orasanu, J., Calderwood, R. and Zsambok, C. 1993, *Decision making in action: Models and methods* (Norwood, NJ: Ablex).

Koch, A. and Peden, W. 1993, *The life and selected writings of Thomas Jefferson* (New York: Random House).

Lorenz, K. Z. 1973, The fashionable fallacy of dispensing with description, *Die Naturwissenschaften, 60,* 1–9.

MacLeod, CM. 1991, Half a century of research on the Stroop effect: An integrative review, *Psychological Bulletin, 109,* 163–203.

Meister, D. 1989, *Conceptual aspects of human factors* (Baltimore: Johns Hopkins University Press).

Neisser, U. 1976, *Cognition and reality: Principles and implications of cognitive psychology* (New York: Freeman).

Reising, D. V. and Sanderson, P. M. 1996, Work domain analysis of a pasteurization plant: Building an abstraction hierarchy representation, in *Proceedings of the Human Factors and Ergonomics Society 40th Annual Meeting* (Santa Monica, CA: Human Factors and Ergonomics Society), 293–297.

Rouse, W. B. 1985, On better mousetraps and basic research: Getting the applied world to the laboratory door, *IEEE Transactions on Systems, Man, and Cybernetics, SMC-15,* 2–8.

Sheridan, T. B. and Hennessy, R. T. 1984, *Research and modeling of supervisory control behavior* (Washington, DC: National Academy Press).

Shiffrin, R. M. 1996, Laboratory experimentation on the genesis of expertise, in K. A. Ericsson (ed.), *The road to excellence: The acquisition of expert performance in the arts and sciences, sports and games* (Mahwah, NJ: Erlbaum), 337–345.

Stokes, D. E. 1997, *Pasteur's quadrant: Basic science and technological innovation* (Washington, DC: Brookings Institution Press).

Stroop, J. R. 1935, Factors affecting speed in serial verbal reactions, *Journal of Experimental Psychology*, 18, 643–662.

Vicente, K. J. 1994, A pragmatic conception of basic and applied research: Commentary on Hoffman and Deffenbacher (1993), *Ecological Psychology*, 6, 65–81.

Vicente, K. J. 1997, Heeding the legacy of Meister, Brunswik, and Gibson: Toward a broader view of human factors research, *Human Factors*, 39, 323–328.

Vicente, K. J., in press, Cognitive engineering research at Riso from 1962-1979, in E. Salas (ed.), *Human/technology interaction in complex systems* (Stanford, CT: JAI Press), in press.

Vicente, K. J. and Burns, C. M. 1996, Evidence for direct perception from cognition in the wild, *Ecological Psychology*, 8, 269–280.

Woods, D. D. 1993, Process-tracing methods for the study of cognition outside of the experimental psychology laboratory, in G. A. Klein, J. Orasanu, R. Calderwood and C. Zsambok (eds.), *Decision making in action: Models and methods* (Norwood, NJ: Ablex), 228–251.

Woods, D. D., Patterson, E. S., Corban, J. M. and Watts, J. C. 1996, Bridging the gap between user-centered intentions and actual design practice, in *Proceedings of the Human Factors and Ergonomics Society 40th Annual Meeting* (Santa Monica, CA: HFES), 967–971.

Woods, D. D., Wise, J. A. and Hanes, L. F. 1982, *Evaluation of safety parameter display concepts: Volume 1* (Final Report NP-2239) (Palo Alto, CA: Electric Power Research Institute).

Zhang, J. and Norman, D. A. 1994, Representations in distributed cognitive tasks, *Cognitive Science*, 18, 87–122.

Zsambok, C. E. and Klein, G. 1997, *Naturalistic decision making* (Mahwah, NJ: Erlbaum).

Zwicky, F. 1967, The morphological approach to discovery, invention, research and construction, in F. Zwicky and A. G. Wilson (eds.), *New methods of thought and procedure* (Berlin: Springer-Verlag), 273–297.

4

Inventing Possibilities

Understanding Work Systems and Tasks

Alex Kirlik

> *Philosophically, one of the deepest discussions in the book is Neiman's*
> *appropriation of Kant's doctrine of freedom. This is a notoriously treacherous*
> *area, but Neiman correctly aligns it with the human capacity for noticing or*
> *inventing (it does not necessarily matter which) possibilities for action. As well*
> *as whatever is the case, we have what might be the case, or what we could make*
> *come about, as well as what ought to be the case. Freedom, in the sphere of action,*
> *is therefore associated with a refusal to accept that what is the case limits and*
> *constrains our possibility for doing the other thing, surprising the psychologist,*
> *as it were.*
>
> Simon Blackburn (2008), Review of Moral clarity:
A Guide for Grown-Up Idealists, by Susan Neiman

Today's human–technology interaction (HTI) researchers and practitioners are increasingly involved in designing novel opportunities for human action and interaction. A core aspect of Vicente's Human-tech approach is that one cannot do so successfully if one limits one's analysis to solely "whatever is the case." In HTI, there is a term for whatever is the case, and that term is *task analysis*, some type of formalized understanding of how people, often experts, go about getting some task accomplished. But design requires us to also consider "what might be the case, or what we could make come about, as well as what out to be the case." Analysis must transcend the study of current practice.

For this purpose, Vicente created the notion of *work domain analysis*, a description of the environment of human work that is complete, yet does not specify the particular tasks a person might perform to achieve his or her goals (also see Bisantz and Burns, 2009). In the article reprinted in this chapter, Hajdukiewicz and Vicente attempt to clarify the distinction between task analysis and work domain analysis, yet show how they interrelate.

I believe Hajdukiewicz and Vicente are correct on the need to maintain a firm distinction between a task analysis, and the analysis and modeling of the system or environment in which a person is performing (in their terms, a "work domain analysis"). So much of the current literature in HTI presumes that, if you want to better support practitioners in some domain, the first thing you need to do is to interview, survey, etc., expert practitioners themselves.

But this approach often starts too far downstream from where one has real design leverage, because one can learn only how practitioners have adapted to the technology through which they currently view their work. They may have no better insights than do novices on the possibilities that might be made available if the mediating technology was designed differently. An analogy is asking a person how to get from point A to point B in a city. If you ask a bike rider, you will get one answer; if you ask a taxi driver, you will get another; and from a subway rider, yet another. But it's the same city—by analogy to HTI, the same "work domain." The answers (your three "task analyses") differ because the three experts in question are using different technologies to mediate their interaction with this domain.

Now, assume you have the job of designing an entirely new form of transportation to help people navigate that city. How helpful is it to know what the bike rider, taxi driver, and subway rider have told you? One can imagine a useful nugget here or there. But a far better starting point is the city map and a representation of any infrastructure that places constraints on acceptable transportation technologies. And, in some cases (the design of future systems for which no expert practitioners yet exist), the expert-interviewing approach is clearly impossible.

In their article, Hajdukiewicz and Vicente do a nice job of making the distinction between task and domain analyses in the context of a laboratory microworld simulation of a power plant. In particular, they provide a good demonstration of how task and work domain analyses are distinct, yet related. However, for readers with backgrounds in primarily psychology or cognitive science, it could be useful to understand how these forms of analysis and modeling relate to more familiar and accessible notions in the literature on cognitive modeling.

For example, it is possible to draw an analogy between Newell and Simon's (1972) "problem spaces" (originally, models of the external task environment—mainly, puzzles and games) and work domain analysis and modeling. In the introduction to their (1972) *Human Problem Solving* book, Newell and Simon noted their debt to Tolman and Brunswik's (1935) *Psychological Review* article, "The Organism and the Causal Texture of the Environment." They did so because they realized that they needed to model the external, environmental constraints on, and opportunities for, behavior that an environment presents to a problem solver. This was the original function performed by their problem spaces, as models of the problem solver's *external* task environment. For Hajdukiewicz and Vicente, this function is performed instead by a hierarchical work domain analysis, a technique inspired by Rasmussen's abstraction hierarchy representation.

Functionally, though, the concepts are similar. Hajdukiewicz and Vicente show how, via a series of transformations, one can move from a work domain analysis to a task analysis (a sequence of actions necessary to achieve a goal), once both initial and goal states are specified. Newell and Simon did likewise. After hand-crafting their problem space representations, Newell and Simon then applied their *general problem solver* algorithm (largely, backward chaining) to derive a sequence of actions that would move an initial state of, say, the Tower of Hanoi to a goal state. Unfortunately, however, cognitive science research in the spirit of Newell and Simon's pioneering work then mis-stepped a bit (for at least 10 or so years) by failing to sufficiently maintain a clear distinction between problem spaces as models of external task environments and problem spaces as internal mental representations.

This led to the well-known "cognitive science has become the psychology of the disembodied intellect" criticism leveled by Donald Norman in the early 1980s. Norman and his student Zhang (Zhang and Norman, 1994) repaired the situation through the use of a clever set of experiments in which they kept the representation of the external task environment clearly separate from what was going on in the head (also see Kotovsky and Simon, 1990). Zhang and Norman constructed different "interfaces" (or isomorphs) for one in the same Tower of Hanoi puzzle by dressing up the problems in different ways. For example, one constraint that is represented in the problem-space model of the Tower of Hanoi is that one cannot put a larger disk upon a smaller disk. Zhang and Norman redesigned the proximal appearance (i.e. the interface design) to the Tower of Hanoi, keeping the puzzle's proximal–distal structure intact. For example, by using teacups instead of disks, participants in their experiments could literally see that they could not put a larger cup on "top" of a smaller cup, and by doing so, they essentially offloaded the obligation to remember and obey this constraint from the problem solver's head to the external world.

One question that arises when pondering this reprint is where and when it is more productive to begin an HTI research project with task analysis as opposed to a work domain analysis. It would seem to depend on the degrees of design freedom available: what has already been fixed in stone and what options are open to influence from HTI—and, also, a prioritization or assessment of the risks associated with not exploring the full space of design options, or of failing to choose wisely among them (see Pew and Mavor, 2007).

Ideally, of course, the design of both technology and human tasks collectively and mutually evolves in collaboration between designers and end users, in what has sometimes been called "participatory design" (Schuler and Namioka, 1993). That is, in the best case, both one's task analysis and work domain analysis are able to co-evolve in a mutually informing manner. Although getting end users involved in the design process continues to remain a challenge in many research-and-development projects, it is hardly a new idea, hardly "rocket science." But it did put a man on the moon (from Sheridan and Gerovitch, 2003):

> **Gerovitch:** Now let's talk about the Apollo project. How did you get involved in it?
>
> **Sheridan:** Jim Nevins, who was the first author on the paper you have [Nevins, Johnson, and Sheridan, 1968; "Man-Machine Allocation in the Apollo Navigation, Guidance and Control System"] was running a small group at Instrumentation Laboratory, which was looking at the human interaction needed for the lunar mission. Stark Draper was originally a regular professor at MIT, in the Aeronautics Department. Then, his laboratory with graduate students got so big, and they were taking on such large contracts, that they broke off from MIT proper. His graduate students

became the team leaders of this operation. They were developing gyroscopes, initially. Those early gyroscopes were used for military systems, to navigate aircraft, and in missile systems. This seemed an obvious way to guide a space rocket to the Moon. Richard Battin, who was one of the senior people in developing space navigation, is still active over in the Aeronautics Department. Battin and Wallace Vandervelde were two early Draper Lab people still active at MIT. . . . Harold Lanning was senior to Battin. The two developed some of the early software for the Apollo system. They were limited to a very small-memory computer. It was incredible what they were doing with that tiny (by comparison to today) computer. Also, it became clear that, for astronauts to interact with that computer, even to do simple things, they had to key-in programs, which was a very different experience for astronauts than flying an airplane. The original astronauts were pilots, and they were used to controlling vehicles by joysticks and pedals. Punching buttons was something that was very strange to them. Programming a computer, punching buttons on a console was something they knew nothing about.

I was then an assistant professor, and I was invited to this group as a consultant. They were looking for someone who knew about human–machine interaction. Draper Lab got the contract to build the guidance and navigation system for Apollo. That system went both into mother ship, the command module, and into the lunar excursion module, the ship that dropped from orbit down to the Moon. That was a big contract. Draper Lab expanded rapidly at that time; they occupied a new building. I can well remember the very first group of astronauts—mostly new Apollo astronauts, but some of the Gemini astronauts were present, too—had a meeting with us to consider the astronaut tasks. Eventually, they had some very fancy simulators to use for design and training, but before we had a simulator, we took the drawings of the design for the console and pasted them on the wall in a small room, and this became our simulator. We said: "Here are the programming procedures you're going to follow." We had the astronauts punching pieces of paper on the wall as a dummy computer simulator.

Gerovitch: Did you register whether they punched correctly or incorrectly at this point?

Sheridan: Early on, no. Eventually, we mechanized it. There came to be some instruments they had to use to navigate—optical instruments, for example, a telescope and a sextant. Those became more than just paper; they weren't quite the real thing, but they were working devices that we attached to the wall. We went from paper to plywood with actual instruments, and eventually worked our way up to the full development technology. Later, we had several other crews of astronauts come in and use these devices to navigate.

At that point, we were taking measurements. One of the things we found was very interesting. First, before we invited the astronauts in, we had the engineers and the secretaries trying it. It was regarded as a fun thing, like a computer game. Everybody wanted to try and see what they could do. So, we got data on the in-house engineers and the secretaries. We thought the astronauts would probably do a little bit better, but on the whole be pretty much the same. But I was astounded that they really were very much better at these tasks. I didn't expect it at all.

One night, we were in the lab with several astronauts, and I had my then 11-year-old son along, and introduced him to the astronauts. Because his father was into this, he was all excited about space. About two or three weeks later, there was a fire in the Apollo capsule during training that killed the whole crew. I recall that my son could not go to school for a whole week, he was so upset by this.

Gerovitch: Were the astronauts who died among those who had worked on the simulator?

Sheridan: Yes, several of those astronauts my son had met. It was quite a traumatic event for him, and of course for others, too.

Gerovitch: Was the purpose of those simulations to train people to use the computer or to improve the design of the computer?

Sheridan: Both. Initially, it was primarily to verify design, to make sure that all the procedures were proper and that everything worked, and to familiarize the astronauts with what it would be, so the astronauts could make comments: I don't like this placed here, I think this procedure looks strange, and so on. We were working with the astronauts in the design phase. Later on, there was some training, but final training really moved down to Houston, where, eventually, there were full training simulators. So, primarily our early simulators were for design and verification purposes.

Gerovitch: Do you recall any specific comments the astronauts made about things they liked or didn't like?

Sheridan: I don't really. One of my jobs that seems very trivial now was the keypad layout for the Apollo computer. We are now accustomed to a telephone keypad, which looks like this:

$$1 \quad 2 \quad 3$$
$$4 \quad 5 \quad 6$$
$$7 \quad 8 \quad 9$$

At the time, that telephone keypad didn't exist. There was a rotary dial. A telephone company was just then experimenting with the pushbutton kind, but it was not in production. Some older calculators started with the bottom:

$$7 \quad 8 \quad 9$$
$$4 \quad 5 \quad 6$$
$$1 \quad 2 \quad 3$$

We had this question: Which way should we arrange the keyboard? We did experiments and had the astronauts try it. It turned out, it really didn't make much difference. They could handle it either way. In the end, we knew the telephone company was going to put out [the former arrangement]; they were closing on this design, so we said we'd just go with that. That wasn't rocket science, but it was something that we had to do.

And there were some really fun aspects. There were questions whether the astronauts could properly line up in front of the sight while in the space suit and helmet and not move too much. If you were bouncing around or moving, you'd lose track of the stars or the Moon. You had to look at the edge of the Moon and then get the star and see how far above the horizon the star was. This looked like a wonderful excuse to take a ride in the zero-gravity airplane called the "vomit comet." We arranged for that, and again, while the test wasn't very profound, everything worked okay, there was no big problem. But we had wonderful time experiencing zero gravity. I took several rides. You can push off and float through space, or do back flips. It gives you about 30–40 seconds of zero gravity. The aircraft dives to the ground, and then you're pinned to the floor of the airplane, and then it does a large parabola. You have 2 g's, then zero, then again 2 g's at the end. I had a good time. Like so much research: you do it partly because it's important, partly because it's fun. Maybe in some cases, more because it's fun than because it's important.

Gerovitch: Did you work mostly on the keyboard and sighting devices, or did you touch on larger issues, like allocation of function between human and machine on board?

Sheridan: The allocation of function at that time was not done by any great scientific method. It was done in committee discussions: Do you think we can have the astronaut do this or that? What would the difficulties be? We were starting from scratch; nobody had done these things before. We thought about airplanes, and we consulted people who knew about airplanes—and we extrapolated to space. The astronauts themselves were experienced pilots. They had a fairly large say in how things were designed, at least from the human factors point of view. That seemed to be realistic, because we had no experience with space. At least one could blame them if it didn't work! In large measure it was a matter of consulting with them on making decisions concerning allocation questions and then setting up simulations to test it out to see if it would work.

A Theoretical Note on the Relationship Between Work Domain Analysis and Task Analysis

John R. Hajdukiewicz and Kim J. Vicente

Abstract

The purpose of this note is to clarify the theoretical relationship between work domain analysis and task analysis, two classes of techniques that

have been used by cognitive engineers to identify information requirements for systems design. The transformation from a work domain analysis to a task analysis (i.e. from a description of the object of control to a
description of control itself) can be conceived as a discrete set of transformations. Work domain analysis identifies the set of all structural
degrees of freedom that are available to any actor. Only a subset of these
will be relevant for a particular context. At any particular point in time,
actors will have to choose which of these relevant degrees of freedom to
utilize. Finally, the utilized degrees of freedom will have a dynamic state
that can usually be described quantitatively. Task analysis is the function
that maps current states onto desired states via a set of human or automated control actions. By making these transformations explicit, the
relevance of work domain analysis to worker (or automation) goals and
actions becomes more clear.

1. Introduction

Cognitive engineers are all familiar with *task analysis* and the role that it
can play in identifying information requirements (Kirwan and Ainsworth,
1992). *Work domain analysis* is a less familiar technique that also aims to
inform systems design and that is receiving an increasing amount of attention (Rasmussen et al., 1994; Vicente, 1999a; Naikar and Sanderson, 1999).
It is important to understand the relationship between these two types of
techniques so that both researchers and designers have a better idea of
their relative advantages and disadvantages for systems design. Several
attempts have been made to compare task analysis and work domain
analysis theoretically (e.g. Vicente 1999a, 1999b). However, these attempts
have not been as clear or as thorough as they could, and should, have
been. In particular, the generalized set of discrete transformations that
link work domain analysis and task analysis have not been fully clarified
in previous work. Consequently, there is still some uncertainty about the
relationship between the two techniques, even among experienced
researchers who have used work domain analysis in their work (e.g. Terrier
et al., 2000).

    The purpose of this note is to resolve this theoretical ambiguity.
First, a case study illustrating how it is possible to transition from a work

domain analysis to a task analysis for a representative laboratory micro-world will be provided. Second, the lessons learned from this case study will be generalized theoretically by induction so that they are applicable to other problem domains. This analysis will show that the relationship between work domain and task analysis can be generically conceived as a series of discrete transformations, each of which has a clear conceptual meaning. At one end, work domain analysis identifies information require-ments that are event- and time-*independent*, providing a robust basis for supporting worker adaptation to novelty and change. At the other end, task analysis identifies information requirements that are event- and time-*dependent*, providing an efficient basis for supporting worker perfor-mance to anticipated situations. The discrete transformations that con-nect these techniques are described, providing a stronger basis for understanding the relationship between work domain and task analysis. The end results are deeper insights into the utility of each technique and an understanding of the relevance of work domain analysis to worker (or automation) goals and actions.

2. Case study

The thermal-hydraulic process control microworld illustrated in Figure 1 will be used as the focus of the case study. This simulation consists of two feedwater systems, which can supply water to two reservoirs. Operators have control over eight valves (six input valves: VA, VB, VA1, VA2, VB1, VB2, and two output valves: VO1 and VO2), two pumps (PA and PB), and two heaters (HTR1 and HTR2) within the numerical ranges specified for each component. The operators are required to achieve the dual purposes of satisfying external, dynamic output demands for water (D1g and D2g) while maintaining each of the reservoirs at their respective temperature goals (T1g and T2g).

2.1. Task analysis

While there are many different ways of doing a task analysis, all of them deal with identifying the goals or actions that need to be pursued by an actor, whether it be a worker or automation. Figure 2 shows a normative

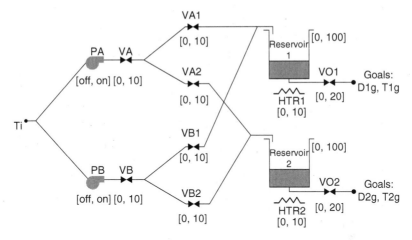

FIGURE 1   A schematic diagram of the process control microworld. The maximum and minimum ranges of each component are shown in square brackets. Adapted from Vicente and Rasmussen (1990).

sequential flow task analysis for starting up the process in Figure 1. This task requires the actor to take the process from a state where all of the components are off and the reservoirs are empty to a steady state where the demand and temperature goals for both reservoirs are all satisfied. If the goal to be achieved were a different one (e.g. shut down the process), then the results of the task analysis could be markedly different. Thus, task analysis is *event-dependent* (Vicente, 1999a). And because the goals that the operator is pursuing change over time, task analysis is also time-dependent.

To simplify the discussion, we will focus only on the mass flow and omit the energy flow aspects of the startup task. Starting from the top left of Figure 2, the actor will need to check the state of the work domain. If the target water demand exceeds the combined capacity of the two feedwater streams (i.e. 20 units/s of flow), then the task cannot be performed. Next, the states of the valves, pumps, and reservoirs are checked. If the process is totally shutdown, then VA, VA1, VA2, VB, VB1, VB2 must be opened to their maximum settings, then pumps PA and PB turned on. Next, the actor must check the level in the reservoir until it exceeds 20% of its capacity. At that point, the actor checks the operating demands again and sets the output valves (VO1 and VO2) to their respective

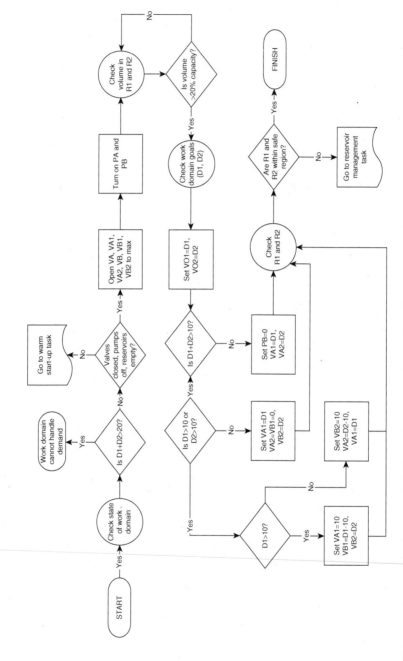

FIGURE 2　An example of a task analysis for starting up the microworld in figure 1.

demand values. Once set, the input valves and pumps need to be config-ured based on the specific demands. As discussed in more detail later, three categories of configurations are possible depending on the values of the demands ($D_1+D_2 \leq 10$; $D_1 + D_2 > 10$, D_1 and $D_2 < 10$; D_1 or $D_2 > 10$). After making the appropriate input valve and pump adjust-ments (see Figure 2), the levels in the reservoirs are checked to ensure that they are within a safe range. If they are, then the startup task is complete.

What is the relationship between this type of analysis—dealing with the familiar conceptual currency of actor goals, tasks, and actions—and a work domain analysis, which does not explicitly represent any of these constructs? To answer this question, we will begin by describing a work domain analysis for the process in Figure 1, and then show how, through a set of discrete transformations, it is possible to eventually connect back to the task description in Figure 2.

2.2. Complete work domain structure

A work domain is the ultimate object of action—the system being controlled, independent of any particular worker, automation, event, task, goal, or interface. Accordingly, work domain analysis identifies the struc-tural constraints associated with the equipment and its functional capa-bilities, showing all of the relevant action possibilities that align with the work domain purposes. Figure 3a provides an outline of the work domain analysis that was developed for the process in Figure 1 (Vicente and Rasmussen, 1990; Bisantz and Vicente, 1992). There are three levels of resolution in this space connected by part-whole links (System, Sub-system, and Component). Also, there are five levels of abstraction con-nected by structural means-ends links (Physical Form, Physical Function, Generalized Function, Abstract Function, and Functional Purpose). The bottom level of Physical Form is not used here because it refers to the physical location and appearance of the work domain, features that are not particularly meaningful in a microworld simulation.

Figure 3a shows that the abstraction and part–whole dimensions, while conceptually orthogonal, are coupled in practice. At higher levels of abstraction (e.g. Functional Purpose), participants tend to think of the work domain at a coarse level of resolution (e.g. System), whereas at lower levels of abstraction (e.g. Physical Function), participants tend to think of the work domain at a detailed level of resolution (e.g. Component). Thus, certain cells in the space are not very meaningful (e.g. Functional Purpose/Component). In the specific case of the process shown in Figure 3a, four cells were identified as being useful for the purposes of process control. Each of these cells contains a different representation of the same work domain. Figure 3b lists the variables associated with each representation, and specific structural (means-ends) links between adjacent levels of abstraction (Hajdukiewicz, 2000).

Accordingly, Figure 3 shows the structural opportunities for aligning action possibilities with the work domain purposes. Any path using these structural links can be used to achieve the stated purposes. This representation is *event-independent* in that it is not contingent on any particular situational context or state in time. Regardless of what the operator's goals happen to be and regardless of what is going on in the process at any particular moment, the structural relationships identified in Figure 3b are the ones that have been built into the process by designers. These action possibilities show the requisite variety of the work domain (Ashby, 1956), and thus represent an unavoidable bedrock of constraint that must be taken into account by any actor, worker or automation.

This event-independence can be made more concrete by developing a phase diagram for each of the levels of abstraction identified in Figure 3. For example, Figure 4 shows a partial phase diagram for the level of Abstract Function for one of the two reservoirs. The horizontal axis represents the mass level (M) and the vertical axis represents its gradient (dM/dt = MI [Mass Input Rate] − MO[Mass Output Rate]). The constraint boundaries are derived from the physical and safety constraints of the process. For example, the pumps and valves have a limited capacity (see Figure 1), defining maximum and minimum values for dM/dt representing how quickly the reservoir level can be increased or decreased, respectively. Similarly, the reservoir has a limited capacity (see Figure 1), defining a maximum value for M representing how much water can be stored without spilling over. These work domain constraints exist, independent of any particular worker, automation, event, task, goal, or interface. They are the fundamental foundation of knowledge for controlling the process. Analogous state space representations could be developed at each of the other levels of abstraction in Figure 3.

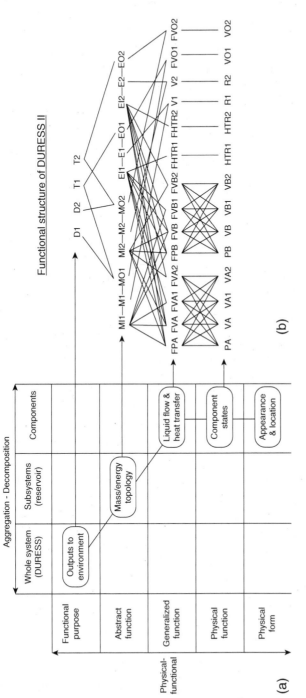

FIGURE 3   Work domain analysis of the microworld (adapted from Bisantz and Vicente, 1992; Hajdukiewicz, 2000).

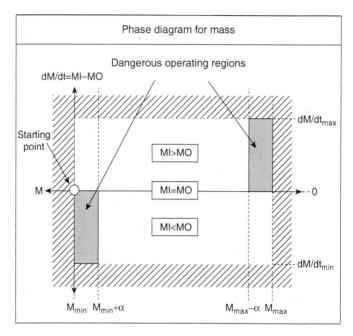

FIGURE 4   Phase diagram for mass in the microworld.

Given that there are no tasks or goals represented in Figures 3 and 4, one might reasonably ask whether a work domain representation is task-relevant, and if so, how?

2.3. Relevant work domain structure

For any category of events, only a subset of the action possibilities in Figure 3b are likely to be relevant. Take the case of a startup task described earlier. The goal in this context is to take the process from a shut down state (i.e. all components turned off and reservoirs empty) and fill the reservoir with water (mass) to a safe level. Note that the heaters, and their associated functions, are not relevant for this context because they cannot be used to change the mass level. Figure 5 shows the subset of the full structural degrees of freedom that are relevant for filling up the two reservoirs. These are the action possibilities available to any actor for this particular task context. Note that the task is still underdetermined— there is more than one way to get the job done.

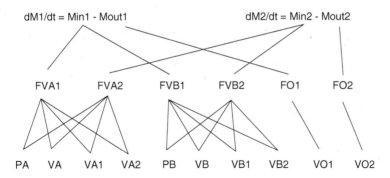

$$dM1/dt = Min1 - Mout1 \qquad\qquad dM2/dt = Min2 - Mout2$$

FVA1   FVA2   FVB1   FVB2   FO1   FO2

PA   VA   VA1   VA2   PB   VB   VB1   VB2   VO1   VO2

FIGURE 5   Structural opportunities to configure the microworld during start-up to control dM/dt for reservoirs 1 and 2.

2.4. Utilized work domain structure

At some point in time, actors must decide which of the structural possibilities in Figure 5 to utilize, given their current task goals. Here too, there are certain constraints that must be obeyed. Particular strategies are feasible for different sets of conditions. Thus, strategies can be seen as categories of action opportunities that further constrain how a task may be accomplished (Vicente, 1999a).

This fact can be illustrated by examining the various ways in which the feedwater streams (i.e. pumps and inflow valves) in Figure 1 can be used to fill up the reservoirs. Figure 6 shows three general configurations that can be utilized depending on the output demands: *single, decoupled, and full* (Vicente, 1999a). The "Description" column describes the configuration strategy. Below this description is a partial AH relevant to the configuration strategy in supporting mass inflow (MI) to each reservoir. The structural links that are utilized are highlighted in this representation. The "Topological Example" column shows an instance for each strategy category, depicting the resultant topological mass flow through the work domain. Many instances can be developed for each category, so the categories still underspecify action.

As shown in Figure 6a, the single feedwater configuration strategy uses only one pump and the valves connected to it to fill both reservoirs. This strategy can be sustained when the outflow demands add up to less than 10 units/s because the capacity of each pump is 10 units/s. As shown in Figure 6b, the decoupled feedwater configuration strategy

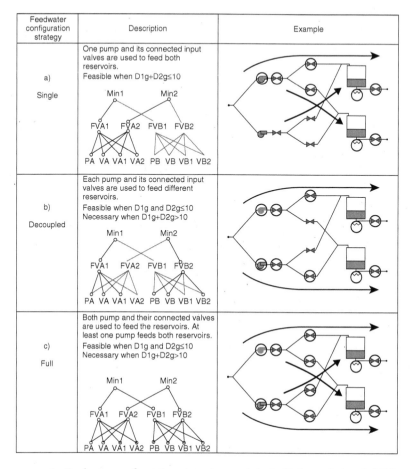

FIGURE 6   Feedwater configuration strategies are a) single, b) decoupled, and c) full (circles represent utilized components). Adapted from Vicente (1999a).

uses both pumps and their connected valves to feed different reservoirs. This strategy can be sustained when the outflow demand for each reservoir does not exceed 10 units/s because the capacity for each pump is only 10 units/s. Finally, as shown in Figure 6c, the full feedwater configuration strategy uses both pumps and their connected valves to feed both reservoirs. This strategy is sustained when the output demands do not exceed 20 units/s in total, since the capacity of the two pumps is 20 units/s in total.

2.5. Current and desired work domain state

Up to this point, we have been describing the qualitative structure of the work domain with an increasing level of specificity. We have not referred to any particular work domain state. In this final step, the degrees of freedom can be narrowed even further by representing a specific work domain state (rather than just structure) at a particular point in time. This involves annotating the nodes in one of the utilized work domain structure diagrams shown in Figure 6 with specific, quantitative values, showing the current state of each component and function. An example is shown in Figure 7. Because this is a state description, it represents what is going on at a particular point in time, and thus, is likely to change from one moment to the next. At this level of description, all of the degrees of freedom for the particular task context of filling up the reservoir will have been resolved—the state is uniquely specified.

An analogous transformation can be used to describe a desired (i.e. goal) state because it too can be represented by annotating the nodes in a utilized work domain structure diagram with specific, quantitative values. The only difference is that, in this case, the desired state of each component and function is shown rather than the current state. However, because desired states will also change over time (e.g. for shutdown vs. startup vs. normal operations), the representation of desired work domain state is also time- and event-dependent. In this way, it is distinctly different from the complete work domain structure described earlier.

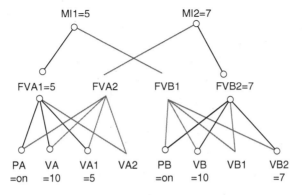

FIGURE 7   Current work domain state for feedwater configuration.

With a quantitative description of both the current and desired work domain states in hand, we are now in a position to close the circle back to the task analysis in Figure 2. The state description in Figure 7 is the input to a task description. For example, the work domain nodes in Figure 7 would serve as the input into the circle labelled "check state of work domain" in Figure 2. Conversely, the state description in Figure 7 is also the output of a task description. For example, the work domain nodes at the bottom of Figure 7 would serve as the output of the box labelled "Open VA,VA1,VA2,VB,VB1,VB2 to max." Finally, the goal state represents a version of Figure 7 that has the desired values in all of the nodes, rather than the current values. Note that the task analysis in Figure 2 does not contain an explicit description of the work domain. It merely refers to work domain nodes and states, not the structure of the work domain itself, as shown in Figure 7. In other words, Figure 2 is a function that maps current work domain states onto desired work domain states via a set of actions.

3. Theoretical generalization

Using the case study described in the previous section, we can describe the relationship between work domain analysis and task analysis in a more generalized fashion. Five levels of analysis were identified and described:

1. Complete work domain structure
2. Relevant work domain structure
3. Utilized work domain structure
4. Current and desired work domain state
5. Final set of actions and work domain states (outputs of a Task Analysis).

As depicted in Figure 8, each level is connected by a discrete transformation. More specifically, the transformation from a complete work domain structure (e.g. Figure 3, showing all relevant action possibilities) to a relevant work domain structure (e.g. Figure 5, showing all relevant action possibilities for a particular category of events) takes us one step away from a work domain analysis and closer to a task analysis, essentially by using a task context as a filter for examining the work domain

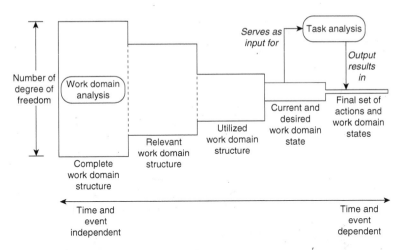

FIGURE 8   Generalized relationship between work domain analysis and task analysis.

representation. The transformation from a relevant work domain structure to a utilized work domain structure (e.g. Figure 6, showing the subset of utilized action possibilities at a particular point in time) takes us a second step away from a work domain analysis and closer to a task analysis, essentially by using the operator's strategy choices as an additional filter for examining the work domain representation. The transformation from a utilized work domain description to a current or desired work domain state (e.g. Figure 7, showing the work domain state at a particular point in time) takes us a third step away from a work domain analysis by using the effects of the actor's actions or goals as a filter for examining the work domain representation. Given these transformations, task analysis is a function that maps current states onto desired states via a set of human or automated actions.

The five levels of analysis just described can probably be applied to any sociotechnical system with a known structure. However, the generalizability of the transformations needs to be determined through additional research. They clearly have a broad range of applicability (e.g. physical engineering systems), but they may require modification or reconsideration for other types of systems (e.g. intentional systems that consist of people rather than physical components; Rasmussen et al., 1994). This remains a topic for future research.

4. Conclusions

Work domain analysis does not explicitly deal with any particular worker, automation, event, task, goal, or interface. These are fundamental concepts in cognitive engineering, so it is reasonable to ask: If work domain analysis does not represent any of these key issues, let alone all of them, then of what use is it? By making the relationship between work domain analysis and task analysis more clear and explicit, the answer to this question becomes apparent.

Work domain analysis represents information that is only implicitly captured, if at all, in a task analysis. And by identifying information requirements that are event- and time-*independent,* work domain analysis provides a robust basis for supporting worker adaptation to novelty and change. This is something that task analysis cannot do, by definition, because a class of events must be explicitly identified (or implicitly assumed) before a task analysis can even be started. There is now a substantial body of research to show that making work domain constraints visible in an interface enhances human performance under unanticipated situations requiring discretionary problem solving (Vicente, 2002; Hajdukiewicz and Vicente, 2002). Therefore, even though it does not deal with goals and actions, work domain analysis can play an important and unique role in shaping how well actors achieve their goals and select their actions.

Acknowledgements

This research was sponsored in part by the Jerome Clarke Hunsaker Distinguished Visiting Professorship from MIT, by a research grant from the Natural Sciences and Engineering Research Council of Canada and by Honeywell International.

References

Ashby, W. R. 1956, *An Introduction to Cybernetics* (London: Methuen).
Bisantz, A. M. and Vicente, K. J. 1994, Making the abstraction hierarchy concrete, *International Journal of Human-Computer Studies,* 40, 83–117.

Hajdukiewicz, J. R. 2000, Adapting to change in complex work environments, *Proceedings of the Conference of Human Factors in Computing Systems (CHI 2000)* (New York: ACM), 89–90.

Hajdukiewicz, J. R. and Vicente, K. J. 2002, Designing for adaptation to novelty and change: The role of functional information and emergent features, *Human Factors*, 44, 592–610.

Kirwan, B. and Ainsworth, L. K. 1992, *A guide to task analysis* (London: Taylor & Francis).

Naikar, N. and Sanderson, P. M. 1999, Work domain analysis for training system definition and acquisition, *The International Journal of Aviation Psychology*, 9, 271–290.

Rasmussen, J., Pejtersen, A. M. and Goodstein, L. P. 1994, Cognitive systems engineering (New York: Wiley).

Terrier, P., Cellier, J.-M. and Carreras, O. 2000, Task analysis does count in making the abstraction hierarchy concrete: Evidence from a pressurized water reactor situation, *Proceedings of the IEA 2000/HFES 2000 Congress, Volume 1* (pp. 161–163) (Santa Monica, CA: HFES).

Vicente, K. J. 2002, Ecological interface design: Progress and challenges, *Human Factors*, 44, 62–78.

Vicente, K. J. 1999a, *Cognitive work analysis: Toward safe, productive, and healthy computer-based work* (Mahwah, NJ: Erlbaum).

Vicente, K. J. 1999b, Wanted: Psychologically relevant, device- and event-independent work analysis techniques, *Interacting with Computers*, 11, 237–254.

Vicente, K. J. and Rasmussen, J. 1990, The ecology of human-machine systems II: Mediating "direct perception" in complex work domains, *Ecological Psychology*, 2, 207–250.

5

Psychological Distance

Manipulating an Interface versus Controlling a System

Alex Kirlik

> *Night vision devices provide a superb form of psychological distance. The complete integration of thermal imaging technology will extend to daylight hours the mechanical distance process that currently exists during the night.... a tank gunner [said] "you see it all as if it were happening on a TV screen.... . I see something running and I shoot at him, and he falls, and it all looks like something on TV. I don't see people, that's one good thing about it."*
>
> (Grossman, 1996: 169–170)

The article by Yu, Lau, Vicente, and Carter reprinted in this chapter, about the effects of various interface designs on the strategies people used to control a simulated powerplant, is probably the subtlest in this book. The point of the article only became clear to me when I happened, upon a second reading of it, to recall an embarrassing incident from my younger days, back when I had more time to fish. And it's an important point.

Proud of my bass fishing skill, I had invited a young woman (let's call her Jenny) that I had been dating for only a few weeks to join me on a weekend camping and fishing getaway. We packed snacks and some food for our lunches, but the general idea was that I would provide the two dinners we would cook on our campfire by catching a hefty stringer of fish each day. I had fished this particular lake many times before, and enjoyed it not only because the fishing was good, but also because it was remote, some 20 miles down dusty or muddy roads to the nearest town. So, I usually had the place pretty much to myself.

Now, with Jenny along, of course I couldn't catch a thing. After eating our second lunch for dinner the first evening, the need to catch some fish became even more important the second day. By late morning,

I was still skunked, and then I saw another boat on the lake with a family out fishing with the kids. When we eventually came within shouting distance, I asked how they were doing, and I was dismayed to see their impressive stringer of fish. I asked the obligatory, "What are you using?" and learned they were using live bait, minnows to be exact.

Now, you have to understand the status culture of bass fishing, at least among my fishing buddies at the time. *Real* bass fisherman use artificial baits or lures meant to mimic prey, and when they use worms, they are plastic. Part of the skill is in tricking the fish, not simply hoping it bites the minnow or worm with your hook in it rather than one of the rest. It's the same sort of pecking order that causes trout fisherman who elegantly and quietly cast fly rods in swiftly flowing streams to look down upon bass fisherman noisily casting clumsy rods and tackle into idle lakes. Hoping that Jenny was unaware of the politics involved, I returned to camp telling her that I had simply forgotten that, at that particular time of the year, that of course the fish would be biting on live bait rather than anything in my tackle box. So, I got out a net buried in the bottom of my box in hopes of netting some minnows of my own.

But before I could get started, the family arrived on shore and walked by us and over to their camper. The father told me that he was driving into town for more live bait for the next day and asked me if I needed anything. Sure, I said, I'd be grateful if you could pick up a few dozen live minnows for me, and handed him some cash. I figured I would use the time until he returned to try to catch some minnows from the lake by tossing my net, but no luck. It was now getting well past lunchtime, and because we had eaten our lunch last night, we were both getting very hungry. And, of course it took dad what seemed like forever to get back to camp. In fact, it was close to dinnertime and beginning to get dark when he did. When he got out of his truck, the kids came running at him, yelling, "McDonalds! McDonalds! McDonalds!" He must have had three bags of the stuff. After doling out the goods, he then walked over to us and handed me a Styrofoam bucket full of minnows.

Then ... inevitably ... from Jenny, came "the look." We packed up camp, headed to McDonalds for a late dinner, and drove home from there, a night before we had originally planned. We agreed that it would probably be a good idea if I just dropped her off at her place.

How could I have been so stupid? Here's is a man offering to drive to a town I know to be full of take-out restaurants, with Jenny and me hungry to the point of colloquially "starving," and I ask him to bring us back food for fish instead of food for people. Figure 3 in the reprint can help us understand the situation, even if it may not fully explain my clueless behavior that day.

As discussed in Chapter 2, Vicente borrowed the abstraction hierarchy (AH) from Rasmussen, who noted that the cognitive activity of operators diagnosing faults in a power plant moves among a hierarchy of abstract representations of the plant and its physics. A nuclear power plant is complex enough to warrant the five levels shown in Figure 3 (b), but the essence of the situation can be captured in the three levels of Purpose, Function, and Physical Form. In the fishing debacle, the level of Purpose would be to relieve hunger. Note that I could be tempted to say that our purpose was to eat, but there are other ways to relieve hunger, however unpleasant. Now, *how* had I decided to achieve this purpose? Use of the word "how" implies function. In my case, I would describe the level of Function as catch and eat fish. Now, at the lowest level of Physical Form, what was I going to use to perform this function? Fishing rod, tackle, bait, and campfire.

With this way of looking at things in place, what was the "fault" in my system? My behavior clearly indicated that I diagnosed the fault to be at the level of Physical Form: I simply had the wrong item filling the variable: bait. I had lures, when I needed minnows. As such, and given this framing, it was only natural (or it seemed so at the time) for me to repair the fault in my system by substituting minnows for bait. In an analogy to the DURESS powerplant microworld discussed in the reprint, I had essentially found a solution to my problem by adjusting a knob on the system interface to alter the value of a variable, without rethinking other possible Functions that could help us meet the Purpose of relieving hunger.

Apparently, it never entered my mind that an alternative "how" (Function) would have let us achieve our Purpose of relieving hunger: McDonalds. There would seem to be a link to the literature on functional fixedness here (e.g., Duncker, 1945), although that term is typically reserved to describe a "mental block" that people display in an inability to use an object in a novel way to solve some problem or achieve some goal. In contrast, my mental block seemed to be an inability to shift my attention away from the level of Physical Form and to consider an alternative, and ultimately, much more attractive Function that could be seized upon to meet our Purpose.

What the reader will see in the reprint is this same general schema at work, but as applied to understanding how different system interfaces for the DURESS microworld prompted different experimental participants to adopt different strategies for performing their task. One of the two interfaces (P + F) presented participants with additional functionally relevant information about the behavior of the controlled system that the other (P) interface did not contain. Vicente and his co-authors found that the participant TL, using the P interface, became locked into an inflexible, feedforward or rule-based strategy for interacting with the simulated plant. That is, the cognitive skill acquired by TL was one of manipulating the interface, rather than controlling the system. TL had ceased to think of his behavior in terms of achieving some ultimate Purpose; rather, he was simply watching and acting upon the interface, much like the tank gunner quoted in the epigraph who reported his experience as shooting at images on TV, not in terms of killing people.

In contrast, participant AV, using the P + F interface, was able to adopt a more flexible and adaptive feedback control strategy, continually monitoring the difference between actual and desired system outputs and taking actions needed to reduce the gap. The strategy of TL would be more accurately described as controlling the system by manipulating the interface. For TL, the ultimate end Purpose always remains foremost in mind: he's not simply an interface or TV viewer.

Returning (regretfully) to the fishing trip fiasco, the analog to the additional F information provided to AV would have been the father telling me, "Hey, it's getting late, and the two of you seem pretty hungry, and I'll be stopping by McDonalds." This likely would have helped by jogging my mind to reconsider my *ultimate* Purpose in that weekend getaway with Jenny ... but no matter now. In some situations, you only get one shot.

Toward Theory-Driven, Quantitative Performance Measurement in Ergonomics Science: The Abstraction Hierarchy as a Framework for Data Analysis

Xinyao Yu, Elfreda Lau, Kim J. Vicente, and Michael W. Carter

Abstract

Measurement in ergonomics science has not kept pace with theorizing. As a result, it is rare to find measures of human performance that are simultaneously objective, quantitative, sensitive, and theoretically grounded. This article proposes a new set of measures, based on the abstraction hierarchy (AH) framework, that satisfies all of these criteria. Each level of the AH can be used to define a quantitative state space that can serve as a frame of reference for objective measurement. These state spaces are complementary because they provide different views of the same human-environment behaviour. Collectively, this set of measures can be used to determine if a participant is strongly or weakly coupled to functional or physical distal properties of the work domain. Data from a longitudinal study are used as a case study to test the value of these novel measures. The empirical results show that these AH-based measures provide unique insight into participants' behaviour that was not revealed by many, more traditional measures of performance. Because it is theoretically grounded, the set of measures proposed here has the potential to be generalized to diverse work domains for which it is possible to develop an AH representation.

1. Introduction

The lack of sophisticated measurement in complex experimental settings poses a significant obstacle to ergonomics science (e.g. Moray et al., 1986; Moray and Rotenberg, 1989; Sanderson et al., 1989; Howie and Vicente, 1998). Traditional measures (e.g. task completion time) are objective, but frequently do not have a compelling theoretical basis and are not sensitive enough to reveal differences between experimental groups. Other measures (e.g. eye movements, verbal protocols) can provide greater scientific insight, but frequently suffer from being extremely time-consuming or subjective to analyse. It would be useful to develop novel empirical measures that are: (a) *objective*, meaning that they can be derived solely from log files of participant actions and system state; (b) *quantitative*, meaning that they can be derived computationally; (c) *theoretical*, meaning that they have a close connection to meaningful constructs; and (d) *sensitive*, meaning that they provide novel empirical insights that cannot be observed using traditional measures. The novel class of measures proposed in this article is based on the abstraction hierarchy (AH; Rasmussen, 1985) and satisfies all four of these criteria, each of which is routinely used to evaluate measurement in many sciences.

The remainder of the article is organized as follows. First, the experimental test-bed used for this research will be introduced. Secondly, the theoretical motivation behind the AH framework will be described. Thirdly, the proposed empirical measures and their connection to the AH will be explained. Finally, the empirical sensitivity of these measures will be illustrated by using data from a 6-month longitudinal study of the impact of interface design on human performance.

2. Experimental test-bed

This research was conducted in the context of the thermal-hydraulic process control microworld illustrated in Figure 1 (Pawlak and Vicente, 1996). This micro-world is a real-time, interactive simulation that was designed to be representative of industrial process control systems,

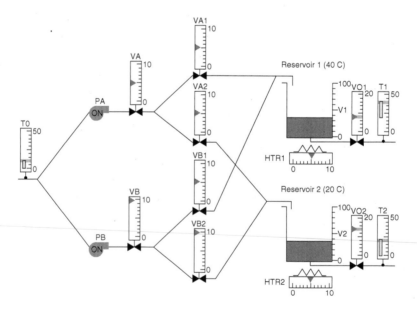

FIGURE 1   Thermal-hydraulic process control microworld (adapted from Pawlak and Vicente 1996).

thereby promoting the generalizability of results from the laboratory to the field (Vicente, 1991).

The microworld consists of two redundant feedwater streams (FWSs) that can be configured to supply water to either, both, or neither of the two reservoirs. Each reservoir has associated with it an externally determined demand for water that can change over time. The work domain purposes are twofold: to keep each of the reservoirs at a prescribed temperature (40 and 20°C), and to satisfy the current mass (water) output demand rates. To achieve these purposes, participants have control over eight valves (VA,VA1,VA2,VO1,VB,VB1,VB2, and VO2), two pumps (PA and PB), and two heaters (HTR1 and HTR2). All of these components are governed by first order lag dynamics, with a time constant of 15 seconds for the heaters and 5 seconds for the remaining components.

A number of other variables, not displayed in Figure 1, can be used to describe the operation of the simulation. Definitions of these variables are provided in Table 1.

The role that these quantitative variables play in the novel measures proposed in this article is discussed later.

3. Theoretical motivation

Explanations of the AH are usually theoretically motivated by psychological theories of human problem solving (e.g. Rasmussen, 1985; Vicente, 1999). However, it is also possible to explain the scientific value of the AH from the theoretical perspective of systems engineering or control theory (Vicente, 1991).

3.1. The inverse dynamics problem

Figure 2 provides one of the simplest possible representations of a human-machine system—a negative feedback control loop. The box labelled *work domain* represents the (forward) dynamics of the controlled system. It is a model of how the actions of the worker are translated into outputs that are relevant to the goal(s) of interest. From the perspective of the worker, however, the important question is "given where I should be, what should I do to get there"? This is frequently referred to as the *inverse*

TABLE I   Definition of microworld process variables.

Variable	Description
Temperature	
T_1	Temperature of res 1
T_2	Temperature of res 2
Output demand	
D_1	Output flowrate for res 1
D_2	Output flowrate for res 2
Mass	
MO_1	Mass output flowrate for res 1
MO_2	Mass output flowrate for res 2
MI_1	Mass input flowrate for res 1
MI_2	Mass input flowrate for res 2
M_1	Mass inventory of res 1
M_2	Mass inventory of res 2
Energy	
E_1	Total energy stored in res 1
E_2	Total energy stored in res 2
EI_1	Energy input flowrate for res 1
EI_2	Energy input flowrate for res 2
EO_1	Energy output flowrate for res 1
EO_2	Energy output flowrate for res 2
Heat transfer	
FH_1	Flow from heater HTR_1
FH_2	Flow from heater HTR_2
Flowrates	
FA_1	Flowrate from valve VA_1
FB_1	Flowrate from valve VB_1
FA_2	Flowrate from valve VA_2
FB_2	Flowrate from valve VB_2
FPA	Flowrate from pump PA
FPB	Flowrate from pump PB
FVA	Flowrate from valve VA
FVB	Flowrate from valve VB
Heaters	
HTR_1	Setting for heater of res 1
HTR_2	Setting for heater of res 2
Pumps	
PA	Setting of pump in fws A
PB	Setting of pump in fws B
Valves	
VA	Setting of initial valve in fws A
VB	Setting of initial valve in fws B
VA_1	Setting of valve 1 in fws A

TABLE I   Definition of microworld process variables. (*Continued*)

Variable	Description
VB1	Setting of valve 1 in fws B
VA2	Setting of valve 2 in fws A
VB2	Setting of valve 2 in fws B
VO1	Setting output valve in res 1
VO2	Setting of output valve 2 in res 2

fws = feedwater stream, res = reservoir.

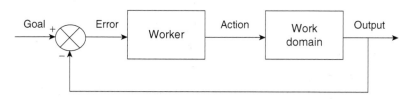

FIGURE 2   A negative feedback control loop.

dynamics problem in systems engineering. As shown in Figure 3(*a*), it involves going from the error signal (i.e. the difference between where you are and where you want to be) to what you should act on (i.e. work domain components). Unfortunately, this mapping is exceedingly complex because there are so many components that can be acted on and many interactions that must be taken into account. It is very difficult for resource-limited actors, such as workers, to solve this inverse dynamics problem unaided.

In the case of the microworld in Figure 1, the inverse dynamics problem requires participants to develop a mapping between two sets of variables, the first describing the four work domain purposes (T1, T2, D1, D2) and the second describing the 12 components that can be acted on (PA, PB, HTR1, HTR2, VA, VA1, VA2, VO1, VB, VB1, VB2, VO2). The decision as to how to act is non-trivial because there seem to be so many degrees of freedom. Furthermore, the relationship between the work domain purposes and the components that can be acted upon is far from obvious. The mapping between the two is essentially a black box from the viewpoint of workers (see Figure 3*a*), unless designers provide some support to help workers solve the inverse dynamics problem. Thus, it is hard for participants to decide what to act on, given knowledge of where they want to be.

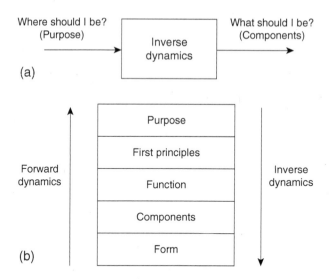

FIGURE 3   (a) The inverse dynamics problem, (b) The AH provides stratified feedback for solving the inverse dynamics problem.

There are at least three different ways for workers to solve this problem (cf. Christoffersen et al., 1997). The first approach, *trial and error*, involves acting on components in a haphazard way, examining the result, and then iteratively making another change. Trial and error is cognitively economic because it does not require much thought, and although it can succeed in the long-run, it is clearly not very efficient. The second approach, *heuristics*, involves developing rules of thumb that map particular states onto particular actions (e.g. if T_1 is too high, then lower HTR_1). Heuristics are also cognitively economic and can be efficient. However, it can take a great deal of practice to acquire heuristics. Furthermore, because they are rules of thumb, heuristics are—by definition—fallible (i.e. they will not always work). The third approach, *model-based derivation*, involves computing the actions to be performed by using a mental model of the work domain dynamics. In the absence of faults, this approach is reliable because it is based on an understanding of the how the work domain functions. However, it is cognitively uneconomic because it requires a great deal of knowledge, memory load and computational power. None of these three approaches to solving the inverse dynamics problem is particularly attractive, because each has important limitations.

In operational settings, workers usually avoid trial and error because the consequences of an error can be quite severe. Model-based derivation is usually avoided because it is not possible to perform, given human information processing capabilities. Thus, workers frequently rely on formal or informal procedures (a form of heuristics) to cope with the inverse dynamics problem in a cognitively manageable, if fallible, way. For example, Table 3 provides an example of the type of heuristics reported by a highly experienced participant in a longitudinal microworld study described later (Christoffersen et al., 1998).

3.2. Abstraction hierarchy

Designers can help workers solve the inverse dynamics problem by providing feedback so as to open up the "black box" in Figure 3a. The AH can be viewed as a modelling framework to do precisely that. Rather than requiring workers to solve the inverse dynamics problem in one complex step—a cognitively daunting task—the AH provides a hierarchically organized set of work domain models that allows workers to transform knowledge of where they should be (i.e. the current state of the purposes) to decisions about what they should do (i.e. how to act on components) in several stratified steps. As shown in Figure 3(b), the top level of the AH provides workers with information about the state of the work domain purposes, whereas the bottom levels provide workers with information about the form of the components on which they can act. The levels in between show how these two entities are structurally related. By providing feedback at each of these levels of abstraction, the black box is now made transparent because the relationship between purpose and form is shown as a stratified hierarchy. Furthermore, the links between levels can guide a workers' search process by showing which lower-level objects are relevant to the current higher-order function of interest. As a result, the inverse dynamics problem is made easier to solve, because it no longer has to be solved all in one complex step. Workers can focus on the high-level objectives to be achieved rather than the myriad specific actions that might be taken in any particular context.

A familiar example is keeping one's car between lane markers while driving. Because the state of the work domain (i.e. the position of the car) is clearly visible with respect to the goal (i.e. the lane markers), experienced drivers do not have to memorize a procedure for how to control the car. Instead, they can just rely on the feedback from the environment to guide their actions directly in a goal-directed fashion. Table 4 provides an example of this type of high-level, functional control reported by a highly experienced participant in a longitudinal microworld study described later (Christoffersen et al., 1998). The contrast with the low-level, action-based heuristic in Table 3 is notable.

In short, the AH framework is intended to provide a mechanism for coping with complexity. The AH is usually used in conjunction with a decomposition (or part–whole) hierarchy that describes the work domain at various layers of resolution. Higher levels describe the work domain at a coarse level, whereas lower levels describe the work domain at a more fine-grained level.

Again, the microworld in Figure 1 can be used to make these ideas more concrete. Figure 4 shows an AH analysis for this microworld (Bisantz and Vicente, 1994). As shown along the top, there are three levels of decomposition for this particular example, each connected by part–whole relations (System, Sub-system, and Component). As shown along the left, there are five levels of abstraction for this example, each connected by structural means-ends links (Functional Purpose, Abstract Function, Generalized Function, Physical Function, and Physical Form). Four cells in Figure 4 have been identified as being useful (the variables at each level are shown in parentheses):

- Functional Purpose/System—outputs to the environment (T_1, D_1; T_2, D_2);
- Abstract Function/Sub-system—mass and energy topologies (MI_1, Ml, MO_1, EI_1, El, EO_1; MI_2, M_2, MO_2, EI_2, E_2, EO_2);
- Generalized Function/Component—liquid flow and heat transfer rates (FPA, FVA, FA_1, FA_2; FPB, FVB, FBl, FB_2; FH_1, FH_2); and
- Physical Function/Component—component settings (PA, VA, VA_1, VA_2; PB, VB, VB_1, VB_2; VO_1, VO_2; HTR_1, HTR_2).

Note that this fourth cell can be considered an *action space*, because it represents the components on which participants can act. The bottom level of Physical Form was not used because the location and appearance of components are not meaningful in a microworld simulation.

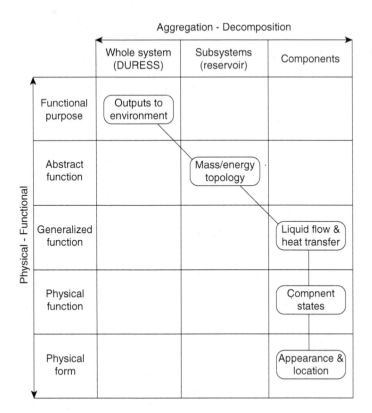

FIGURE 4   Representation of thermal-hydraulic process control micro-world in abstraction/decomposition space (adapted from Bisantz and Vicente 1994).

4. Quantitative measurement

The AH has been used for a wide number of purposes in ergonomics science, including protocol analysis, interface evaluation, interface design, database design, training, and worker role allocation (Vicente, 1999). However, before this research, it does not appear to have been used to identify objective, quantitative measures that can illuminate human performance.

4.1. A stratified hierarchy of state spaces

Each of the four cells in Figure 4 contains a different representation of the very same work domain, each being a different frame of reference, or state space, for measuring performance. Thus, the participant-environment behaviour during any one trial in an experiment can be plotted as a trajectory over time. However, because each level of the AH defines a different state space, each trial will be revealed as a different trajectory, depending on the level of abstraction chosen for measurement.

Consequently, each frame of reference can be used to conduct a different data analysis. For example, at the Functional Purpose/System level, the microworld in Figure 1 can be described in a four-dimensional state space (not including the time dimension) defined by the four outputs: T_1, D_1, T_2, D_2 (see Table 1). The behaviour of the simulation during one trial for one participant can be plotted as a trajectory in this state space. For a successfully completed startup trial, this trajectory would start at the origin of the space (because the process is initially shutdown) and would end at the area defined by the particular set-point values (and tolerances) for that trial.

If we take a block of trials for one participant, we get a series of trajectories in the same state space, one for each trial. It is then possible to calculate the multidimensional variance of these trajectories, using the formula shown in the appendix. This variance is a quantitative measure of consistency at this level of the AH. For example, if the path that a participant takes is exactly the same for each trial when plotted in this state space, then the variance would be zero. However, if the path that a participant takes in this state space is wildly different from trial to trial, then the variance would be quite large. Therefore, in the language of dynamical systems theory (Port and van Gelder, 1995), this measure of variance in trajectories across a block of trials can be considered to be a relative measure of *coupling* to the distal properties of the work domain. If participants exhibit low variance, then they are strongly coupled to this level of the AH. If participants exhibit high variance, then they are weakly coupled to this level of the AH. While the construct of coupling is frequently used in the ergonomics science literature, it is rarely defined computationally and measured quantitatively as it is here.

The very same block of trials can be plotted as trajectories at any of the levels of the AH. Moreover, it is possible to calculate the variance of that block of trajectories at any level of the AH in a manner that is analogous to that just described for the Functional Purpose level (see the appendix). And, because each level of the AH represents a different state space for the same work domain, the same block of trials will be represented as a different set of trajectories at each level of the AH. Thus, it is possible for the same participant to exhibit high variance at one level and low variance at another. Such a pattern of results allows us to make inferences about the relative degree of coupling for a particular participant as a function of level of the AH. For example, one participant may be more strongly coupled to a higher level of the AH, suggesting that they are focusing on the functions to be satisfied. Another participant may be more strongly coupled to a lower level of the AH, suggesting that they are focusing on a particular sequence of quantitative component settings (e.g. like a detailed procedure consistently followed by rote).

In the remainder of this article, we will show that this quantitative set of measures may reveal important differences between participants, even after extensive experience.

5. Case study

5.1. Longitudinal experiment on interface design

The measures just defined will be illustrated with data from a longitudinal experiment investigating the impact of interface design on human performance (Christoffersen et al., 1996, 1997, 1998). Two interfaces were tested using a between-participants design (see Pawlak and Vicente [1996] for a detailed description of the interfaces). The P group used an interface that only presented *physical* information (i.e. the state of the components and the overall purposes to be achieved), much like the situation depicted in Figure 3a. Based on the earlier discussion, one might expect that participants would have to engage in lower-level control based on heuristics to do well with this interface. The P + F group used an interface that presented both *physical* and *functional* information (i.e. all levels of the AH), much like the situation depicted in Figure 3b. Based on the earlier discussion, one might expect that participants would have to engage in higher-level control based on feedback to do well with this interface. Unfortunately, it is difficult to test these hypotheses using traditional measures of performance.

5.2. Previous analyses

Only normal (i.e. non-fault) trials will be analysed here. The primary performance measure that had been used to investigate performance under normal trials was total trial completion time. Previous analyses using this measure had shown that there was no significant mean difference between interface groups, but that the P group was significantly more consistent than the P + F; P participants occasionally took twice as long as usual to complete the required tasks, even after 5.5 months of quasi-daily practice (Christoffersen et al., 1996). Table 2 provides a summary of the mean completion times for each participant for the first and last block of normal trials over the course of the 6-month long experiment.

These data show that participants AV and TL were the most proficient in their respective interface groups. They were clearly better than the other participants and not unlike each other, except for the difference in completion time variability. Analyses using other measures showed a similar pattern (Yu et al., 1997). On many measures, AV and TL seemed very alike and better than everyone else.

There was one strong exception to this pattern. When participants were asked to write down how they controlled the microworld, AV and TL reported using qualitatively different procedures (Christoffersen et al., 1998). As shown in Table 3, TL reported following a rote set of precise actions on components (e.g. "set HTR2 to 3 1/3"; "it might not make sense but it works"). However, as shown in Table 4, AV reported

TABLE 2   Average startup task completion time for first 22 and last 20 normal trials (from Christoffersen *et al.* 1998).

Group	Participant	Trials 1–22		Trials 196–217	
		M	SD	M	SD
P + F	AS	860.2	441.3	437.2	31.3
	AV	517.3	149.0	353.5	16.1
	IS	644.4	125.8	399.0	17.5
P	ML	660.3	261.8	390.2	48.0
	TL	493.6	80.2	357.5	20.5
	WL	624.3	170.4	437.2	97.9

TABLE 3   Last control recipe for TL on P interface (Christoffersen *et al.* 1998).

(1) Open valves VB2 and VB to their maximum (10) and start PB. Set HTR2 to 4.5.

(2) Set VA1 to 7, VA to maximum (10), and start PA. Set HTR1 to 10.

(3) As the temperature in Res 2 reaches to lower end of the desired range, set HTR 2 to 3 1/3; then set VO2 to desired level.

(4) Set VO1 to desired level. As the temperature in Res 1 reaches the lower end of the desired temperature range, set VA1 to level 10.

(5) As the resevoirs reaches level 60, adjust VA1 to equal VO1 and VB2 to equal VO2. Modify heater settings as necessary.

Hint: HTR1 should be at same numerical setting as VA1, and HTR2 at 1/3 of VB2 (it might not make sense, but it works).

If the demand on res 2 is greater than 10:
Follow steps (1), (2) and (3) above, then:

(4) Set VA2 such that the total water input into res 2 is one level above VO2. Set VA1 such that VA1 +VA2= 10. Set heater levels as defined in the hint section above.

(5) As the resevoir reaches level 60, adjust values so that VA1 = VO1 and VA2 +VB2 = VO2. Modify heater settings as required.

TABLE 4   Last control recipe for AV on P + F interface (experimenter notes are in brace brackets).

Turn PA & PB on
Turn VA & VA1 on (max)
Turn HTR1 on (max)
Turn VB & VB1 & VA2 on (if necessary)
{arrow underneath text, from parenthetical phrase to VA2}
Turn HTR2 on (max)
Adjust VO1 & VO2 to output
Adjust VA & VA1, VB & VB1 & VA2 to necessary input.
Adjust HTR1 & HTR2 For the inputs
Do some fine tuning. END

focusing on the functions to be achieved (e.g. "necessary input") and did not list many precise actions. If we believe these subjective data, then AV and TL were controlling the process in qualitatively different ways. TL's knowledge about the process seems to be action-based, while AV's seems to be function-based. Yet, the mean trial completion time analysis and many of the other measures that we investigated did not uncover this difference. Instead, they suggested that TL and AV were comparable and quite proficient in their control performance. Is this another case of dissociation between subjective reports and behavioural performance, or are the traditional measures failing to pick up a difference that really exists? We hypothesized that the quantitative measures based on the AH could shed some objective, quantitative light on the relative difference between TL and AV.

5.3. Abstraction hierarchy measures

The variability in the trajectories for each participant was calculated at each level of the AH described above, by block (see the appendix for the mathematical formulae). We will begin by discussing the results from the Functional Purpose/System level, illustrated in Figure 5. These trajectories were normalized with respect to the set-point values for each trial, thereby allowing us to meaningfully compare trajectories across trials. The graphs in Figure 5 show the variability in trajectories for each participant over the course of the entire experiment, as a function of 11 blocks of ~20 trials each. After the initial part of the experiment, the variances for TL and AV are about the same, and they exhibit very consistent trajectories at this level of the AH. This is not surprising, given that both participants were the most proficient in their respective groups. Thus, according to this measure, TL and AV behaved in the same fashion. As already mentioned, the Physical Function/Component cell in Figure 1 represents an action space because it presents the low-level component states. The variability of trajectories in this level was computed in the same manner except that the trajectories were not normalized with respect to the set-point values for each trial. Such a normalization is not possible because there is no direct relationship between set-point values

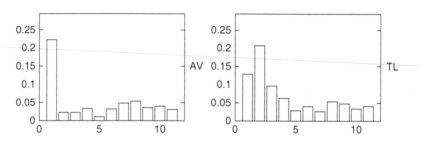

FIGURE 5   Variance at functional purpose/system.

and component settings. Thus, the variability analysis at this level is based on absolute setting values (with a compensation for the fact that different components have different scale values; see the appendix). Figure 6 compares the action variability for AV and TL during the last four blocks of the experiment. These data show that TL's behaviour is consistently less variable than AV's at this level of the AH. This result is consistent with the observation that TL's behaviour is driven more by a fixed set of specific actions than AV's (compare Tables 3 and 4). Thus, this finding provides support for the expectations generated by the subjective data reported by these two participants.

Figure 7 shows the results of the variability analysis at the Generalized Function/Component level. The trajectories in this frame of reference were also not normalized with respect to the set-point values for each trial for the reasons stated above. The results are very similar to those of the previous analysis because there is a strong correlation between these two levels of the AH. By inspecting the equations describing the process dynamics, we can see that there is a direct correspondence between these two sets of variables after the transient produced by a change in component setting. In other words, if we are given the component settings we can usually uniquely derive the liquid flow rates and heat transfer rates (for normal trials). The only times during which this relationship is weakened is during the transient period after a control action. Thus, this analysis does not provide any new insights.

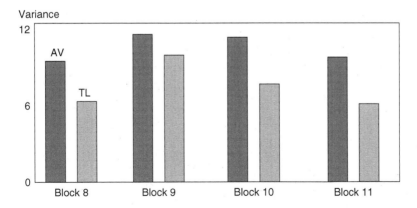

FIGURE 6   Comparison of variance at physical function/component at the last four blocks.

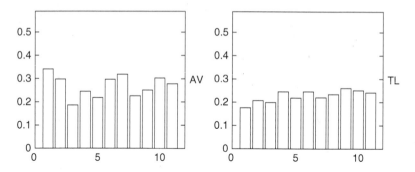

FIGURE 7   Variance at generalized function/component.

The final set of AH variance analyses was conducted at the Abstract Function/Sub-system level. There are two important differences between this frame of reference and the last two just described. First, the measurement is taking place at an aggregate level. We are now examining variables at the Sub-system level, which are aggregates of the variables that were examined at the level of Components (see Figure 4). Secondly, measurement at this level is in terms of variables that describe the system in terms of first principles (i.e. mass and energy conservation laws). In this sense, this frame of reference is a privileged level of description. The first analysis conducted at this level was based on trajectories that were not normalized for the particular set-point values for different trials. In this case, the calculations are based on absolute data values (except for a compensation for the fact that different components have different scale values; see the appendix). The results from this analysis are presented in Figure 8. It is difficult to discern any patterns in the data.

There is another way to look at these data, however. Because each trial has a different set of setpoints, we would expect there to be variance in the trajectories for this reason alone. Although the trajectory for each trial begins at the origin, the end point for each trajectory will be different for each trial as a function of the setpoint for that trial. If we assume that participants try to stabilize both volume and temperature for each reservoir, then it is possible to correct the trajectories for differences in setpoint values across trials. This is accomplished by dividing the mass

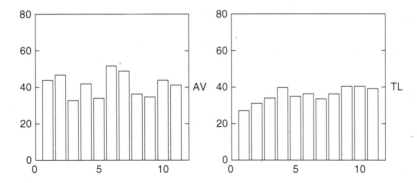

FIGURE 8   Variance at abstract function/sub-system (normalized by scale only).

input and output flowrates by the demand setpoints, and dividing the energy input and output flowrates by the product of the demand set-points and the temperature set-points (see the appendix). Normalizing the trajectories in this fashion eliminates any variability caused solely by differences in setpoints across trials.

The results from this second analysis are presented in Figure 9. Several interesting findings emerge from this alternative way of looking at the data. The most important of all is the large difference between the variances for TL and AV. From the beginning of the experiment,

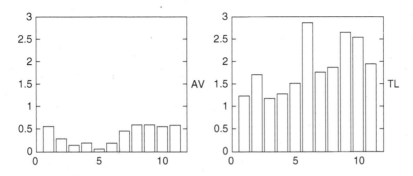

FIGURE 9   Variance at abstract function/sub-system (normalized by both scale and goals).

but especially in the second half, the trajectory variance for AV is much lower than that for TL. This result provides objective validation of the subjective report data in Tables 3 and 4. AV is thinking about and controlling the process at a high level of abstraction, focusing on the mass and energy level. Moreover, he contextualizes his control at this level based on the setpoint values for each trial. This can be observed by the noticeable difference in the data in Figures 8 and 9 for AV. It is only when we compensate for differences in setpoint values that we see that, at a high level of abstraction, AV is acting in a consistent fashion across trials. In contrast, the regularities in TL's behaviour are more at the action level (Figure 6), where he exhibited a lower variance than AV. Because TL's actions are relatively similar for trials with different setpoints, his behaviour is not as contextualized (or situated) as AV's. Thus, when we examine TL's data at a contextualized, functional level of abstraction, he exhibits less structure than does AV.

5.4. Discussion

Subjective report data had suggested that AV and TL controlled the process in qualitatively different ways (see Tables 3 and 4). However, these differences had not been confirmed by many other objective measures of performance that had been used to analyse the data from this experiment (Yu et al., 1997). The AH-based measures proposed in this article offered unique insight by providing objective, quantitative evidence about the important differences between these two participants. Furthermore, these insights were consistent with the subjective report data. At the lowest level of the AH (i.e. the action space), TL exhibited less variability in his trajectories than AV. Because TL thought about the process in terms of specific actions on components, it makes sense that the regularities in his behaviour appear at this low level of abstraction. Conversely, at a high level of abstraction, AV exhibited less variability in his trajectories than TL. Because AV thought about the process in terms of functions, it makes sense that the regularities in his behaviour should appear at a high level of abstraction.

Perhaps most importantly of all, these findings are consistent with the theoretical rationale behind the AH, given the different interfaces used by

TL and AV. AV used the P + F interface which presented him with both physical and functional information (see Figure 3*b*), thereby providing some help in solving the inverse dynamics problem. Because he could see the state and structure of the system, he did not have to memorize a set of procedures. Instead, he could use the information in the P + F interface as an error signal to generate actions that were appropriate to the current context. Thus, there was a stronger coupling between AV's actions and the micro-world, as shown by the AH analysis at the level of first principles in Figure 9. This stronger coupling also led to a larger degree of context-conditioned variability (Turvey et al., 1982). Because different trials had different goal setpoint values, AV's actions were more variable across trials (see Figure 6).

TL used the P interface, which only displayed physical information (see Figure 3*a*), making it more difficult to solve the inverse dynamics problem. Although the P interface provided TL with enough feedback to control the system efficiently, it does not reveal all of the interactions that govern the microworld. As a result, TL could not rely primarily on the feedback in the interface to generate his actions. Instead, he had to acquire a rote set of detailed actions that he used as a script for each trial. Thus, TL's actions were less variable across trials because they seemed to be governed more by the steps in his procedure than by what was presently going on in the process. Consequently, TL exhibited a weaker coupling to the first principles of the microworld (see Figure 9). The regularities in his control were at the action level (see Figure 6).

This theoretical interpretation of the differences between AV and TL is only possible because there is a very strong connection between the objective, empirical measures described in the appendix and the theoretical constructs of the AH framework.

6. Conclusions

This article has made a novel contribution to performance measurement in ergonomics science. A novel set of measures have been proposed based on the AH framework. As far as we know, this is the first time that the AH has been used for this purpose. In addition to being theoretically driven, these measures benefit from being objective and quantitative, thereby improving the rigour of ergonomics science. The measures were also sensitive enough to identify behavioural differences between participants in a longitudinal study of interface design. These differences had not been objectively identified by many other analyses using more traditional measures, such as task completion time.

The primary limitation of this work is that these novel measures were only applied to two participants in one experimental setting. Analogous measures can be derived for other work domains for which it is possible to develop an AH representation. Although the content of the levels of the AH will differ for various work domains, the relationship between levels will be the same. The key empirical question for future research is whether such measures will lead to important and unique insights in other contexts, as they have here. Accordingly, it is important that the AH be used as a measurement tool in diverse application domains to assess the generalizability of the approach proposed here.

Acknowledgements

This research was sponsored by a contract from the Japan Atomic Energy Research Institute. We would like to thank Dr. Fumiya Tanabe (contract monitor), Greg Jamieson, Klaus Christoffersen, and Chris Hunter for their contributions.

Appendix

Functional purpose/system

This measure shows the consistency in subjects' performance across trials, at the level of goal variables (outputs). The state of the four goal variables, $(\overline{MO_1}(t), \overline{MO_2}(t), \overline{T_1}(t), \overline{T_2}(t))$ can be plotted against time, creating one trajectory in five-dimensional space for each trial. The variance in these trajectories within a block of trials is then calculated.

The variance of goal variables over a block of trials is defined as follows:

1. *Time shift:* Generally, there is a delay between the beginning of a trial and the time of the first action by the participant. The magnitude of this delay varies across participants, and within-participants across trials. For the purposes of this analysis, this idiosyncratic response delay is noise, so it should be removed. If there is a time delay, τ for the trial, then the four goal variables T_1, T_2, MO_1, MO should be shifted by τ so that they all start at time 0. This leads to functions $T_1(t-\tau)$, $T_2(t-\tau)$, $MO_1(t-\tau)$, and $MO_2(t-\tau)$, respectively.

2. *Normalization:* For each trial, the four goal variables:
   $MO_1(t-\tau)$, $MO_2(t-\tau)$, $T_1(t-\tau)$, $T_2(t-\tau)$ are normalized with respect to their set points, which leads to $\overline{MO_1}(t-\tau)$, $\overline{MO_2}(t-\tau)$ $\overline{T_1}(t-\tau)$, and $\overline{T_2}(t-\tau)$ respectively. Normalization allows us to compare all of the variables across trials from a common reference scale.

3. *Linear interpolation:* The microworld simulation only logs its state at the time of a participant action rather than at a constant sampling interval. Thus, if there is a long time between actions, then the state of the process during this time will be unknown and must be derived. To recover these data, $\overline{MO_1}(t-\tau)$, $\overline{MO_2}(t-\tau)$, $\overline{T_1}(t-\tau)$, $\overline{T_2}(t-\tau)$ are linearly interpolated every 3 seconds over the first 300 seconds of a trial (the minimum duration of a trial). This interpolation interval was chosen based on knowledge of the bandwidth of the micro-world dynamics. Thus, we get

$$\overline{MO_1}(t_i),\ \overline{MO_2}(t_i),\ \overline{T_1}(t_i),\ \overline{T_2}(t_i) \text{ with } t_1 = 0,\ t_2 = 3,\ t_3 = 6;...;\ t_{101} = 300.$$

4. *The multi-dimensional, time-wise variance at each t_i is calculated by:*

$$\text{var}(t_i) = \frac{\sum_{j=1}^{n}(\overline{MO_1}^j(t_i) - ave_{\overline{MO_1}(t_i)})^2 + (\overline{MO_2}^j(t_i) - ave_{\overline{MO_2}(t_i)})^2 + (\overline{T_1}^j(t_i) - ave_{\overline{T_1}(t_i)})^2 + (\overline{T_2}^j(t_i) - ave_{\overline{T_2}(t_i)})^2}{n-1}$$

where $\overline{MO_1}^j(t_i)$, $\overline{MO_2}^j(t_i)$, $\overline{T_1}^j(t_i)$, $\overline{T_2}^j$ are normalized outflow rates and temperatures at time t_i of trial j within the block of sampled trials. $ave_{\overline{MO_1}(t_i)}$, $ave_{\overline{MO_2}(t_i)}$, $ave_{\overline{T_1}(t_i)}$, $ave_{\overline{T_2}(t_i)}$ are the average values of

$\overline{MO}_1^j(t_i), \overline{MO}_2^j(t_i), \overline{T}_1^j(t_i), \overline{T}_2^j(t_i)$ respectively, over the same block of trials. For example,

$$ave_{\overline{MO}_1(t_i)} = \sum_{j=1}^{n} \overline{MO}_i^j(t_i)/n.$$

5. *The multi-dimensional variance* over the entire 300 s span can then be calculated as follows:

$$\text{variance} = \frac{\int_0^{300} \text{var}(t)dt}{300} \approx \frac{\sum_{i=0}^{300} \text{var}(3i) \times 3}{300}.$$

Abstract function/sub-system

At this level of the AH, there are 12 variables that describe the state of the microworld: MO1, EI1, EO1, Ml, El, MI1, MO2, EI2, EO2, M2, E2, and MI2 (see Bisantz and Vicente, 1994). With the addition of time, they form a 13-dimensional space. Multi-variance is defined in the same way as variance at the goal level, except that the variables are normalized with respect to their maximum possible scale values. This normalization process removes any artificial, differential-weighting effects caused by heterogeneous numerical scales across variables.

There are actually two ways to calculate variance at this level of the AH, one that is context-sensitive and another that is not:

1. The first way is by normalization with respect to the setpoint variables (D1, T1, D2, and T2), as well as scale (shown in Table A1).
2. The second method is by normalization with respect to scale only (shown in Table A2).

Generalized function/component

At this level of the AH, there are 10 variables that describe the state of the process: FA, FA$_1$, FA$_2$, FB, FB$_1$, FB$_2$, FO1, FO2, HTR$_1$, and HTR$_2$. Including time, they form an 11-dimensional space. As before, the variables are

TABLE A1

For reservoir 1:	For reservoir 2:
$\overline{MO}_1 = MO_1/D_1$	$\overline{MO}_2 = MO_2/D_2$
$\overline{EI}_1 = EI_1/D_1 \times T_1 \times 2{,}090{,}000$	$\overline{EI}_2 = EI_2/D_2 \times T_2 \times 2{,}090{,}000$
$\overline{EO}_1 = EO_1/D_1 \times T_1 \times 2{,}090{,}000$	$\overline{EO}_2 = EO_2/D_2 \times T_2 \times 2{,}090{,}000$
$\overline{M}_1 = M_1$	$\overline{M}_2 = M_2$
$\overline{E}_1 = E_1/168{,}000{,}000$	$\overline{E}_2 = E_2/168{,}000{,}000$
$\overline{MI}_1 = MI_1/D_1$	$\overline{MI}_2 = MI_2/D_2$

TABLE A2

For reservoir 1:	For reservoir 2:
$\overline{MO}_1 = MO_1$	$\overline{MO}_2 = MO_2$
$\overline{EI}_1 = EI_1/2{,}090{,}000$	$\overline{EI}_2 = EI_2/2{,}090{,}000$
$\overline{EO}_1 = EO_1/2{,}090{,}000$	$\overline{EO}_2 = EO_2/2{,}090{,}000$
$\overline{M}_1 = M_1$	$\overline{M}_2 = M_2$
$\overline{E}_1 = E_1/168{,}000{,}000$	$\overline{E}_2 = E_2/168{,}000{,}000$
$\overline{MI}_1 = MI_1$	$\overline{MI}_2 = MI_2$

normalized with respect to their maximum values before calculating the variance in trajectories.

Physical function/component

In the fourth level of the AH for this micro-world, there are 12 different components that participants can act on: PA, PB, VA, VA1, VA2, VB, VB1, VB2, VO1, VO2, HTR1, and HTR2. With time, these variables form a 13-dimensional action state space. Multi-variance is defined in the same way as variance at the functional purpose level, except that: (a) the variables are normalized with respect to their maximum settings; and (b) time is represented on an ordinal scale (e.g. time of first action, time of second action, etc.) rather than on an interval scale. The latter decision was made because the order of actions seemed to be more important and more meaningful than their precise timing.

References

Bisantz, A. M. and Vicente, K. J. 1994, Making the abstraction hierarchy concrete, *International Journal of Human-Computer Studies*, 40, 83–117.

Christoffersen K., Hunter, C. N. and Vicente, K. J. 1996, A longitudinal study of the effects of ecological interface design on skill acquisition, *Human Factors*, 38, 523–541.

Christoffersen K., Hunter, C. N. and Vicente, K. J. 1997, A longitudinal study of the effects of ecological interface design on fault management performance, *International Journal of Cognitive Ergonomics*, 1, 1–24.

Christoffersen K., Hunter, C. N. and Vicente, K. J. 1998, A longitudinal study of the impact of ecological interface design on deep knowledge. *International Journal of Human-Computer Studies*, 48, 729–762.

Howie, D. E. and Vicente, K. J. 1998, Measures of operator performance in complex, dynamic microworlds: Advancing the state of the art, *Ergonomics*, 41, 485–500.

Moray, N. and Rotenberg, I. 1989, Fault management in process control: Eye movements and action, *Ergonomics*, 11, 1319–1342.

Moray, N., Lootsteen, P. and Pajak, J. 1986, Acquisition of process control skills, *IEEE Transactions on Systems, Man, and Cybernetics*, 16, 497–504.

Pawlak, W. S. and Vicente, K. J. 1996, Inducting effective operator control through ecological interface design, *International Journal of Human-Computer Studies*, 44, 653–688.

Port, R. F. and Van Gelder, T. 1995, *Mind as motion: Explorations in the dynamics of cognition* (Cambridge, MA: MIT Press).

Rasmussen, J. 1985, The role of hierarchical knowledge representation in decision making and system management, *IEEE Transactions on Systems, Man, and Cybernetics*, 15, 234–243.

Sanderson, P. M., Verhage, A. G. and Fuld, R. B. 1989, State-space and verbal protocol methods for studying the human operator in process control, *Ergonomics*, 32, 1343–1372.

Turvey, M. T., Fitch, H. L. and Tuller, B. 1982, The Bernstein perspective: I. The problems of degrees of freedom and context-conditioned variability, in J. A. S. Kelso (ed.), *Human motor behavior: An introduction* (Hillsdale, NJ: Erlbaum), 239–252.

Vicente, K. J. 1991, Supporting knowledge-based behaviour through ecological interface design. Unpublished doctoral dissertation, University of Illinois at Urbana-Champaign, Urbana, IL.

Vicente, K. J. 1999, Cognitive work analysis: Toward safe, productive, and healthy computer-based work (Mahwah, NJ: Erlbaum).

Yu, X., Chow, R., Jamieson, G. A., Khayat, R., Lau, E., Torenvliet, G. L., Vicente, K. J. and Carter, M. W. 1997, Research on the characteristics of long-term adaptation, JAERI Final Report, CEL 97-04, Cognitive Engineering Laboratory, University of Toronto.

6

Statistics for Human-tech Research

Alex Kirlik

> *If science ceases to become a rebellion against authority, then it does not deserve the talents of our brightest children. I was lucky to be introduced to science at school as a subversive activity of the younger boys. We organized a Science Society as an act of rebellion against compulsory Latin and compulsory football. We should try to introduce our children to science today as a rebellion against poverty and ugliness and militarism and economic injustice.*
>
> Freeman Dyson, *The Scientist as Rebel* (p. 7)

I have long thought that human–technology interaction (HTI) requires a textbook on indigenous research methods, especially when it comes to experimental design and statistics. Education on these topics is often outsourced to those teaching them from a purely psychological science perspective, as opposed to those viewing experimentation and data analysis within some larger, practically relevant problem-solving context. The article (by Vicente and Torenvliet) reprinted in this chapter makes the argument that "the statistical analysis techniques that are most familiar to, and most frequently used by, ergonomics scientists and practitioners have important limitations that could be overcome if we also relied on alternative methods of statistical inference." There is little to disagree with in the authors' rebellious stature toward what they take as entrenched statistical practice in the social and behavioral sciences, but I would add that I have seen many improvements along the lines the authors advocate in the years since this article was originally published.

The authors also make the point that their purpose "is *not* to make an original technical contribution to this literature nor is it to dismiss the use of the traditional techniques. Instead, the aim is to bring the practical implications of this literature to the attention of the ergonomics science community, so that we can suggest some complementary ways of analyzing data statistically." This is also one purpose of this book, and I suggest that the reprint may make useful reading especially for those who are unfamiliar with the recent, voluminous literature on the relative merits of null hypothesis statistical testing (NHST) versus other forms of statistical inference.

Especially for HTI researchers, other salient critiques are also relevant here. Wickens (1998), for example, cogently argues that HTI researchers need to better understand and appreciate the difference between a statistically significant effect and an important or useful one. Wickens also provides an informative discussion of the different implications of Type I and Type II errors, in practically relevant, as opposed to basic, research contexts. For example, if a cure for cancer is found to be significant at the $p < .10$ instead of $p < .05$ level—a typical publication threshold—should that research not be communicated? Conversely, if a design or training intervention in an HTI context results in, on average, reduction in reaction time to an email alert of 21 ms, this finding may be statistically significant while having little significance in a broader sense.

Chapter 2 introduced the concept of Kenneth Hammond's "Law of the Laboratory." Vicente relied on this notion to present his continuum, which ranges from "controlled, but unrepresentative" (traditional laboratory experiments") to "representative but uncontrolled" (field studies). As noted in Chapter 2, Hammond presented his "Law of the Laboratory" as a *false* dichotomy. Why?

Following Hammond (1989, and Brunswik, 1956), it is important to note that agriculture provided the inspiration for Fisherian statistics and analysis of variance (ANOVA; inferential techniques discussed at length in the reprinted article). One applies one "treatment" to 100 samples of a population (in psychology, to 100 subjects or participants; in agriculture, to 100 plants) and a different (or no) treatment to 100 other samples drawn from the same populations. ANOVA is a technology for ensuring generalization from the samples observed (subjects, plants) to the remainder of the (unobserved humans and plants) comprising the population from which the samples were drawn. Yet, it provides no parallel assurance for generalizing beyond the treatment conditions used in the experiment. That is, ANOVA provides absolutely no resources to answer the question: "Other than in your laboratory, where else in the world might we expect to observe these fascinating phenomena?"

Why? Farmers require no *statistical* generalization for this. Instead, they *physically* generalize the results of their experiments: they simply apply the treatment (e.g. a fertilizer shown to prove effective) directly to the entire population of plants from which they drew a sample for experimentation. The results of the experiment generalize beyond the experiment because the farmer *makes* them generalize. As Brunswik (and Hammond) have observed, this dis-analogy is one primary reason that many so many "findings" from psychological research are so fragile, and have no guarantee of having implications beyond the confines of the laboratory.

Brunswik's (1956) representative design is essentially a logical basis for trying to guarantee that experimental findings generalize to conditions beyond the laboratory, by ensuring that laboratory conditions are representative of specified external conditions. Adhering to representative design is difficult, but it provides an alternative to Hammond's Law of the Laboratory. It is a methodology for achieving simultaneously reasonable levels of experimental control and experimental rigor in detecting cause–effect relations.

Representative design has its limits, but it has clear implications for any HTI research aiming for practical relevance. Albeit imperfect and incomplete, the collection of studies appearing in our volume *Adaptive Perspectives in Human-Technology Interaction* (2006) were intended to demonstrate that one does not have to view experimental control and representative complexity as a zero-sum game (every study collected in that volume relied on data collected via either field observation or representatively through design simulators or microworlds). In addition, each contributing author to that volume also explicitly framed his or her research using the terminology of Brunswikian theory and method.

In concluding, I would like to also try to make obvious a point that I have found is hardly obvious to my many colleagues in the social and behavioral sciences, even those who wish their research to be relevant to design. That is, it is the farmer's style of generalization—physical generalization—that now largely runs the show in determining the design of the tools and technologies comprising our artifactual ecology. Physical generalization is just another word for technology, and by far, technology is the most successful and prevalent manner of generalizing the results of scientific research. Medical researchers may use ANOVA in analyzing the results of their clinical trials testing the efficacy of pharmaceuticals. But neither ANOVA nor any article in a medical journal ever healed a patient.

Instead, the positive effects of new pharmaceuticals change the world for the better by the same mechanism used by the farmer—by physically generalizing the treatment to the wider population of people (in this case, those afflicted with some disease or unhealthy condition) not included in the clinical trial. Generalization of results from experiment to patient is carried by the pharmaceutical (i.e. technology) itself.

Apple, Inc., may have done an experiment or two in designing the iPod and iPhone (although I have reasons to suspect not). But the huge impact that Apple has made on our modern technology has been enabled by the same old techniques used in agriculture, with a dash of clever marketing added to the mix. Unless the future Human-tech professional is trained in skills such as conceiving and prototyping his or her own novel designs (in addition to being trained in the experimental design and statistical methods needed to evaluate them) I do not see a bright future for Human-tech research.

The Earth Is Spherical ($p < 0.05$): Alternative Methods of Statistical Inference

Kim J. Vicente and Gerard L. Torenvliet

Abstract

A literature review was conducted to understand the limitations of well-known statistical analysis techniques, particularly analysis of variance. The review is structured around six major points: (1) averaging across participants can be misleading; (2) strong predictions are preferable to weak predictions; (3) constructs and measures should be distinguished conceptually and empirically; (4) statistical significance and practical significance should be distinguished conceptually and empirically; (5) the null hypothesis is virtually never true; and (6) one experiment is always inconclusive. Based on these insights, a number of lesser-known and less-frequently used statistical analysis techniques were identified to address the limitations of more traditional techniques. In addition, a number of methodological conclusions about the conduct of human factors research are presented.

1. Introduction

In ergonomics science, the statistical analysis of data almost always relies on analysis of variance (ANOVA), which is a particular type of null-hypothesis significance testing (NHST). All have been taught these techniques and they are so commonly used and so widely accepted that they are frequently applied to data without a second thought. And, because the formulae for these statistical procedures have been embedded in easy-to-use software, their application is faster and less effortful than ever before. Having said that, consider the following quotations:

> Null-hypothesis significance testing is surely the most bone-headedly misguided procedure ever institutionalised in the rote training of science students (Rozeboom 1997: 335). The physical sciences, such as physics and chemistry, do not use statistical significance testing to test hypotheses or interpret data. In fact, most researchers in the physical sciences regard reliance on significance testing as unscientific.
>
> (Schmidt and Hunter 1997: 39)

> I believe that the almost universal reliance on merely refuting the null hypothesis as the standard method for corroborating substantive theories … is a terrible mistake, is basically unsound, poor scientific strategy, and one of the worst things that ever happened in the history of psychology.
>
> (Meehl 1978: 817)

These quotes are extreme, but the undeniable scientific point is that the statistical analysis techniques that are most familiar to, and most frequently used by, ergonomics scientists and practitioners have important limitations that could be overcome if we also relied on alternative methods of statistical inference.

Critiques of NHST and ANOVA go back at least to the 1960s (e.g. Rozeboom, 1960; Bakan, 1966; Meehl, 1967; Lykken, 1968), resurfaced periodically in the 1970s and 1980s (e.g. Meehl, 1978; Hammond et al., 1986, 1987; Rosnow and Rosenthal, 1989), and have appeared with increasing frequency and cogency during the past decade (e.g. Cohen, 1990, 1994; Meehl, 1990; Loftus, 1991, 1993b, 1995, 2001; Loftus and Masson, 1994; Hammond, 1996; Thompson, 1996; Harlow et al., 1997;

Loftus and McLean, 1997). These critiques have been met with rebuttals (e.g. Serlin and Lapsley, 1985; Chow, 1996; Abelson, 1997; Hagen, 1997; Harlow et al., 1997). The discussion has grown to the point where several journals have dedicated special sections to discussing the pros and cons of this issue (e.g. Thompson, 1993; Shrout, 1997; Chow, 1998).

There is now a growing consensus that there are sound reasons to justify discontent with sole reliance on traditional methods of statistical data analysis. This dissatisfaction has led some journal editors to take significant actions to remedy the situation. As editor of *Memory & Cognition,* Loftus (1993a) strongly encouraged authors to adopt non-traditional data analysis and presentation methods. The editors of *Educational and Psychological Measurement* (Thompson, 1994), *Journal of Applied Psychology* (Murphy, 1997), and *Journal of Experimental Education* (Heldref Foundation, 1997) went further, by requiring that authors report alternative statistical results. The editor of the *American Journal of Public Health,* the top journal in that discipline, even went so far as to ban statistical significance testing and any reference to p-values for a couple of years (Shrout, 1997). More recently, the American Psychological Association Board of Scientific Affairs struck a Task Force on Statistical Inference consisting of a number of world-class researchers in both psychology and statistics "to elucidate some of the controversial issues surrounding applications of statistics including significance testing and its alternatives; alternative underlying models and data transformation; and newer methods made possible by powerful computers" (Wilkinson et al., 1999: 594). There must be some substantive issues at stake for several scholars and organizations to take such strong actions.

The authors' experience has been that most ergonomics scientists are unaware of the controversy surrounding traditional methods of statistical inference, of the important limitations of these methods, and that alternative methods can be adopted to overcome some of these limitations (this opinion is empirically substantiated later, albeit informally). The purpose of this article is to discuss all of these issues in the context of ergonomics science. To be clear, the purpose is *not* to make an original technical contribution to this literature nor is it to dismiss the use of the traditional techniques. Instead, the aim is to bring the practical implications of this literature to the attention of the ergonomics science community, so that we can suggest some complementary ways of analysing data statistically.

2. Six issues in statistical inference

This literature review is organized into six sections, each of which identifies a major issue in statistical inference and a corresponding set of alternative methods. Although some of these points may seem self-evident, the review will show that they are frequently not heeded by ergonomics scientists. By making each of these points explicit, new ways of analysing data can be identified. These lesser-known statistical analysis techniques may, in turn, provide a different, and sometimes perhaps more valuable, set of insights into data.

Before proceeding, several caveats need to be mentioned. First, some of the limitations of ANOVA that are discussed are found only in more modern treatments and usages, and not in the original Fisherian formulation. But, since it is the former, rather than the latter, that is familiar to and generally adopted by most of the intended readers, it seems nevertheless worthwhile to discuss these limitations. Secondly, several of the alternative data analysis techniques discussed can be, but are not usually, derived from information generated by an ANOVA. However, regardless of how they are calculated, one of the main points is that alternative methods of statistical inference provide valuable information that is complementary to that which is usually reported using traditional techniques. Thirdly, in some cases, the limitations identified are not as much with ANOVA itself but rather with the way in which it is generally used. For example, there is no reason why the information usually provided by ANOVA cannot be supplemented by some of the complementary measures identified. The main point is that this practice is not usually followed in the human factors community, and that there are good reasons to change the way in which we currently analyse our data. Finally, we do not claim to have identified a panacea for the problems with traditional techniques. The alternative methods proposed, whilst useful and complementary, are not perfect. Furthermore, there is no substitute for having a clear idea of a study's objectives before determining the right mix of statistical techniques to apply to the data.

2.1. Averaging across participants can be misleading

We will begin by discussing an issue with which many researchers are familiar but that is, nevertheless, frequently overlooked. ANOVA involves averaging across participants. As a result, it is commonplace for ergonomics scientists to assess statistical significance at an aggregate level of group means. Yet, taking an average only makes statistical sense if the samples being aggregated are qualitatively similar to each other. Without looking at each participant's data individually, we do not know if the group average is representative of the behaviour of the individuals. In fact, it is possible for a group average to be a "statistical myth" in the sense that it is not indicative of the behaviour of any single participant in the group.

Data from a 6-month longitudinal study conducted by Christoffersen et al. (1994) can be used to illustrate this point in a salient fashion. Figure 1 shows a learning curve illustrating the average time to complete a task as a function of experience. The curve is based on data averaged over six participants. A power law fit has been superimposed on the aggregate data. Based on visual inspection alone, it can be seen that there is a good fit between the data and the power law curve. A regression analysis showing a substantial r^2 value of 0.74 confirms this impression. One might conclude from this aggregate-level analysis that these data provide support for the power law of practice (Newell and Rosenbloom, 1981). However, such a conclusion could be premature. Without looking

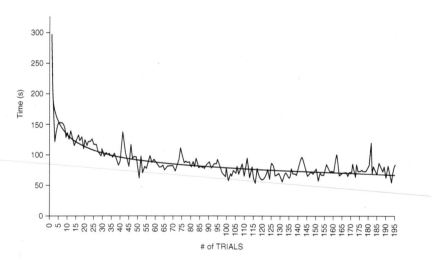

FIGURE 1   Learning curve averaged over six participants (Christoffersen et al. 1994).

at each participant's data it cannot be known whether the elegant, aggregate power curve fit would provide an equally good account of the skill acquisition of each individual.

Figure 2 shows the learning curve data for one of the six participants. Again, a best fit power law curve has been superimposed, but this time on the raw data of an individual, not the mean data of the group. The degree of fit between the power law of practice and this participant's data is obviously poor. Thus, to use the group average as a basis for generalizing to individuals would be quite misleading in this case.

Plateaus in learning curves and the dangers of aggregating data over participants are hardly new insights (Bryan and Harter, 1897, 1899; Woodworth, 1938). Yet, as Venda and Venda (1995) pointed out, these insights are still frequently ignored by many, although by no means all, ergonomics scientists. It is believed that, in part, these oversights result from the fact that ANOVA encourages the aggregation of data over participants. Consequently, a special, added effort must be made to examine the data for each individual to see if what is true of the group is also true of the individual.

Taking the dangers of aggregating over participants to heart can actually lead to new and perhaps more compelling ways of analysing data. Several statistical methods can be used to address the aforementioned problems,

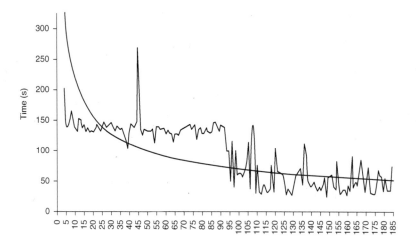

FIGURE 2   Learning curve for one of the six participants (Christoffersen *et al.* 1994).

but here only one is discussed. In cases where a within-participants design is adopted, each individual can be viewed as an experiment and see if the theoretical predictions being tested hold for each person. An example of this type of test is provided by Vicente (1992), who compared the performance of the same participants with two different interfaces, one labelled P and the other labelled P + F. There were theoretical reasons for hypothesizing that the P + F interface would lead to better performance than the P. However, rather than just seeing if the group means of the two conditions differed, Vicente also conducted a more detailed analysis to see if the theoretical prediction held for each and every participant. The number of participants for whom the hypothesized relationship (P + F > P) held was counted and then this count was analyzed statistically by conducting a sign test (Siegel, 1956). In one analysis, the P + F interface led to better performance than the P for 11 out of 12 experts, a statistically significant result.

This example is important for two reasons. First, in at least some applied situations, it may be more important for ergonomics scientists and practitioners to know how often an expected result is obtained at the level of the individual than at the level of an aggregate. For example, say the performance impact of an advanced control room for a nuclear power plant is being tested. Are we only interested in knowing whether the mean performance of the new control room is better than that with the old, or are we also interested in knowing the proportion of operators for which performance with the new control room is better? It seems that the latter is also valuable. After all, an ANOVA could show that the new interface leads to a statistically significant improvement in performance, but an analysis like the one conducted by Vicente (1992) might reveal that the new interface only leads to better performance for half of the operators (a nonsignificant result with a sign test). In this case, the aggregate level analysis is misleading, just as the aggregate data in Figure 1 are. And, because of the potential hazard involved, designers might be wary about introducing a new control room that will result in a performance decrement for half of its operators. Secondly, this example also shows that non-parametric tests (e.g. the sign test and the c^2 test), that are statistically less powerful than parametric tests, can actually be used in innovative ways to test strong predictions. This topic is discussed in more detail next.

2.2. Strong predictions are preferable to weak predictions

Empirical predictions can be ordered on a continuum from strong to weak (Vicente, 1998). At the strong end, there are *point* predictions. To take a hypothetical example from physics, a theory might predict that the gravitational constant, *G*, should be $6.67 \times 10^{-11} \mathrm{Nm}^2/\mathrm{kg}^2$. An experiment can then be conducted to see how well the data correspond to this point prediction. Slightly farther along the continuum, *interval* predictions are found. To continue with the same example, a different theory might only predict that $6 \times 1^{-11} \mathrm{Nm}^2/\mathrm{kg}^2 < G < 7 \times 10^{-11} \mathrm{Nm}^2/\mathrm{kg}^2$. An interval prediction is weaker than a point prediction because it is consistent with a wider range of results. Still farther towards the weaker side of the continuum, *ordinal* predictions are found. For example, a third theory might only predict the direction of the force of gravity. In this case, all one would know is that gravity pulls objects towards, rather than away from, the earth. Finally, at the weak end of the continuum, *categorical* predictions are found. For example, a very primitive theory might merely predict that the force of gravity on the earth is statistically significantly different from zero, regardless of its direction (i.e. that gravity exists).

Meehl (1967, 1978, 1990) has repeatedly pointed out that a mature science should strive to make predictions towards the strong end of this continuum, but that psychology has generally failed to do so. The same claim can generally be made for ergonomics science, although there certainly are exceptions. According to Meehl, one of the causes of this lack of maturity is that researchers have let the constraints of the statistical analysis techniques with which they are most familiar (i.e. ANOVA) govern the strength of the predictions they make. And, because ANOVA is usually used by behavioural researchers to determine if an effect is significantly different from zero (i.e. if the independent variable has no effect whatsoever), ergonomics scientists frequently restrict themselves to testing categorical predictions. This area is the weakest on the continuum and is, thus, indicative of a comparatively immature scientific practice. Because we are so accustomed to following this procedure, we may not even be aware that we are merely testing a categorical prediction. However, the hypothetical example cited above shows just how weak such a test really is. Merely predicting that gravity exists does not seem like an impressive scientific achievement. Granted, pairwise comparisons of means can be used to test ordinal predictions at an aggregate level, but this is still a far cry from the interval and point predictions located on the strong end of the continuum described above.

It could be argued that most areas of human factors research have not reached the level of theoretical maturity to make point or interval predictions. There is merit to this objection, but, even so, it does not follow that we cannot or should not be more ambitious than we have been in the past. Rather than letting familiar statistical analysis techniques keep us from achieving a mature science, we should instead seek out a different set of techniques that can be used to test stronger predictions, whenever they can be made. For a practical science like ergonomics, the value of quantitative prediction is particularly important. Engineering design always involves tradeoffs, so, in making the case for ergonomics science, it is invaluable to know how big an impact a particular design intervention will have on performance or safety (Chapanis, 1967).

The innovative work of Hammond et al. (1987) provides an example of how ergonomics scientists can begin to make stronger predictions and how these can be tested using untraditional statistical analysis techniques. Hammond et al. were interested in comparing the efficacy of intuitive and analytical cognition in expert judgement. Accordingly, they conducted an experiment to investigate the impact of two independent variables, depth task characteristics and surface task characteristics, on the level of performance and the type of cognitive processing (i.e. intuition vs. analysis) of 21 professional highway engineers. There were three levels for the depth task characteristics dimension: (a) an aesthetics task that was intended to induce intuition; (b) an highway capacity calculation task that was intended to induce analysis; and (c) a safety judgement task that was intended to induce a hybrid of intuition and analysis. Each of these tasks was presented in three different formats, each with a different set of surface characteristics: (a) film strips that were intended to induce intuition; (b) formulae that were intended to induce analysis; and (c) bar graphs that were intended to induce a hybrid of intuition and analysis. Each of the 21 highway engineers experienced each of the nine combinations of depth and surface task characteristics.

From a traditional perspective, this experimental design fits neatly into a within-participants 3 × 3 randomized block factorial ANOVA.

However, analysing the data in this fashion would only allow the experimenters to test null hypotheses. Such a test only amounts to an evaluation of a categorical prediction (equivalent to the fact that gravity exists). Furthermore, the ANOVA would only evaluate the results at an aggregate level of analysis, and, thus, could mask some important individual differences (see the previous section).

Hammond et al. (1987) addressed these deficiencies in three ways. First, instead of evaluating the NHSTs associated with ANOVA, they instead tested the prediction that the results from the nine experimental conditions should occur in a particular order predicted by the theory motivating their research. Note that this is a much stronger prediction. Instead of just hypothesizing that the effect was different from zero, Hammond et al. were committing to one specific ordering of their experimental conditions. Also, because there was a total of nine conditions in their experiment, there are many possible orderings that could conceivably occur (9! = 362 880). Only one of these orderings is perfectly consistent with the prediction they were making. Secondly, instead of testing this ordinal prediction at the level of a group aggregate, they tested it individually for each of the 21 participants. That is, Hammond et al. (1987) predicted "the exact order of appearance of a specific type of cognitive activity for each engineer separately, over a set of nine conditions, each of which included a sample of 40 highways. Thus, there were in effect 21 individual experiments, each of which tested the ... theory" (p. 769). Because of the level of specificity involved, the risk of being wrong is again greater than with ANOVA, thereby resulting in a stronger set of predictions. Thirdly, to test the predicted ordering on a participant-by-participant basis, Hammond et al. relied on correlational analysis and χ^2-based order table analysis. The technical details can be found in Hammond et al.'s article, but the basic rationale is similar to that for the Vicente (1992) study described in the previous section. Non-parametric tests were used to determine how often the predicted order of results was observed at the level of individuals rather than at the aggregate level of the group.

The study conducted by Hammond et al. (1987) provides a role model to show how the maturity of ergonomics science can be enhanced by using alternative statistical analysis techniques to test stronger predictions than those that are usually assessed using ANOVA alone.

2.3. Constructs and methods for measurement should be distinguished conceptually and empirically

Even if we were able to make and evaluate stronger predictions, the level of science is only as good as the empirical methods used. Of particular importance is the relationship between the constructs that are used to make predictions and the methods of measurement that are used to evaluate those predictions. This linkage is one of the key epistemological foundations supporting any kind of scientific activity, including ergonomics science (cf. Xiao and Vicente, 2000). As Campbell and Fiske (1959) pointed out in their seminal article over 40 years ago, there are certain basic criteria that must be met before a pattern of experimental results can be interpreted in a meaningful fashion. *Reliability* refers to the extent to which similar results are obtained when the same construct is assessed using the same method of measurement under comparable conditions. If results cannot be replicated, then there is a lack of reliability. *Convergent validity* refers to the extent to which similar results are obtained when the same construct is assessed using different methods of measurement under otherwise comparable conditions. If different methods give different results, then the pattern of findings is contaminated, and, thus, difficult to interpret. Instead of observing the effects of the construct of interest, you are instead observing the effects of the way in which the construct was measured—a much less interesting phenomenon, unless you are a methodologist. Finally, *discriminant validity* refers to the extent to which distinct results are obtained when different constructs are assessed using the same measurement method under comparable conditions. If different constructs lead to similar results, then the pattern of findings is again contaminated, and, thus, difficult to interpret. Instead of observing differential effects across the various constructs of interest, you are instead observing similar effects caused by the method of measurement.

A few hypothetical ergonomics science examples can help make these abstract concepts more concrete. If an empirical investigation of the interaction between spatial ability and mental workload for a particular work context were being performed, how could the three criteria identified by Campbell and Fiske (1959) be operationalized? Beginning with the issue of reliability, whatever method used to measure each construct should lead to consistent results under comparable conditions.

For example, the test for spatial ability should have a high test–retest correlation. Otherwise, we cannot have much confidence in our knowledge of one of the key constructs in the experiment. Moving on to convergent validity, different methods of measuring the same construct should lead to consistent results under comparable conditions. For example, if there were two different methods for measuring mental workload (e.g. a computer-based version and a paper-based version of the same subjective rating scale), it would be ideal if those methods were to give the same results for the same participant for a particular trial. If the two methods give different results, then the variance in the data is being caused by the method of measurement. In such a case, confident inferences cannot be made about the item of interest, namely the construct of mental workload. As for the third criterion of discriminant validity, the same measurement methods should lead to distinct results for different constructs of interest. For example, a computer-based test of spatial ability should be more strongly correlated with a paper-based test of spatial ability than with a computer-based assessment of mental workload. If this criterion is not met, then there is too high a correlation between tests that are intended to measure different constructs. Once more, such a result would provide a very shaky foundation for scientific knowledge.

In each of these three cases, the key objective is to determine whether the results observed can be safely attributed to the content of the constructs of interest rather than the form of the methods that are used to measure those constructs. Campbell and Fiske (1959) refer to the latter as "methods variance." To make sure that methods variance is not contaminating the results, a way is needed to evaluate reliability, convergent validity, and discriminant validity empirically. To achieve this goal requires that any one experiment has at least two constructs and at least two methods of measurement. Using these insights, Campbell and Fiske proposed an analysis technique that can allow experimenters to determine if they are measuring the construct in which they are interested, rather than something entirely different. This technique, called the Multitrait-Multimethod Matrix (MTMM), was originally developed for the specific case of investigating individual differences (thus, the emphasis on traits). More recently, the technique was extended by Hammond et al. (1986) so that it can be applied to a much wider range of behavioral phenomena.

Campbell and Fiske (1959) used the MTMM technique to review the literature on individual differences. Their analysis painted "a rather sorry picture" (p. 93) of the validity of the measures that had been used in that literature. Most of the results that had been generated were more likely to have been determined by the methods used for measurement than by the traits that had been hypothesized to account for the results. The MTMM technique provides a way of identifying such situations. However, as Hammond et al. (1986) pointed out, the technique is rarely used in experimental psychology. The same is true of ergonomics science; although some researchers have investigated convergent validity using other techniques, studies of all three threats to validity using the MTMM technique are exceedingly rare. Researchers tend to analyse their data using other more familiar techniques, such as ANOVA. However, those techniques do not provide an analytical means for evaluating reliability, convergent validity, and discriminant validity, as does MTMM. As a result, researchers cannot know if their results are being caused by methods variance. Hammond et al. make a very strong case that this situation makes it exceedingly difficult to develop a cumulative scientific knowledge base. Instead, the result is conflicting findings because researchers have not determined empirically that the preconditions for sound scientific knowledge have been satisfied in their experiments. The MTMM technique and its extensions provide a systematic means of remedying this situation.

Lee's (1992; Lee and Moray, 1994) investigation of the relationship between operator trust, self-confidence, and the use of automation is the only application of MTMM in the ergonomics science literature of which we are aware. As such, it can be used to illustrate the value of conceptually and empirically distinguishing between constructs and methods of measurement. In Lee's study, there were two constructs of interest, the operators' trust in the automation's ability to control a process and the operators' self-confidence in their own ability to control a process. There were also two methods of measurement, ratings on a subjective scale and the frequency of operators' monitoring behaviour. The matrix shown in Table 1 can be built from this experimental design. Note that Lee did not present the same conditions more than once, so it is not possible to assess the reliability values along the diagonal of Table 1.

TABLE I   A multitrait-multimethod matrix relating trust and self confidence measured by subjective scales and frequency of monitoring behaviour for Lee's (1992, Lee and Moray 1994) study.

		Trust		Self-confidence	
		SS	MB	SS	MB
Trust	SS				
	MB	✓			
Self-confidence	SS	×	×		
	MB	×	×	✓	

✓: a high correlation is expected in that cell (i.e. convergent validity).
×: a very low correlation is expected in that cell (i.e. divergent validity).
SS: subjective scales.
MB: monitoring behaviour.

Nevertheless, it is possible to use MTMM to assess discriminant and convergent validity. Convergent validity is exhibited if different methods lead to similar results for the same construct under comparable conditions. There are two cells in Table I that are relevant to assessing this criterion. The first is the cell in the second row and first column of Table I. One should expect to see a high correlation value in this cell (indicated by a '✓') because trust measured by monitoring behaviour should lead to results that are comparable to those obtained by measuring trust with a subjective scale. The second relevant cell is in the fourth row and third column of Table I. One should also expect to see a high correlation value in this cell because self-confidence measured by monitoring behaviour should lead to results that are comparable to those obtained by measuring self-confidence with a subjective scale.

Divergent validity is exhibited if the same or different methods lead to different results for different constructs under comparable conditions. The remaining four cells in the bottom left corner of Table I are relevant to assessing this criterion. One should expect to see lower correlation values (indicated by a ×) in these cells. For example, ratings of self-confidence on a subjective scale and ratings of trust on a subjective scale should be weakly correlated, if at all, because they are measuring different constructs. If the data turn out to be strongly correlated, then one can infer that methods variance is at play (i.e. that the results are determined more by the fact that a subjective rating scale is being used as a method of measurement than by the constructs that are of real interest).

Table 2 shows the results that Lee (1992) obtained using the MTMM technique. A cursory examination shows that the criteria of discriminant and convergent validity were not consistently met in this study. For example, the highest correlation in Table 2, 0.42, is that between two different constructs (trust and self-confidence) when they were measured with a common method (subjective scales). One would expect to see a low correlation here because different constructs should lead to different results. The fact that there is a comparatively large correlation suggests that methods variance is contaminating the results. As another example, there is a very low correlation, 0.04, between the two methods of measuring self-confidence. One would expect to see a high correlation here because different methods for measuring the same construct should lead to the same results. The fact that there is a very low correlation suggests that methods variance is again contaminating the results.

This example provides a concrete illustration of how the MTMM technique can be used to evaluate discriminant and convergent validity in ergonomics science. Unless these criteria are satisfied, the results obtained from any study cannot lead to sound scientific knowledge. If the results obtained by Lee (1992; Lee and Moray, 1994) and those reviewed by Campbell and Fiske (1959) and Hammond et al. (1986) are any indication, then the ergonomics science literature is likely to be full

TABLE 2   A multitrait-multimethod matrix relating trust and self confidence measured by subjective scales and frequency of monitoring behaviour (Lee 1992, Lee and Moray 1994). The values are the means of z-transformed correlation coefficients of individual operators. Abbreviations are as in table 1.

		Trust		Self-confidence	
		SS	MB	SS	MB
Trust	SS				
	MB	0.15(✓)			
Self-confidence	SS	0.42	0.04(×)		
	MB	−0.07	−0.08(×)	0.04(v)	

✓: a high correlation was expected in that cell (a sign of convergent validity).
×: a very low correlation was expected in that cell (a sign of divergent validity).

of results that are caused by methods variance rather than by the substantive, theoretical issues that motivated the research. The MTMM technique provides a means of identifying, and, thus, beginning to remove, such obstacles to scientific progress.

2.4. Statistical significance and practical significance should be distinguished conceptually and empirically

It is a truism in ergonomics science and practice that statistical significance is not the same as practical significance (Chapanis, 1967). This truism has a sound basis in statistics (although, as will be discussed shortly, it is frequently ignored). For example, the NHSTs that are usually associated with ANOVA are measures of statistical significance, or, more precisely, the probability that the data could have arisen, given that the null hypothesis is true. This type of test does not tell us much that is likely to be very useful in determining the practical significance of a finding. To assess the latter, information is needed about magnitude, and it is useful to distinguish between two types: (a) measures of association strength; and (b) measures of effect size (Snyder and Lawson, 1993). Using measures of magnitude and some criterion from the domain of interest regarding what magnitude is important for applied purposes, it is possible to assess the practical significance of a result. Such pragmatic information is of great importance to an intrinsically applied discipline, like ergonomics science. Nevertheless, it is much more common to see tests of statistical significance than tests of strength of association or effect size reported in the literature. In this subsection, the value added provided by data analysis techniques that provide magnitude information will be discussed.

Because of the central role that they play in multiple linear regression, measures of *association strength* are probably more familiar to readers, so will be discussed first (see Snyder and Lawson, 1993, for more details). The most common statistic (and the simplest to calculate) is the proportion of the total variance explained by a particular effect, usually referred to in ANOVA as eta-squared. Despite the fact that eta-squared is easy to calculate from the information in an ANOVA table (it is simply a ratio of sums of squares), it is rare to see such information reported. Moreover, because the emphasis has been on significance tests, ergonomics scientists sometimes only report the result of the .F-test and do not provide the information from the ANOVA table that could be used by other researchers to calculate the strength of association. This practice is unfortunate because an F- or p-value does not provide any information about the magnitude of an effect. In contrast, eta-squared provides an estimate of how strong the association is between the independent variable(s) of interest and the dependent variable chosen. When combined with criteria from a particular domain of interest, this statistic can help in making inferences about practical significance.

For example, if one is interested in the ergonomics science problem of worker selection, it is known from the individual differences literature that it is unusual for a particular selection test to account for say 20% of the variance in the data. Thus, if an eta-squared value is obtained that is greater than this benchmark value, then it is known that the result is practically significant (i.e. it may be used to develop a better basis for worker selection). Note that the result may or may not be statistically significant. If the sample size is small, it is possible to have a comparatively large eta-squared value (e.g. a selection test accounting for more than 20% of the variance) and results that are not statistically significant. Such a result could, nevertheless, be considered practically significant. Conversely, if the sample size is large, it is possible to obtain statistically significant results and yet have a comparatively very low eta-squared value (e.g. a selection test accounting for only 1% of the variance). Such a result would be of little practical value (i.e. it could not be used to develop a useful basis for worker selection). The bottom line is that measures of association strength, like eta-squared, provide a more complementary set of insights into the results than do the statistical significance tests that are typically reported with ANOVA.

There are various types of statistics that can be used to obtain information about association strength. For example, omega squared is an estimate of the population strength of association. It can be computed from knowledge of the F-statistic, number of treatment levels (p), and sample size (n) as follows:

$$\omega^2 = \frac{(P-1)(F-1)}{(p-1)(f-1)+np}.$$

Some sample statistics of association, like eta-squared, are biased esti-mates, meaning that they tend to overestimate systematically the propor-tion of variance explained. To be conservative, it is more appropriate to use unbiased estimates of strength of association that compensate for this tendency to overestimate. Snyder and Lawson (1993) describe several such statistics, and readers are referred there to obtain more details. But, regardless of the particular measure used, the fundamental point remains the same—measures of association strength provide information that complements that provided by statistical significance tests, and the former information is of greater interest in determining practical significance.

A similar argument holds for the second type of magnitude infor-mation. *Effect size* (Cohen, 1988, 1990, 1994; Rosnow and Rosenthal, 1989; Abelson, 1995; Rouanet, 1996) is a measure of the magnitude of an effect, and, thus, can also be used along with domain-specific criteria to indicate the degree of practical importance of ergonomics science results. Note that effect size and statistical significance provide complementary information: "it is very important to realize that the effect size tells us something very different from the *p*-level. A result that is statistically significant is not necessarily practically significant as judged by the mag-nitude of the effect" (Rosnow and Rosenthal, 1989: 1279).

In an applied science like ergonomics, effect size plays a critical role. As Chow (1996: 8) observed: "a significant result may be a trivial one in practical terms. Alternatively, an important real-life effect may be ignored simply because it does not reach the arbitrary chosen level of statistical significance." Despite this truism, an informal survey of the ergonomics science literature (see below) reveals that statistical significance is reported far more frequently than is effect size. Once again, it is believed that this is indicative of an over-reliance on NHST and ANOVA. Neither of these statistical techniques provides direct measures of effect size.

Because of the foundational importance of practical significance to ergonomics science, it is important that effect sizes are calculated in addi-tion to assessing statistical significance. Several ways of calculating effect size have been proposed in the literature. For example, Cohen (1988) has proposed the standardized mean difference statistic, *d,* as a generalizable measure of effect size. Based on the results that are typically found in behavioural research, Cohen has suggested that $d = 0.2$ is indicative of a small effect, $d = 0.5$ is indicative of a medium sized effect, and that $d = 0.8$

is indicative of a large effect. These nominal values provide a starting point for evaluating the practical significance of research results.

Like the other points made earlier, the distinction between statistical significance and effect size is best conveyed by an example (adapted from Rosnow and Rosenthal, 1989). Consider two hypothetical experiments, both conducted to evaluate the impact of two types of training programmes, T_1 and T_2, on human performance. In one experiment (with $n = 80$), T_1 is found to lead to significantly better performance than T_2 ($t(78) = 2.21; p < 0.05$). In another experiment (with $n = 20$), no significant difference between T_1 and T_2 is observed ($t(18) = 1.06, p > 0.30$). By relying solely on these tests, we might be tempted to conclude that the second experiment failed to replicate the results of the first. Such a conclusion would cast doubt on the practical impact of T_1 on human performance.

Calculating effect size adds new information that can help put the results in a more realistic light. In this hypothetical example, the magnitude of the effect is actually the same for both experiments ($d = 0.50$), despite the fact that the p-values for the two experiments differed considerably. How is this possible? Because the second experiment had a smaller sample size, the power to reject the null hypothesis at $\alpha = 0.05$ was very low, only 0.18. In contrast, the first experiment had a much larger sample size, and, thus, its power was 0.6—over three times greater than that in the second experiment. These results clearly show the difference between statistical significance and effect size, and, thus, why it is important to calculate effect size.

2.5. The null hypothesis is virtually never true

There is another reason for not relying solely on the results produced by NHST and ANOVA. As odd as it may sound, there are very good reasons to argue that the null hypothesis is almost never really true in behavioural research. This point has been made by many noted researchers (e.g. Meehl, 1967, 1978, 1990, 1997; Cohen, 1990, 1994; Loftus, 1991, 2001; Abelson, 1995; Thompson, 1996; Steiger and Fouladi, 1997), but its implications have not been taken as seriously as they should be in ergonomics science.

Consider a typical ergonomics experiment comparing the effect of two treatments (e.g. two interfaces, two training programmes, or two selection criteria) on human performance. One group of participants is given Treatment X, whereas another is given Treatment Y. The null hypothesis in such a study is that there is no difference whatsoever between the population means for the two treatment groups. Can we really consider such a hypothesis seriously? For example, can we realistically expect that the effects of two different interfaces are exactly the same to an infinite number of decimal points? Meehl (1967) was perhaps the first of many to point out that the answers to questions such as this one are almost sure to be "no":

> Considering ... that everything in the brain is connected with everything else, and that there exist several "general state-variables" (such as arousal, attention, anxiety and the like) which are known to be at least slightly influenceable by practically any kind of stimulus input, it is highly unlikely that any psychologically discriminable situation which we apply to an experimental subject would exert literally zero effect on any aspect of performance. (p. 162)

One way to illustrate the implausible nature of the null hypothesis is to consider the insight that is gained by using NHST with very large sample sizes. Meehl (1990) describes a data set obtained by administering a questionnaire to 57 000 high school seniors. These data were analysed in various ways using χ^2 tables, with each analysis looking at the interaction between various categorical factors. In each case, the null hypothesis was that there was no interaction between the categories being compared. A total of 105 analyses were conducted. Each analysis led to statistically significant results, and 96% of the analyses were significant at $p < 0.000\ 001$. As Meehl observed, some of the statistically significant relationships are easy to explain theoretically, some are more difficult, and others are completely baffling. To take another example, with a sample size of 14 000, a correlation of 0.0278 is statistically significant at $p < 0.001$ (Cohen, 1990). Figures such as these show that the scientific knowledge that is gained solely by refuting the null hypothesis is minimal, at best. The same types of problems can occur in studies with low sample size as well (Chapanis, 1967).

If the null hypothesis is almost always false, then the act of conducting a NHST means something very different than what we usually thinks it means. Rather than being a generator of scientific insight, the NHST instead becomes an indirect indicator of statistical power. For example, if a data set does not yield results that are significant at $p < 0.05$, then the likely interpretation is not that the alternative hypothesis is incorrect, but that the sample size of the experiment was too low to obtain an acceptable level of power. After all, as the Meehl (1990) and Cohen (1990) examples show, if one has the fortitude and resources to include enough participants in experiments, then virtually any null hypothesis can be rejected. Thus, the value of just conducting a NHST is minimal. As Cohen (1994: 1001) has pointed out, "if all we ... learn from a research is that A is larger than B ($p < 0.01$), we have not learned very much. And this is typically all we learn."

Accepting the fact that the null hypothesis is virtually never true in behavioural research, what are the implications for the statistical analysis of data? The short answer is that it would be useful to have other data analysis techniques that offer more insights than a NHST or ANOVA alone. Two related techniques have frequently been suggested to fulfil this role, power analysis and confidence intervals (Cohen, 1990, 1994; Loftus, 1993b, 1995, 2001; Loftus and Masson, 1994; Abelson, 1995; Meehl, 1997; Steiger and Fouladi, 1997).

Rather than using the results of a NHST as a surrogate measure of statistical power, researchers would be better off if they calculated power directly before an experiment is conducted to obtain a proper sample size. The resulting measure provides an explicit indication of the sensitivity of an experiment to detect an effect of interest. In addition to its preferred *a priori* role in determining the sample size for a planned experiment, the calculation of power is also valuable in a *post hoc* role where the failure to reject the null hypothesis is used as evidence to falsify a particular theory. In these situations, it is essential that statistical power be calculated. After all, the failure to reject the null hypothesis could simply be caused by the fact that too small a sample size was used to detect the effect of interest. Therefore, to keep ergonomics scientists from "falsifying" theories simply by not including enough participants in their experiment, it would be useful to present calculations of power. Doing so would provide additional information over that obtained just by conducting a NHST or ANOVA.

Confidence intervals provide another data analysis technique that can be used to obtain greater insight into experimental results. Whereas the results of a NHST merely show the probability that the data could have arisen given that the null hypothesis were true, confidence intervals directly provide information about the range of values within which population parameters are likely to be found. As such, they have several advantages over NHST. First, confidence intervals provide a graphical representation of results rather than an alphanumeric representation (see the example, below). This format makes it easier for researchers to extract information from their data analysis. Secondly, the width of a confidence interval provides an indication of the precision of measurement. Wide confidence intervals indicate imprecise knowledge, whereas narrow confidence intervals indicate precise knowledge. This information is not provided by the p-value given by a NHST. Thirdly, the relative position of two or more confidence intervals can provide qualitative information about the relationships across a set of group means. If two confidence intervals do not overlap, then the means are significantly different from each other statistically, otherwise they are not. Whilst this information can be gained from a standard NHST, confidence intervals add information about the order of means across groups, information that cannot be found in, for instance, an ANOVA table. Finally, confidence intervals also allow us to assess the statistical significance of individual effects. If a confidence interval on a group mean includes zero, then the treatment did not have a significant effect. (To achieve a similarity between NHST and confidence intervals, the type I error rate for the NHST should be equal to 1—the confidence coefficient.) Therefore, the plotting of confidence intervals provides researchers with more insights into their data than could be obtained by NHST or ANOVA alone.

The informativeness of confidence intervals can be illustrated with a simple example borrowed from Steiger and Fouladi (1997). Figure 3 shows data from three hypothetical experiments, each consisting of two conditions. Thus, each confidence interval in the figure is for the difference between a pair of means. Each experiment was performed in the same domain and using measures with approximately the same amount of variability. Note that the confidence intervals from experiments 1 and 3 do not include zero. In these two cases, a NHST would indicate that the difference in means is significantly different from zero, leading to a

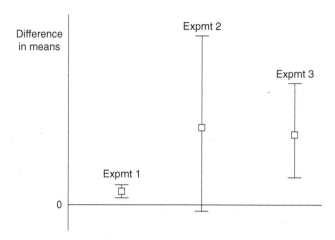

FIGURE 3   Hypothetical example showing how confidence intervals reflect different degrees of measurement precision (adapted from Steiger and Fouladi 1997).

decision to reject the null hypothesis. In experiment 2, the confidence
interval includes zero. Thus, in this case, a NHST would indicate that the
difference in means is not significantly different from zero. Thus, the
confidence intervals in Figure 3 provide all the information that can
be obtained directly from a NHST, the difference being that that information is presented graphically.

However, additional information not directly available from a NHST
can also be obtained from confidence intervals. For example, based on
the results presented above, the NHST might lead us to believe that the
results from experiment 2 do not agree with those from the other two
experiments. The confidence intervals provide a graphical basis for reaching a different interpretation. Experiment 1 had a very large sample size
and a very high level of precision, resulting in a very narrow confidence
interval band. However, precision should not be confused with magnitude. Figure 3 clearly shows that the effect size in experiment 1 is comparatively very small. The only reason why the null hypothesis was
rejected was because the measurement precision was so great. Thus, the
results from experiment 1 are precise but small in magnitude.

In contrast, experiment 2 has a very wide confidence interval band
that indicates poor measurement precision. However, it could very well
that the magnitude of the difference in means in experiment 2 is larger
than that in experiment 1, but that the power was just inadequate to detect

that effect. Thus, the results from experiment 2 are imprecise, and, thus, it is not known with any certainty if they are large or small in magnitude.

Finally, experiment 3 also has a relatively wide confidence interval band indicating poor measurement precision. Nevertheless, this confidence interval does not overlap with that from experiment 1, indicating that the magnitude of the difference in means in experiment 3 is greater than that in experiment 1. Thus, the results from experiment 3 are comparatively imprecise but larger in magnitude.

The important point to take away from this hypothetical example is that confidence intervals provide much more information than do NHSTs alone. Furthermore, that information is provided in a graphical format, thereby making it easier for ergonomics scientists and practitioners to pick up meaningful patterns perceptually (e.g. width of bands, overlap across bands, inclusion of the zero point). In this hypothetical example, the added information leads to a very different interpretation than may have been obtained by reliance on NHST alone.

In summary, power analysis and confidence intervals are rarely-used, but very valuable, statistical analysis techniques. Together, they allow us to gain richer insights into data, and thereby allow us to go beyond merely rejecting the null hypothesis. Note that confidence intervals can be calculated for effect sizes and measure of strength of association as well, thereby combining the respective advantages of each of these techniques into one statistical procedure (Fowler, 1985; Rosnow and Rosenthal, 1989; Cohen, 1990, 1994). In this way, information would be obtained about the precision of knowledge of effect size or strength of association, information that is surely to be of practical value in ergonomics science and practice (see previous subsection).

2.6. One experiment is always inconclusive

This final point cuts across the comparative advantages and disadvantages of any particular set of statistical analysis techniques. No matter how carefully it is designed, no matter how sophisticated the equipment, no matter how clever the researcher, and no matter what statistical analysis techniques are used, any one experiment alone can never provide definitive results. The origin of this limitation is a logical one. Empirical research relies on inductive inference, and as any philosopher or logician knows, induction provides no guarantees.

The same conclusion can be obtained empirically from the history of science. To take but one example, several times experimental results were obtained that supposedly falsified Einstein's special theory of relativity (Holton, 1988). Each time, subsequent research revealed that it was the experiments and not the theory that were at fault. The important point, however, is that this conclusion was not apparent at the time that the results were generated. For example, 10 years passed before researchers identified the inadequacies of the equipment used in one of the experiments that had supposedly falsified special relativity. By implication, when an anomalous result is first obtained, only additional research can determine how best to interpret the result. In Einstein's words: "whether there is an unsuspected systematic error or whether the foundations of relativity theory do not correspond with the facts one will be able to decide with certainty only if a great variety of observational material is at hand" (cited in Holton, 1988: 253). In short, despite widespread belief to the contrary, there is no such thing as a "critical experiment" because empirical knowledge is inductive and, thus, quite fragile when viewed in isolation (Chapanis, 1967). Like the other points that are reviewed above, this insight is far from new, but it too has not been given the attention that it deserves.

As several authors have pointed out (e.g. Dar, 1987; Rosnow and Rosenthal, 1989; Cohen, 1990; Thompson, 1996; Rossi, 1997; Schmidt and Hunter, 1997), the way in which NHST and ANOVA are used in practice tends to cause researchers to overlook this epistemological limitation. In the extreme, the attitude is: "if a statistical test is significant at $p < 0.05$, then the research hypothesis is true, otherwise it is not." If valid, such an inferential structure would make life easier for researchers. Unfortunately, what NHST really evaluates is the probability that the data could have arisen given that the null hypothesis were true, *not* the probability that the null hypothesis is true given the data that were obtained (Cohen, 1994). Although both of these quantities are conditional probabilities, they are logically very different from each other. NHST only allows us to make inferences of the first kind. Therefore, as surprising as it may sound, "significance tests cannot separate real findings from chance findings in research studies" (Schmidt and Hunter, 1997: 39), a statistical fact that should really give us considerable pause.

Researchers frequently ignore the fact that there is no objective, mechanical procedure for making a dichotomous decision to evaluate the validity of research findings (e.g. Chow, 1996, 1998). This attitude can unwittingly have a devastating effect on a body of literature. A case study described by Rossi (1997) provides an incisive, if somewhat depressing, example. He reviewed the literature on a psychological phenomenon known as "spontaneous recovery of verbal associations." During the most intensive period of), about 40 articles were published on this topic. However, only about half of these studies led to a statistically significant effect of spontaneous recovery. Consequently, most textbooks and literature reviews concluded that the data were equivocal, and, thus, that the empirical evidence for spontaneous recovery was unconvincing. Eventually, the collective wisdom became that spontaneous recovery was an ephemeral phenomenon, and, as a result, research in the area was essentially abandoned.

Rossi (1997) conducted a retrospective analysis of the collective findings in this body of literature. Data from 47 experiments with an aggregate of 4926 participants were included in the analysis. Only 43% of these studies reported statistically significant results at $p < 0.05$. This low percentage of significant results led researchers to doubt the existence of the spontaneous recovery effect. However, when the experiments were analysed as a whole, there was statistically significant evidence in support of the spontaneous recovery effect ($p < 0.001$). Rossi also conducted an effect size analysis and a power analysis across these studies. The results indicate that the average effect size was relatively small ($d = 0.39$) and that the average power was quite low (0.38). Together, these findings explain why the significant effects were in the minority. Because researchers were dealing with a small effect and their studies had low power, many experiments failed to detect a statistically significant effect.

Together, these facts add up to a fascinating illustration of how naive attitudes about both statistical tests and the value of replication can have a deep impact on a body of literature. As Rossi (1997) pointed out, researchers did not report any effect sizes, so they did not know that they were dealing with a small effect. Similarly, no study reported power, so researchers were not aware that their experiments had low power. With this veil of ignorance as background, researchers (incorrectly) interpreted the results from each experiment using a dichotomous decision criterion: if $p < 0.05$, then the result is valid, otherwise it is not. However, as Rosnow and Rosenthal (1989: 1277) have observed, "dichotomous significance testing has no ontological basis ... surely, God loves the 0.06 nearly as much as the 0.05" (see also Cowles and Davis, 1982). Because of the combination of small effect and low power, 57% of the experiments did not generate results that passed the naive (and indefensible) dichotomous decision criterion. This, combined with a lack of appreciation for the importance of replication across studies, led researchers to abandon what turned out to be a legitimate, albeit small, psychological effect.

What can be concluded from the spontaneous recovery case study? First, the case shows, once again, the value of calculating effect size and power so that researchers can better interpret their results. Secondly, the case also illustrates how misleading and unproductive it is to use the $p < 0.05$ criterion (or any other dichotomous decision rule) as the gatekeeper of scientifically acceptable knowledge. As Rossi (1997: 183) pointed out, "the inconsistency among spontaneous recovery studies may have been due to the emphasis reviewers and researchers placed on the level of significance attained by individual studies .... A cumulative science will be difficult to achieve if only some studies are counted as providing evidence." Thirdly, and relatedly, the spontaneous recovery case study also brings home the importance of replication across multiple studies. It is the pattern of results across studies that is most important for building scientific knowledge. In the words of Abelson (1995: 77), "Research conclusions arise not from single studies alone, but from cumulative replication." Even if no single result reaches statistical significance at the $p < 0.05$ value, the entire pattern of results can still be statistically significant when viewed as a whole. The converse point is equally valid: "A successful piece of research doesn't conclusively settle an issue, it just makes some theoretical proposition to some degree more likely. Only successful future replication in the same and different settings ... provides an approach to settling the issue" (Cohen 1990: 1311).

How many cases like the one reviewed by Rossi (1997) are there in the ergonomics science literature? It is very difficult to answer this question. Nevertheless, there is one thing of which we can be sure: Making decisions on a dichotomous basis using NHST alone will only make it more likely for such problems to plague the ergonomics science literature. It is for this reason that an increasing number of noted researchers have felt the need to point to the importance of replication to building sound, cumulative knowledge (e.g. Rosnow and Rosenthal, 1989; Meehl, 1997;

Schmidt and Hunter, 1997). This lesson is perhaps the most important one of all amongst the ones that have been reviewed.

3. Is all of this obvious?

Seasoned ergonomics scientists might object that the six points in the previous section are obvious, and, thus, that this review does not make a significant contribution to the literature. If this is indeed the case, then one would expect that the vast majority of the empirical articles published in *Human Factors*, the flagship journal of the discipline in the US, would exhibit an awareness of most of these points. To test this hypothesis empirically, an informal review was conducted of all of the articles published in volume 40 of *Human Factors*.

3.1. Method

For each of the empirical articles in that volume, the number that reported: (a) an individual participant analysis of any kind (corresponding to point 1 in the literature review); (b) an analysis of a particular order of means, an interval magnitude, or a point prediction (point 2); (c) an MTMM analysis (point 3); (d) an analysis of association strength or effect size (point 4); and (e) power or confidence intervals (point 5) were counted. This procedure is not fool-proof (e.g. MTMM is not the only way to assess reliability, convergent validity, and discriminant validity), but it provides a more than adequate basis for an informal survey.

3.2. Results

Figure 4 illustrates the number of articles that used various data analysis methods in the sample. A number of patterns clearly stand out. First, ANOVA is, by far, the most frequently used method of data analysis. It was used in 33 of the articles that were surveyed, twice as frequently as the next most popular method of data analysis. Secondly, only one study reported an individual analysis of each participant's behaviour as opposed to relying just on group means, thereby showing that point 1 in this review is rarely recognized in practice. Thirdly, only a handful of articles

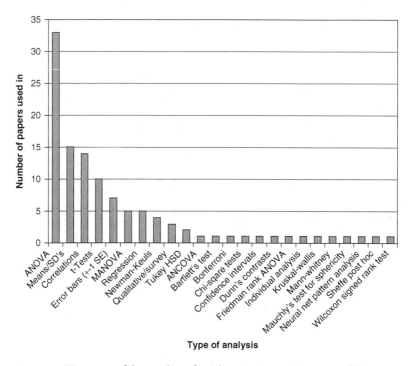

FIGURE 4   Histogram of the number of articles reporting various types of data analysis methods in volume 40 of *Human Factors.*

used non-parametric tests, and, even in these rare cases, the tests were not used to make more stringent predictions, thereby showing that point 2 is not widely put into practice. Fourthly, no article reported a MTMM analysis, thereby suggesting that point 3 in this literature review is not put into practice. Fifthly, no article reported an analysis of effect size or association strength, thereby suggesting that point 4 is also not put into practice. Finally, only one article presented a graph of confidence intervals and no article presented a power analysis, thereby showing that point 5 is also rarely put into practice.

3.3. Discussion

Perhaps seasoned ergonomics scientists are indeed aware of all of the points in this review, but, if so, then this informal survey convincingly shows that there is a discrepancy between what is acknowledged to be true and the way in which we behave (the authors include themselves in this lot). The recommendations made in this article have very rarely found their way into ergonomics science. Even with all of the important limitations that are associated with it, ANOVA remains far and away the *de facto* standard for data analysis in ergonomics science.

4. Conclusions

The purpose of this literature review is not to point a finger at ergonomics scientists who have relied solely on NHST or ANOVA to analyse data. The authors are just as guilty of uncritically using traditional methods of data analysis as anyone else. After all, these are the techniques that have been taught, are well known by journal editors and reviewers, and are supported by software packages. Thus, there are numerous pressures that cause many to continue to use the traditional methods. Nevertheless, one of the main points of this article is that, by following these pressures, ergonomics scientists are—perhaps in many cases unknowingly—incurring a substantial scientific cost:

> When passing null hypothesis tests becomes the criterion for successful predictions, as well as for journal publications, there is no pressure on the ... researcher to build a solid, accurate theory; all he or she is required to do, it seems, is produce "statistically significant" results.
>
> (Dar 1987: 149)

The data analysis methods advocated here can lead to a more mature science of ergonomics, but they require one to follow a path of greater effort. For example, some of the methods reviewed require that experiments are designed differently. If we are going to conduct individual level analyses like Hammond et al. (1987) did, then we need to rely more on within-participants designs. If we are going to use the MTMM advocated by Campbell and Fiske (1959), we need to include multiple constructs and multiple methods in a single experiment. If we are going to be able to make point or interval predictions, we need to develop stronger theories to guide experimentation. If we are going to develop a more cumulative knowledge base, we need to engage in more replication than done in the past. Thus, a change in data analysis techniques is not a cosmetic modification to be taken lightly. Instead, it requires some deep changes in the ways in which ergonomics science is conducted. Because of the enormity of this task, most ergonomists typically find it easier to stick to that with which they are most comfortable. Meehl (1990) describes a typical reaction to the critiques of NHST and ANOVA that he has made over the years:

> Well, that Meehl is a clever fellow and he likes to philosophize, fine for him, it's a free country. But since we are doing all right with the good old tried and true methods of Fisherian statistics and null hypothesis testing, and since journal editors do not seem to have panicked over such thoughts, I will stick to the accepted practices of my trade union and leave Meehl's worries to the statisticians and philosophers. (p. 230)

In short, to effect a change in the way ergonomics scientists and practitioners analyse their research data will not be easy.

In this article, a step has been taken toward facilitating positive change by: (a) describing the limitations of traditional methods of analysis, especially ANOVA; (b) explaining why those limitations are relevant to ergonomics science and practice; (c) describing other methods of data analysis that address some of those limitations; and (d) citing many references that readers can consult to obtain the mechanical details on how to perform these less-familiar analyses (see Bailar and Mosteller, 1988, and Wilkinson et al., 1999, for additional guidance and explanations). It is the authors' hope that ergonomics scientists and practitioners will consider using some of these techniques the next time that they conduct empirical research. Although the effort required will admittedly be higher than usual, through such incremental efforts we can progress toward more sound and cumulative scientific knowledge.

5. Postscript

> "Much of what we have said has been said before, but it is important that our graduate students hear it all again so that the next generation of … scientists is aware of the existence of these pitfalls and of the ways around them." (Rosnow and Rosenthal 1989: 1282)

Acknowledgements

This research project was sponsored by a contract from the Japan Atomic Energy Research Institute (Dr. Fumiya Tanabe, contract monitor), and a research grant from the Natural Sciences and Engineering Research Council of Canada. We would like to thank Ian Spence, Fumiya Tanabe, Bill Howell, and especially the anonymous reviewers for their contributions and help.

References

Abelson, R. P. 1995, *Statistics as principled argument* (Hillsdale, NJ: Lawrence Erlbaum Associates).

Abelson, R. P. 1997, On the surprising longevity of flogged horses: Why there is a case for the significance test, *Psychological Science,* 8, 12–15.

Bailar, J. C, III and Mosteller, F. 1988, Guidelines for statistical reporting in articles for medical journals: Amplifications and explanations, *Annals of Internal Medicine,* 108, 266–273.

Bakan, D. 1966, The test of significance in psychological research, *Psychological Bulletin,* 66, 423–437.

Bryan, W. L. and Harter, N. 1897, Studies in the physiology and psychology of the telegraphic language, *The Psychological Review,* 1, 27–53.

Bryan, W. L. and Harter, N. 1899, Studies on the telegraphic language: The acquisition of a hierarchy of habits, *The Psychological Review,* 6, 347–375.

Campbell, D. T. and Fiske, D. W. 1959, Convergent and discriminant validation by the Multitrait-Multimethod Matrix, *Psychological Bulletin,* 56, 81–105.

Chapanis, A. 1967, The relevance of laboratory studies to practical situations, *Ergonomics,* 10, 557–577.

Chow, S. L. 1996, *Statistical significance: Rationale, validity, and utility* (London: Sage).

Chow, S. 1998, Précis of statistical significance: Rationale, validity, and utility, *Behavioral and Brain Sciences,* 21, 169–239.

Christoffersen, K., Hunter, C. N. and Vicente, K. J. 1994, *Research on factors influencing human cognitive behaviour (I) (CEL 94-05)* (Toronto: University of Toronto, Cognitive Engineering Laboratory).

Cohen, J. 1988, *Statistical power analysis for the behavioral sciences,* 2nd edn. (Hillsdale, NJ: Lawrence Erlbaum Associates).

Cohen, J. 1990, Things I have learned (so far), *American Psychologist,* 45, 1304–1312.

Cohen, J. 1994, The earth is round ($p < .05$), *American Psychologist,* 49, 997–1003.

Cowles, M. and Davis, C. 1982, On the origins of the .05 level of statistical significance, *American Psychologist,* 37, 553–558.

Dar, R. 1987, Another look at Meehl, Lakatos, and the scientific practices of psychologists, *American Psychologist*, 42, 145–151.

Fowler, R. J. 1985, Point estimates and confidence intervals in measures of association, *Psychological Bulletin*, 98, 160–165.

Hagen, R. L. 1997, In praise of the null hypothesis statistical test, *American Psychologist*, 52, 15–24.

Hammond, G. 1996, The objections to null hypothesis testing as a means of analysing psychological data, *Australian Journal of Psychology*, 48, 104–106.

Hammond, K. R., Hamm, R. M. and Grassia, J. 1986, Generalizing over conditions by combining the Multitrait-Multimethod Matrix and the representative design of experiments, *Psychological Bulletin*, 100, 257–269.

Hammond, K. R., Hamm, R. M., Grassia, J. and Pearson, T. 1987, Direct comparison of the efficacy of intuitive and analytical cognition in expert judgment, *IEEE Transactions on Systems, Man, and Cybernetics*, 17, 753–770.

Harlow, L. L., Mulaik, S. A. and Steiger, J. H. 1997, *What if there were no significance tests?* (Mahwah, NJ: Lawrence Erlbaum Associates).

Heldref Foundation 1997, Guidelines for contributors, *Journal of Experimental Education*, 65, 95–96.

Holton, G. 1988, *Thematic origins of scientific thought: From Kepler to Einstein*, revised edn (Cambridge, MA: Harvard University Press).

Lee, J. D. 1992, Trust, self-confidence, and operators' adaptation to automation. Unpublished doctoral dissertation, Urbana, IL: University of Illinois at Urbana-Champaign, Department of Mechanical & Industrial Engineering.

Lee, J. D. and MORAY, N. 1994, Trust, self-confidence, and operators, adaptation to automation, *International Journal of Human-Computer Studies*, 40, 153–184.

Loftus, G. R. 1991, On the tyranny of hypothesis testing in the social sciences, *Contemporary Psychology*, 36, 102–105.

Loftus, G. R. 1993a, Editorial comment, *Memory and Cognition*, 21, 1–3.

Loftus, G. R. 1993b, A picture is worth a thousand p values: On the irrelevance of hypothesis testing in the microcomputer age, *Behavior Research, Methods, Instruments, & Computers*, 25, 250–256.

Loftus, G. R. 1995, Data analysis as insight: Reply to Morrison and Weaver, *Behavior Research Methods, Instruments, and Computers*, 27, 57–59.

Loftus, G. R. 2001, Psychology will be a much better science when we change the way we analyze data, *Current Directions in Psychological Science*, in press.

Loftus, G. R. and Masson, M. E. 1994, Using confidence intervals in within-subject designs, *Psychonomic Bulletin & Review*, 1, 476–490.

Loftus, G. R. and Mclean, J. E. 1997, Familiar old wine: Great new bottle, *American Journal of Psychology*, 110, 146–153.

Lykken, D. T. 1968, Statistical significance in psychological research, *Psychological Bulletin*, 70, 151–159.

Meehl, P. E. 1967, Theory testing in psychology and physics: A methodological paradox, *Philosophy of Science*, 34, 103–115.

Meehl, P. E. 1978, Theoretical risks and tabular asterisks: Sir Karl, Sir Ronald, and the slow progress of soft psychology, *Journal of Consulting and Clinical Psychology*, 46, 806–834.

Meehl, P. E. 1990, Why summaries of research on psychological theories are so often uninterpretable, *Psychological Reports*, 66, 195–244.

Meehl, P. E. 1997, The problem is epistemology, not statistics: Replace significance tests by confidence intervals and quantify accuracy of risky predictions, in L. L. Harlow, S. A. Mulaik and J. H. Steiger (eds.), *What if there were no significance tests?* (Mahwah, NJ: Lawrence Erlbaum Associates), 175–197.

Murphy, K. R. 1997, Editorial, *Journal of Applied Psychology*, 82, 3–5.

Newell, A. and Rosenbloom, P. S., 1981, Mechanisms of skill acquisition and the law of practice, in J. R. Anderson (ed.), *Cognitive skills and their acquisition* (Hillsdale, NJ: Lawrence Erlbaum Associates), 1–53.

Rosnow, R. L. and Rosenthal, R. 1989, Statistical procedures and the justification of knowledge in psychological science, *American Psychologist*, 44, 1276–1284.

Rossi, J. S. 1997, A case study in the failure of psychology as a cumulative science: The spontaneous recovery of verbal learning, in L. L. Harlow, S. A. Mulaik and J. H. Steiger (eds.), *What if there were no significance tests?* (Mahwah, NJ: Lawrence Erlbaum Associates), 175–197.

Rouanet, H. 1996, Bayesian methods for assessing importance of effects, *Psychological Bulletin*, 119, 149–158.

Rozeboom, W. L. 1960, The fallacy of the null-hypothesis significance test, *Psychological Bulletin*, 57, 416–428.

Rozeboom, W. W. 1997, Good science is abductive, not hypothetico-deductive, in L. L. Harlow, S. A. Mulaik and J. H. Steiger (eds.), *What if there were no significance tests?* (Mahwah, NJ: Lawrence Erlbaum Associates), 335–391.

Schmidt, F. L. and Hunter, J. E. 1997, Eight common false objections to the discontinuation of significance testing in the analysis of research data, In L. L. Harlow, S. A. Mulaik and J. H. Steiger (eds.), *What if there were no significance tests?* (Mahwah, NJ: Lawrence Erlbaum Associates), 37–64.

Serlin, R. C. and Lapsley, D. K. 1985, Rationality in psychological research: The good-enough principle, *American Psychologist*, 40, 73–83.

Shrout, P. 1997, Should significance tests be banned? Introduction to a special section exploring the pros and cons, *Psychological Science*, 8, 1–2.

Siegel, S. 1956, *Nonparametric statistics for the behavioral sciences* (New York: McGraw-Hill).

Snyder, P. and Lawson, S. 1993, Evaluating results using corrected and uncorrected effect size estimates, *Journal of Experimental Education*, 61, 334–349.

Steiger, J. H. and Fouladi, R. T. 1997, Noncentrality interval estimation and the evaluation of statistical models, in L. L. Harlow, S. A. Mulaik and J. H. Steiger (eds.), *What if there were no significance tests?* (Mahwah, NJ: Lawrence Erlbaum Associates), 221–257.

Thompson, B. 1993, Foreword, *Journal of Experimental Education*, 61, 285–286.

Thompson, B. 1994, Guidelines for authors, *Educational and psychological measurement*, 54, 837–847.

Thompson, B. 1996, AERA editorial policies regarding statistical significance testing: Three suggested reforms, *Educational Researcher*, 25, 26–30.

Venda, V. F. and Venda, V. Y. 1995, *Dynamics in ergonomics, psychology, and decisions: Introduction to ergodynamics* (Norwood, NJ: Ablex).

Vicente, K. J. 1992, Memory recall in a process control system: A measure of expertise and display effectiveness, *Memory & Cognition*, 20, 356–373.

Vicente, K. J. 1998, Four reasons why the science of psychology is still in trouble, *Behavioral and Brain Sciences*, 21, 224–245.

Wilkinson, L. and Task Force on Statistical Inference, APA Board of Scientific Affairs 1999, Statistical methods in psychology journals: Guidelines and explanations, *American Psychologist*, 54, 594–604.

Woodworth, R. S. 1938, *Experimental psychology* (New York: Holt).

Xiao, Y. and Vicente, K. J. 2000, A framework for epistemological analysis in empirical (laboratory and field) studies, *Human Factors*, 42, 87–101.

7

Constructing the Subject

Cognitive Modeling

Alex Kirlik

Exhibit A

The more we learn of human behavior and the more we observe the users of technology, the more we think it necessary to guard against generalizing the assumption of regular and mechanistic behavior from well-defined tasks to other aspects of life. We must not let convenient engineering abstractions dull our awareness of the complex cultural, emotional, and spiritual life in which task performance is embedded and in terms of which it has, or all too often lacks, meaning for the individual. We believe that the engineer who deals with human performance should avoid two faults that have made the "efficiency expert" one of the most hated in industry: (1) the neglect of personal and of social variables, and (2) the use of people as means to ends they do not share and do not determine. If a person is to design tasks for others, he has the responsibility to attempt to see the tasks and their implications in a wider context and to attempt to ensure that they are life-enhancing. This is not easy to do, nor are the criteria clear cut. It requires that the designer himself close feedback loops with reality at several levels, not only at the level of specific performance criteria of the given system or of the human task which are part of it, but also at the level of his own personal values. This, in the long run, is the demand of good engineering. The human use of man–machine systems is just the human use of human beings.

Sheridan and Ferrell, 1974: 18-19

Exhibit B

Retailers Reprogram Workers in Efficiency Push

Retailers have a new tool to turn up the heat on their sales people: computer programs that dictate which employees should work when, and for how long. . . . Such "workforce-management" systems are sweeping the industry as retailers fight to improve productivity and cut payroll costs. Limited Brands Inc., Gap Inc., Williams-Sonoma Inc., and GameStop Corp. have all installed them recently.

Some employees aren't happy about the trend. They say the systems leave them with shorter shifts, make it difficult to schedule their lives, and unleash Darwinian forces on the sales floor that damage morale. . . . "There's been a natural resistance to thinking about human beings as pieces in a puzzle rather than individuals," (sic) says John M. Gibbons, a senior research adviser at the Conference Board and a former director of human resources at Gap. "When you have those clear methods of measurement, and just-in-time delivery for supply-chain management, it's a natural transition to apply it to human resources as well." . . . Ann Taylor calls its system the Ann Taylor Labor Allocation System—Atlas for short. It was developed by RedPrairie Corp., a retail-operations software firm based in Waukesha, Wisc. "We liken the system to an airplane dashboard with 100 different switches and levers and knobs," said Ann Taylor's Mr. Knaul. "When we launched that, we messed with five of them." Giving the system a nickname, Atlas, he said, "was important because it gave a personality to the system, so [employees] hate the system and not us."

The Wall Street Journal, September 10, 2008,
Reported by Vanessa O'Connell

The article reprinted in this chapter (by Vicente, Mumaw, and Roth) presents a qualitative cognitive model of a nuclear power plant operator's monitoring activities. The final word in the previous sentence is key: one of the most important findings was that monitoring a power plant is anything but passive. Instead, via extensive field observations, Vicente and his colleagues found that the operator engages in a rich set of *activities*, displaying a diverse cognitive and behavioral repertoire. The operator often actively interrogates the plant, and his or her own active structuring of the workplace plays a key role in supporting these activities. Unlike most laboratory tasks that have provided the lion's share of data guiding modeling in cognitive science, a power plant is both dynamic (changes state autonomously) and interactive (can be interrogated).

Modeling human cognition in such situations with computational formalisms is a rapidly growing human–technology interaction (HTI) research area. As such, there exist many points of resonance between the qualitative cognitive model, grounded in a substantial field study and presented in the reprinted article, and my own and some others' modeling research. My goal in this chapter is to use the observations and findings presented in the reprint, and related modeling research conducted in dynamic and interactive settings, to attempt to influence the computational cognitive modeling research community. As Sheridan and Ferrell point out, it can be very tempting to infer that success at cognitive and performance modeling, owing largely to experiments that tightly constrain the behavior of people providing the behavioral data for modeling, implies that one has understood human performance in its entirety. These successes give rise to a conception of human work as machine work, the perils of which are amply illustrated by the design of the "workforce management" technologies now being used by retailers such as the Limited, the Gap, and Williams-Sonoma. Perhaps the modeler, when the target of modeling is a person, has an ethical obligation to communicate, along with his or her model, all of the dimensions of human behavior and existence that are *not* represented in his or her model. This would seem to be required to help ensure that our models, our mechanistic conceptions, are not put to evil purposes.

Additionally, many, if not most, researchers in computational cognitive modeling would like their models to have engineering implications, or to be useful in the system design process (in some fashion), but are facing difficult challenges in getting their models—grounded largely in data from cognitive psychology laboratories—to (using their words) "scale up" to the realities of dynamic, interactive systems and operational environments. As such, my hope is that this chapter will also play a useful role in informing the modeling community about some key (and, in many cases, as-yet unmet) challenges associated with computationally modeling cognition in these environments or systems, and at least a few insights into how these challenges may be overcome. A second goal for this chapter is to introduce those interested in a Human-tech approach to the motivation for adding cognitive modeling to one's methodological toolbox, and the advantages that can be gained by doing so.

Some background: In March 2005, I was asked by Wayne Gray, who was then leading up an effort to establish a new Technical Group (TG) of the Human Factors and Ergonomics Society on "Human Performance Modeling," to attend a workshop he was organizing on "Integrated Models of Cognitive Systems." Gray, who had recently contributed his chapter to my (2006) *Adaptive Perspectives on Human-Technology Interaction* volume, knew that, unlike most of the cognitive scientists attending the workshop, I brought an ecological approach to modeling, and he asked me to speak on essentially what that meant. To be frank, *part* of what that meant was that, based on my previous research, I brought a skeptical attitude toward much of the research I expected to be presented at that workshop. More pointedly, I found the body of research on "computational cognitive architectures," motivated almost entirely by data collected in cognitive psychology laboratories, to be less than fully compelling, or at least less than totally convincing. But perhaps attending Gray's workshop might convince me? In any event, I accepted Gray's generous offer, and the fruits of my labor appeared as a chapter (Kirlik, 2007) titled "Ecological resources for modeling interactive behavior and embedded cognition" in the resulting volume *Integrated Models of Cognitive Systems* (Gray, 2007).

As my chapter title hopefully suggests, even though I held a skeptical attitude toward much of the cognitive modeling research going on at the time, I had long since realized that the majority of scientific debates are fruitless. Instead (and by seeking to emulate more senior researchers I viewed as having made valuable contributions), I approached the task of speaking at Gray's workshop and writing my chapter as if the burden was very much on me to clarify, and make more directly available, the added resources or insights that one could obtain by viewing modeling from an ecological perspective. I crisply identified what taking such a perspective meant: Taking the human–environment *system*, rather than the human mind, brain, or nervous system alone, as one's unit of analysis and object of study. As such, the tone of both my talk and my chapter was not "this is wrong" but rather, "this is one possible way out of some of your pressing problems."

One reason I thought I might have something to offer along these lines was that I had recently completed a 5-year, NASA-sponsored research project jointly with Mike Byrne of Rice University on computational cognitive modeling (Byrne and Kirlik, 2005; Byrne, Kirlik, and Fick, 2006; Byrne, Kirlik, and Fleetwood, 2008). Like the power plant operators described in the reprint, Byrne and I were modeling operators of dynamic, interactive systems, namely, commercial aviation pilots in both ground (taxi) and airborne (approach and landing) operations. NASA, which had collected these data in high-fidelity simulations of these operations (Foyle and Hooey, 2008), provided us with data sets to both inform and validate our models.

I had sought out Byrne as a collaborator on this project because I knew that he had recently completed a 3-year post-doc working on the computational cognitive architecture ACT-R in John Anderson's laboratory at Carnegie Mellon University. While there, Byrne had played a leading role in bringing ACT-R a few steps closer to the world by providing it with the computational equivalents of eyes and hands. Many years earlier, Byrne had been a student in my graduate cognitive engineering course at Georgia Tech, a few weeks of which were devoted to cognitive modeling. At the time, I shared with the class my assessment that one factor that kept the cognitive models of that time from being more useful for design was that none of them had resources for representing the external world (e.g. a design) and how a person interacts with that world.

Perhaps prodded by these discussions, Byrne did an outstanding class project examining the effects of supplementing a cognitive model called CAPS (Just and Carpenter, 1992) with (computational) eyes and hands as well. In this project, Byrne showed how the predictions of his model (again, of an airline pilot) regarding the memory demands associated with following a preflight checklist, were quite different (significantly lower) when the model was supplied with a "computational thumb" to move down the checklist (to keep track of the current step in the checklist) and an eye for both viewing this thumb and for reading off the checklist items. At the time, all computational cognitive architectures would have had to perform all of the cognitive functionality performed by these activities via operations on an internal representation of the checklist (in the mind's eye, so to speak). Byrne later fleshed out this research and provided what he called a "situated" computational cognitive model, S-CAPS (Byrne, 1994).

In 1999, when Byrne and I began working on our NASA project, trying to bring the current version of ACT-R to bear on the NASA data sets, we immediately realized that we needed to bring ACT-R even closer to reality. To get a handle on many of the timing issues associated with modeling visual attention allocation and dynamic decision making, we realized that we would have to find a way to hook our ACT-R model of a pilot up to a high-fidelity, PC-based flight simulator, the latter representing the pilot's external environment.

Viewing human behavior as mutually constrained by both internal cognition and the external environment, as the ecological approach does, this model of the pilot's external environment was essential. In fact, this model was likely to have played just as important a role in determining what was in our NASA data sets as the role played by pilot cognition in the NASA simulator studies. At one point, we created a video game–style cable and communications protocol for ACT-R and our PC-based flight simulator (X-Plane) to pass data back and forth from the computer running ACT-R and the computer running X-Plane.

In retrospect, it may be obvious that we would need to model the integrated human–environment system in this fashion if we were to model the pilot. That is, it should be obvious that we would need to take an ecological (or systems) approach. But I knew this was far from obvious to the audience to whom I would be speaking at Gray's workshop and writing to in Gray's book. Unless one has directly experienced the challenge of modeling cognition in dynamic and interactive situations, why should the need to take an ecological or systems perspective in doing so be intuitive, much less obvious? As such, I took as my goal in writing my chapter for Gray's volume to communicate the value of an ecological approach to cognitive modeling, illustrating the general approach with three examples from our prior research. Each of those examples demonstrated the utility of creating functional-level models of both the human performer and the dynamic and interactive environment in which they were working. The three resulting models thus represented human–environment interaction as a single, integrated system composed of two interacting subsystems.

Interestingly, and far from coincidentally given the context studied, the qualitative cognitive model presented in the article to be reprinted in this chapter is largely consistent with, and thus provides additional evidence for observations such as those provided in my chapter. Although a complete coverage of research on this problem is beyond the current scope, I should mention other, related research attempting to bring computational cognitive models into more intimate contact with the world: For example, research by Salvucci (e.g. Salvucci, 2006) on modeling driving, by Gray (2006) and Gray and Boehm-Davis (2000) on modeling interactive behavior, by Ritter and his colleagues (e.g. Ritter, Baxter, Jones, and Young, 2000; Ritter, Van Rooy, St. Amant, and Simpson, 2006) on modeling human–computer interaction, by Ritter, Kukeja and St. Amant (2007) on modeling teleoperation, and by Fu (e.g. Fu, 2005) and Pirolli (2007) on modeling ecologically-adaptive (and in some cases, maladaptive) information search strategies. Hopefully, all of these efforts are leading toward cognitive modeling that captures more and more aspects of cognition and behavior, as well as the environmental factors that play a crucial role in shaping cognition and behavior. Might we live to see the day when the designers of "workforce management" systems could use a computational human performance model that could have predicted many of the negative consequences their technology would have on retail workers?

But, just consider how much work remains to be done. In his book, *A Mind So Rare* (2001), the senior cognitive scientist Merlin Donald provides a thoughtful, and I think insightful, treatment of the fact that much recent current research in experimental psychology (e.g. visual cognition, attention allocation, working memory, and the like), as well as much current thought in the philosophy of mind (e.g. by Daniel Dennett), finds little, if any, functional role for consciousness. Donald himself notes that he had made a career's worth of contributions to this tradition as an experimentalist, but is now, upon reflection and near retirement, unable to swallow the implications of this line of work.

Donald then offers a resolution. Could this huge body of experimental findings be flawed in some way? No, he concludes. This body of findings, and the philosophical ponderings motivated by them, are not flawed, he observes, but instead simply *irrelevant* to the molar aspects of everyday life. He characterizes the body of experimental psychology research conducted in this tradition as the study of "minimalist people." He suggests that consciousness may still have a functional role in human life, but at longer time spans than tolerated by, or at least characteristic of (most) experimental psychology research.

To illustrate, he asks the reader to consider the cognitive demands associated with participating in an hours-long restaurant discussion of a movie that he and seven other participants are having, after watching a controversial, emotionally charged movie (Spielberg's *Saving Private Ryan*). Four different languages are spoken, most participants knowing only one or two of them. The group has very different levels of cinematic knowledge, and conflicting views, values, and agendas. They also need to keep their behavior appropriate to the setting: food must be ordered and eaten, and bills must be settled. If not fully convincing that such a conversation could not be managed without something very much like what we call consciousness, Donald is fully convincing (to me, at least) that one should be extremely wary of generalizing the findings of even thousands of experiments on "minimalist people" to everyday life situations.

A signpost: near the end of a long and distinguished career as a psychologist and cognitive scientist, Merlin Donald has (re)discovered representative design. The idea that, if one does not build *directly into one's experimental methodology* a logic for generalizing experimental findings beyond the laboratory, there is simply no guarantee of generalization, and thus of societal or practical relevance. Donald also notes the significant risks, and possibly even waste, entailed by research focused largely on what is proximally convenient, rather than distally important.

Much in the spirit of Donald's observations, I should note that some cognitive HTI researchers have noted something very much like the disconnect between much current formal modeling and human cognition in naturalistic, rather than laboratory, contexts. In doing so, these researchers have been motivated by a need to coin a new term—*macrocognition*—to describe longer-term, molar cognitive activities such as those discussed in the reprint (Klein, Ross, Moon, Klein, Hoffman, and Hollnagel, 2003). It is still too soon to tell whether this construct and line of research will bear fruit in providing a scientific account of these activities superior to folk psychology or qualitative models grounded in folk psychological concepts (see Stich, 1983, 1996). Macrocognition researchers often suggest that the only way these kinds of cognitive activities can be studied is through naturalistic observation. However, although research might naturally begin in the field, it cannot stop there. It must ultimately seek to provide justified abstractions of actual work contexts if any two research problems are ever be seen as the same, or even similar, and thus amenable to similar approaches or solutions.

A great amount work lies before us to give computational cognitive modeling the ability to represent the full richness of human cognition and performance in actual HTI settings, so that the resulting models call attention to the entire range of positive contributions workers provide. These models would then make it more likely for those in business and technology to think of workers as individuals and less likely as merely "pieces in a puzzle." A similar amount of work also lies ahead to bring the results of naturalistic studies of macrocognition in actual HTI contexts to the level of abstraction and formality required to inform this modeling. One can at least hope that researchers coming from the perspectives of both formal modeling and naturalistic observation will eventually meet in a much-needed middle ground.

Operator Monitoring in a Complex Dynamic Work Environment: A Qualitative Cognitive Model Based on Field Observations

Kim J. Vicente, Randall J. Mumaw, and Emilie M. Roth

Abstract

Complex and dynamic work environments provide a challenging litmus-test with which to evaluate basic and applied theories of cognition. In this work, we were interested in obtaining a better understanding of dynamic decision making by studying how human operators monitored a nuclear power plant during normal operations. Interviews and observations were conducted *in situ* at three different power plants to enhance the generalizability of results across both individuals and plants. A total of 38 operators were observed for approximately 288 hours, providing an extensive database of qualitative data. Based on these empirical observations, a cognitive model of operator monitoring was developed. This qualitative model has important theoretical implications because it integrates findings from several theoretical perspectives. There is a strong human information processing component in that operators rely extensively on active knowledge-driven monitoring rather than passively reacting to changes after they occur, but there is also a strong distributed cognition component in that operators rely extensively on the external representations to offload cognitive demands. In some cases, they even go so far as to actively shape that environment to make it easier to exploit environmental regularities, almost playing the role of designers. Finally, expert operators use workload regulation strategies, allowing them to prioritize tasks so that they avoid situations that are likely to lead to monitoring errors. These meta-cognitive processes have not received much attention in the human information processing and distributed cognition perspectives, although they have been studied by European psychologists who have studied cognition in complex work environments. Collectively, these findings shed light on dynamic decision making but they also serve an important theoretical function by integrating findings from different theoretical perspectives into one common framework.

1. Introduction

The history of science is replete with examples of fundamental discoveries that were derived by adopting practical problems of social significance as a vehicle for research. Perhaps one of the most salient examples is Louis Pasteur's discovery of the germ theory of disease. This work represents a landmark contribution to basic science, but much of the work was conducted in the context of practical problems, such as improving the technology of fermentation and preventing the spoilage of foods and drinks (Stokes, 1997).

The same approach has been adopted with great success in cognitive science, albeit infrequently. Perhaps the most notable example is Hutchins' (1995a, 1995b) work on distributed cognition. That research was conducted in a practical context, namely maritime navigation on board U.S. Navy ships. However, the primary goal was to make a fundamental contribution to cognitive science, not to solve a practical problem. The strong influence of Hutchins' work on the cognitive science community shows that practical problems can provide a productive stimulus for discovery. Such problems provide a litmus test for existing theories of cognition (Gibson, 1967/1982), and can lead to new theories that are more comprehensive in scope.

Complex dynamic work environments can play this function in fundamental research in cognitive science and cognitive engineering (Patel et al., 1996). They provide rich settings in which many processes of interest to basic researchers can be studied (e.g. monitoring, perception, attention, diagnosis, problem solving, decision making, planning, expertise). In this article, we focus on one particular complex dynamic work

environment—human operator monitoring in nuclear power plants—-
and use it as a litmus test of some existing theories in cognitive science.
In previous phases of this research program, we conducted a number of
field studies of operator monitoring under normal operating conditions
(Vicente and Burns, 1996; Mumaw et al., 2000;Vicente et al., 2001). In
this article, we integrate those field data into a qualitative cognitive model
of this phenomenon. This model brings together, under one framework,
aspects of human cognition that have been emphasized by different theoretical approaches (e.g. human information processing, distributed cognition), and which thus, have not yet been integrated theoretically in the
literature. Accordingly, the primary contribution of this research is to
take a small step towards a more comprehensive and integrated theory of
human cognition that is relevant to applied concerns.

The remainder of the article is organized as follows. In section 2, the
field studies that provided the empirical foundation for the modeling
effort are summarized. In section 3, a qualitative cognitive model of
operator monitoring is presented. The different categories are explained
and a few examples of how the model captures operator activity are presented. In section 4, the relationship between this model and related
work in cognitive science and cognitive engineering is explained.

2. Empirical foundation for modeling: field research

The model presented later is based on qualitative data collected from
several field studies of operator monitoring in nuclear power plants. The
methodology, results, and applied contributions of those field studies
have already been described in detail elsewhere (Vicente and Burns,
1996; Mumaw et al., 2000;Vicente et al., 2001). Therefore, in this article,
we merely provide a summary account of these field studies to serve as
the context for interpreting the detailed description of the model in the
next section.

2.1. The field setting: nuclear power plants

Nuclear power plants are complex dynamic work environments that
impose very challenging demands on human cognition. The plants

themselves are composed of literally thousands of different components. There are many interactions between components, making it difficult for operators to anticipate all of the side effects of their actions. In addition, the behavior of the plant is dynamic. Even if operators feel mentally overwhelmed and want to take a break, the pace of events is externally determined, so operators must try to keep up. The dynamics also have lags, which means that operator and machine actions do not have immediate effects. Operators must learn to anticipate by timing their actions appropriately to have the desired effect. Being too late or too early can result in a failure to achieve important tasks. Furthermore, operators have to cope with both normal and abnormal operations, on-line in real-time. Failure to cope with abnormalities effectively can pose tremendous threats to the public and the environment. This great hazard potential puts a heavy burden on operators. There is also a great deal of uncertainty about the true state of the plant because of incomplete and noisy information. Sensors sometimes fail, some goal-relevant information cannot be sensed, and even under the best of circumstances, sensors have measurement error. This uncertainty complicates the cognitive process of situation assessment. Finally, the plants that we studied are also highly automated which, paradoxically, can also introduce an element of complexity. Most of the time, the operators work in a supervisory control mode (Sheridan, 1987), monitoring the status of the plant while it is being controlled by automation. This task is challenging because operators are not actively in the loop controlling the plant. Nevertheless, they must try to be attentive and make sure that the plant and automation are both behaving as intended and as expected. These daunting cognitive demands are typical of those associated with other complex, dynamic work environments, such as aviation, medicine, and petrochemical processes (Woods, 1988; Vicente, 1999).

2.2. The human-machine interface: control room designs

The operators we studied worked in the main control rooms of their respective plants. These control rooms provide literally thousands of displays, controls, and alarms that operators can use to do their job. In each of the three plants we visited, the main control rooms had four control units (each controlling its own nuclear reactor). Figure 1 shows the panels

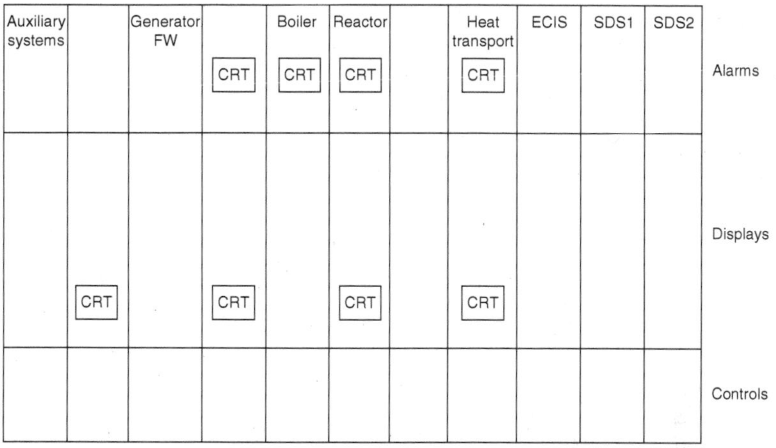

Auxiliary systems	Generator FW		Boiler	Reactor		Heat transport	ECIS	SDS1	SDS2	
		CRT	CRT	CRT		CRT				Alarms
										Displays
	CRT		CRT		CRT		CRT			
										Controls

FIGURE 1   The main control room for one of the nuclear power plants we studied.

on a single unit from the newest of the three plants we studied. A single operator runs each unit, although there are other workers in the control room and out in the plant serving support roles.

The control room for each unit consists of stand-up control panels, displays and alarm overviews, an operator desk, several printers, and bookshelves for procedures and other operations documents. In the two older plants, the control panels are made up primarily of traditional analog meters, strip-chart recorders, and control devices, whereas in the newest plant (shown in Figure 1), there is a greater reliance on computer technology to display information. Alarms (primarily those that are safety-related) are presented as a series of tiles at the top of the control panels that light up and provide an audio tone if an alarm condition occurs. Some instrumentation is located outside of the main control room.

2.3. The task: monitoring under normal operations

Operators in nuclear power plants encounter many different types of situations and are responsible for many different tasks. To provide a focus for our research, we chose to study how operators monitor the plant during normal operations.

The primary reason for doing so was that most of the previous work in this area had studied operators during abnormal conditions (e.g. Roth et al., 1992; Vicente et al., 1996). This emphasis is understandable given the safety-critical nature of these plants, but the unintended side effect was that little was known about normal operations. At the same time, studying monitoring under normal operations also provided us with an opportunity to study various cognitive processes that are of interest to basic researchers. One hypothesis we had was that the primary challenge to monitoring is operator vigilance. After all, large-scale accidents, such as those that occurred at Three Mile Island and Chernobyl, are rare, leading to an often-heard characterization of process control tasks as "99% boredom and 1% sheer terror." Minor failures occur more frequently but are still relatively rare. An alternative hypothesis was that the primary demands in monitoring relate to selective attention. Given that a nuclear power plant control room consists of thousands of indicators, one might think that the difficulty is in choosing what to attend to and what to ignore—a virtually impossible selective attention task. A third hypothesis was that the major difficulty in monitoring is one of visual perception. Because the control room is so large and consists of so many instruments, the key to monitoring may be to develop the visual acuity and discrimination skills that are required to detect changes and read indicators accurately. As the remainder of this article shows, none of these hypotheses does justice to the richness of the phenomena we observed. Although vigilance, attention, and visual perception are all relevant issues, we found that there is much more to monitoring than meets the eye.

2.4. Methodology: observation and interviews in situ

Interviews and observations were conducted *in situ* at three different nuclear power plants to enhance the generalizability of results across both individuals and plants. A total of 38 operators were observed for approximately 288 hours, providing an extensive database of qualitative data.

The methodology that we used was iterative and informal, in keeping with the qualitative and descriptive nature of a field study approach (Lorenz, 1973). Initially, our observations were open-ended. Several different operators were observed over a period of approximately 8 hours out of a 12-hour shift. Both day and night shifts were sampled. The goal in this initial phase of data collection was to get an overall understanding of the work environment, leading to a preliminary model of operator monitoring. Additional observations were then made at the same plant using a somewhat more focused set of issues based on the understanding developed in the earlier phase. In particular, we were interested in seeing if the categories in the preliminary model were able to account for the events we observed. Modifications and additions to the model were made, as necessary. More observations were then made at two other plants to test for generalizability across operators and plants. The methodology was similar to that used in the first plant. Again, modifications and additions to the preliminary model were made, as necessary. The final research product was a qualitative cognitive model of operator monitoring that accounted for the activities of dozens of operators observed over hundreds of hours across three different plants with varying levels of computer technology.

3. Qualitative cognitive model of operator monitoring: overview

3.1. Major elements

The Operator Monitoring Model is shown in Figures 2 and 3. Each of these two figures represents one half of the complete model; the right side of Figure 2 connects to the left side of Figure 3. The model is in the language of the nuclear domain because it was intended to be used as an organizing framework for the findings from our field studies.

The model has four major elements: initiating events, cognitive activities, facilitating activities, and monitoring activities. *Initiating events*, represented at the leftmost side of Figure 2, identify the three types of triggers that initiate monitoring. Some of these triggers are periodic (i.e. not tied to the occurrence of a specific event) and others are directly related to a particular event, such as an alarm. Once initiated, monitoring can be sustained over an indefinite period, or it can be altered and adapted via the various paths through the model. Also, multiple initiating events may be in effect at the same time, requiring the operator to time-share several monitoring activities.

The *cognitive activities* are those activities inside the large, shaded box in Figure 2—activities outside of this box are interactions with the

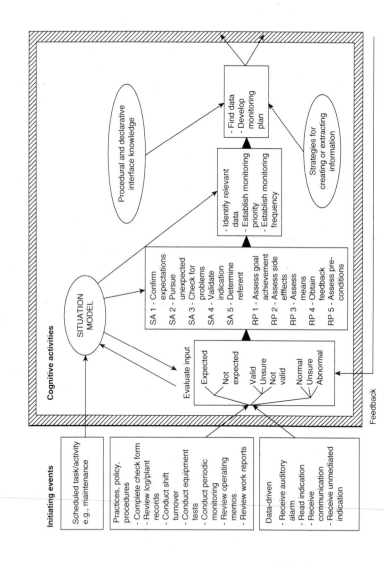

FIGURE 2   Left half of the operator monitoring model.

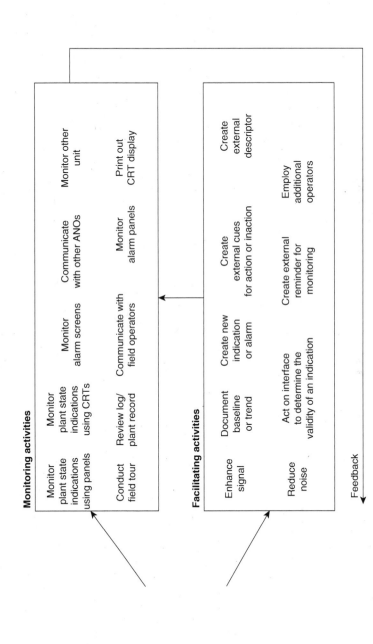

FIGURE 3   Right half of the operator monitoring model.

"world" (the control room interface, the plant, other personnel, etc.). The cognitive activities, which are in the smaller rectangular boxes, are action statements (i.e. verb–object form). Various types of knowledge that serve as inputs to the cognitive activities are shown in three ellipses. A major element that drives cognitive activities is the situation model, which is represented by the ellipse at the upper-left side of the cognitive activities box. The cognitive activities are used to identify the data that should be monitored, determine the priority and frequency of monitoring, and determine how that monitoring can be achieved.

Figure 3 shows the two remaining activities. *Facilitating activities* are actions taken by the operator to facilitate monitoring; these activities provide a set of options for configuring the interface or acting on the control room environment in other ways to make a specific monitoring task easier. In some cases, facilitating activities are not needed, and the operator can directly select an appropriate monitoring activity.

The *monitoring activities* box shows the set of resources for monitoring. The operator must select one or more of these resources to actually obtain an indication. The set of resources listed in Figure 3 represents all of the options that are available in the three control rooms we observed in our field studies. Note also that there is a feedback loop from monitoring activities to the input to cognitive activities. This feedback loop allows the operator to update the situation model after monitoring and either maintain monitoring or adapt it according to new requirements.

This brief overview of the major elements of the model is expanded in section 4 to provide a more detailed account of how the model works. Prior to that expanded account, however, it is important to describe more fully the situation model, which plays a major role in the cognitive activities box.

3.2. Situation model

The *situation model* is an incomplete mental representation that integrates the operator's current understanding of the state of both physical and functional aspects of the plant and the automated control systems. This model supports a number of general cognitive activities:

- it captures the operator's knowledge of the plant's physical systems and their characteristics and interconnections;

- it supports the operator in developing cause-and-effect relationships in explaining plant behavior and indications;
- it supports the operator in integrating separate indications and accounting for all data;
- it aids the operator in generating expected values (with more or less precision) for unmonitored parameters;
- it aids the operator in developing a description that captures plant state at a higher level than individual indications (i.e. system performance, process performance, goal achievement, etc.);
- it allows the operator to "run" mental simulations of the plant to anticipate future states of the plant, or to evaluate plant performance under various configurations.

As shown in Figure 4, an operator's training will develop a mental model of a somewhat idealized plant during basic training, which focuses on original plant design and theoretical foundations. Over time, as an operator becomes familiar with the plant through actual operation, his mental model will continue to evolve to better reflect the current plant (e.g. original systems may have been removed or replaced). Finally, the operator must adjust his mental model at the beginning of a shift by updating system status, operating mode, on-going maintenance activities, etc. This up-to-the-minute mental model is what we refer to as the situation model that plays such a prominent role in monitoring.

Another important input into the situation model is episodic knowledge (Tulving, 1983), which captures real and simulated operating experience with the plant. Episodic knowledge should be contrasted to knowledge of facts and static relationships, such as "valve 29 is a motor-driven valve," "system x connects to system y at valve 23." Episodic knowledge captures dynamic aspects of the plant, such as "a large LOCA produces symptoms first in the x indications," "it takes roughly x seconds before there is a noticeable response after taking the x action." This type of knowledge comes from actual operating experience and from training scenarios. The training scenarios in the full-scope simulator are important because they may be the only source for this type of knowledge about certain abnormal events. Thus, both episodic and declarative knowledge are critical in developing a situation model that supports the full range of cognitive activities listed above.

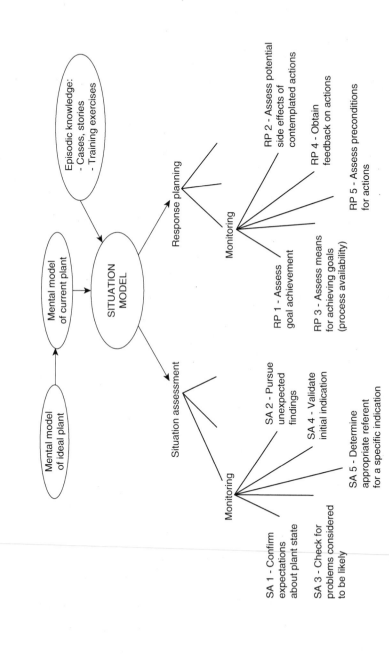

FIGURE 4   Role of the situation model.

At a high level of description, all operator cognitive activity can be split into situation assessment and response planning. As Figure 4 shows, the situation model supports both of these activities. *Situation assessment* refers to the process of constructing an explanation to account for observations. Studies show that operators actively develop a coherent understanding of the current state of the plant (e.g. Roth et al., 1994). Situation assessment is similar in meaning to "diagnosis" but is broader in scope. Diagnosis typically refers to searching for the cause(s) of abnormal symptoms (e.g. a malfunctioning piece of equipment). Situation assessment encompasses explanations that are generated to account for normal as well as abnormal conditions.

We believe that some monitoring activities serve this situation assessment activity. Note that, in Figure 4, there are placeholders under situation assessment for other unspecified activities that comprise situation assessment. We have chosen to restrict our scope by leaving those unspecified. However, all of the categories listed in Figure 4 were observed during our field studies. We have identified five types of monitoring that support situation assessment (SA).

1. *Confirm expectations about plant state (SA1)*—the operator can have expectations regarding plant response (to a change in the system, etc.) or regarding unmonitored indications. In both cases, the operator has developed an expectation about some indications, and monitoring serves to obtain those indications to either confirm or disprove the expectation.

2. *Pursue unexpected findings (SA2)*—an operator will occasionally encounter an indication that he believes to be valid but is unexpected. In these cases, the operator will actively direct monitoring to seek other indications that might help him understand the unexpected indication.

3. *Check for problems considered to be likely (SA3)*—the operator is a central element of plant operations and is continuously aware of the set of maintenance, test, and repair activities being carried out on his unit. The operator understands that certain activities create the potential for particular problems (e.g. a particular malfunction in a system, or a vulnerability to a particular type of error), and he needs to be vigilant

to such problems. Therefore, monitoring is actively directed to indications that can reveal the occurrence of a likely problem.

4. *Validate initial indication (SA4)*—in general, control room and interface technology are not perfectly reliable, and operators are often unwilling to trust any single indication. Therefore, an operator will sometimes locate and monitor indications that can validate or invalidate the veracity of an initial indication.

5. *Determine an appropriate referent for a specific indication (SA5)*—there are some cases for which the operator obtains an indication but does not have a clear reference value for the indication. The reference value serves to give meaning to the indication (e.g. normal or abnormal). When an appropriate referent is not provided with the indication, the operator must actively seek other indications to establish that referent.

Response planning refers to deciding on a course of action, given a particular situation assessment. In general, response planning involves identifying goals, generating one or more alternative response plans, evaluating the response plans, and selecting the response plan that best meets the goals identified. In general, operators have formal written procedures that guide their response, but studies show that operators do not execute procedures purely on faith (Roth et al., 1994). Operators continue to identify appropriate goals based on their own situation assessment, evaluate whether the actions they are taking based on the procedure are sufficient to achieve these goals, and adapt the procedure to the situation if they decide it is necessary to do so. As shown in Figure 4, we have identified four types of monitoring that support response planning (RP).

1. *Assess goal achievement (RP1)*—operator actions are taken in order to achieve some operational goal. As an operator moves through a procedure, he needs to determine whether the intended goal is being achieved, and he must actively identify and monitor indications that can aid the assessment of goal achievement.

2. *Assess the potential side effects of contemplated actions (RP2)*—an important activity for operators is ensuring that their actions, and the actions of others working on the unit, do not have side effects (unintended consequences). While the situation model is the primary tool for

assessing the potential for unintended consequences, monitoring is required to support the mental simulation.

3. *Assess means for achieving goals (i.e. evaluate process availability) (RP3)*—an activity related to the previous activity (RP2) is assessing the availability of plant systems that can be used for achieving operational goals. In response planning, the operator needs to consider the possibility that a process could fail and an alternative process would be required. Thus, active monitoring is needed to support the evaluation of process availability.

4. *Obtain feedback on actions (RP4)*—as actions are taken, the operator needs to obtain feedback that the intended action was indeed carried out (e.g. the valve did close, the pump did start) and that relevant parameters are responding in appropriate ways (e.g. pressure is decreasing, level is increasing). Active monitoring is required to obtain this feedback.

5. *Assess pre-conditions for action (RP5)*—In some cases, particular actions can only be taken after certain pre-conditions are satisfied. Thus, operators will monitor the plant with the specific intent of assessing the status of those pre-conditions.

These nine types of monitoring are all various forms of knowledge-driven monitoring that are generated from the situation model. Top-down, knowledge-driven monitoring can be contrasted to bottom-up, data-driven monitoring. *Data-driven monitoring* is affected by the form of the information, its physical salience (size, brightness, loudness, etc.) and its behavior (e.g. bandwidth and the rate of change of the information signal) (Moray, 1986). For example, a signal that is changing rapidly may be sampled more frequently by the observer. In the extreme, this type of monitoring can be viewed as "passive" in that the operator's monitoring behavior is driven solely by the characteristics of the information. *Knowledge-driven monitoring*, on the other hand, can be viewed as "active" monitoring in that the operator is not merely responding to characteristics of the environment that "shout out," but is deliberately directing attention to areas of the control room environment that are expected to provide specific information that can be used to achieve specific goals. These specific goals are captured by the nine types of monitoring enumerated above and illustrated in Figure 4. We will return to this distinction again later, as we describe the operator monitoring model in more detail.

4. Qualitative cognitive model of operator monitoring: overview: detailed description

Our description of the model will follow the layout from left to right in Figures 2 and 3, beginning with initiating events, followed by cognitive activities, facilitating activities, and finally the monitoring activities themselves. At the end of this section, we will also show how the concepts in this qualitative cognitive model capture the activities in two specific instances of monitoring practice that we observed in the field. Because our model is in domain specific terms (in contrast to frameworks, like cognitive work analysis (Vicente, 1999), which are stated in domain-independent terms), we would expect the detailed behaviors it represents to differ across domains. However, the general types of activities and the cognitive functions they support have the potential to be generalized across other domains of expertise (see section 6).

4.1. Initiating events

We have identified three types of triggers that initiate monitoring. The first category, *data-driven* events, are not actively sought by the operator, but are rather prompted by changes in the environment. Four cases of this category were noted:

- *Receive auditory alarm*—when an alarm is triggered, an auditory signal is emitted in addition to a visual indication of the alarm. Thus, the control room interface "alerts" the operator that a significant event has occurred. The operator obtains the alarm message, and must now evaluate the meaning and importance of the alarm.
- *Read indication*—as an operator scans the control room interface (e.g. a panel of meters) to locate a particular indication, he/she may unintentionally read other indications in the same area. There are cases in which one of these indications "jumps out" at the operator. Often, the operator notices an abnormal or unusual reading.

- *Receive communication*—there are many other people involved with running and maintaining a unit, as well as equipment common to all units. These personnel (e.g. field operators, maintenance workers) may identify a situation that they want to let the operator know about. The operator can receive a communication from these other workers by phone, in person, or by radio transmission.
- *Receive "unmediated" indication*—the designers of the plant have placed sensors throughout the plant to measure various aspects of the process performance (e.g. pressure, temperature). These sensors are ultimately connected to indicators on the control room interface. Thus, the sensed information is mediated by technology and brought to the interface. However, there are cases in which the operator receives information through his own senses (vision, hearing, feeling, smelling) instead of through the interface (Vicente and Burns, 1996). This information is not "mediated" by technology.

The second category of initiating events shown on the left of Figure 2 are those that are defined by *standard operator practices*, *plant policy*, or *plant procedures*. In general, these events are designed to ensure that operators stay in touch with the state of the plant. Typically, these are events that are required periodically. Note that these are considered knowledge-driven. The full set of initiating events in this category are:

- *Complete check form*—check forms are used periodically by field operators to document the status of certain variables. To fill out these forms, field operators must go out into the field to see the information and the component. These forms are subsequently reviewed by the operator in the main control room, enabling him/her to monitor parameters in the field indirectly.
- *Review log/plant records*—the log is a hand-written, chronological record of notable activities (not necessarily abnormal) that have occurred during a shift, and can include tests completed, significant alarms, deficiency reports, work permits, jumpers, changes in reactor power, which channels were refueled, pieces of equipment taken out of service, etc. This is a short-term record of the unit's history, as opposed to the longer-term events logged in the long-term status binder. The log is reviewed during the shift turnover, but it can also be consulted during a shift to remind the operator of what had been

done on the previous or even earlier shifts. The log provides a means by which operators can be aware of the recent status of a unit (e.g. what components are not working, which meters are not working, what is currently being repaired, etc.). This provides a valuable context for monitoring and interpreting information on a shift.

- *Conduct shift turnover*—an operator arrives in the control room approximately 15 to 30 minutes before his/her shift is scheduled to begin. At this time, he/she conducts a shift turnover with the operator he is relieving. The turnover consists of several activities. Perhaps most importantly, there is a discussion between operators regarding the state of key variables, any unusual alarms, jobs completed and jobs outstanding, plans that are active, variables that need to be monitored more closely than normal, which field operators or technicians are working on which components, what the field operators are aware of, any significant operating memos, and a review of the log. After these discussions, the operator coming on shift will also look at the call-up sheets to see what tests are scheduled for that shift, and the daily work plan that documents upcoming maintenance and call-ups. He/she will also review the computer summaries and alarms. At this point, the operator will try to explain every alarm until he/she has a satisfactory understanding of why these alarms are in. Operators are also required to execute a formal panel check procedure that involves following a check sheet that requires making checks of specific values on the control panels to determine whether they are in an acceptable state. Some operators were also observed to conduct an informal panel walkthrough before beginning the required turnover activities. They would walk by the panels and quickly scan them to get a general feel for the status of the unit and review any tags. Finally, operators who were not intimately familiar with a particular unit would review the long-term status binder that documents the "quirks" of that unit.

- *Conduct equipment tests*—a number of equipment tests are scheduled on every shift. The purpose of these tests is to ensure that back-up systems and safety systems are in an acceptable state, should they be required. These tests provide operators with a means by which they can monitor the status of these systems (e.g. which safety systems are working properly, how quickly they are responding, which meters are working, etc.).

- *Conduct periodic monitoring*—a standard operating practice is to conduct a review of plant indications on a regular basis. Operators can scan the control panel and CRT indications from their desks, or they may walk down the panels on a periodic basis.
- *Review operating memos*—a tag is placed on a control to indicate that a temporary procedure has been developed to govern that control device. This temporary procedure is either not yet in the procedure manual, or it temporarily supersedes the procedure in the manual. Operators review the new operating memos early in a shift.
- *Review work reports*—work reports describe major maintenance and testing activities on a unit. The operator needs to be aware of these activities because they can remove equipment from operation or set up other situations that may make some safety systems temporarily unavailable. Also, the operator must be concerned with violations of the technical specifications, which can result from interactions between multiple work activities.

The third category of initiating events in the top left of Figure 2 are *scheduled tasks and activities* that are to be carried out on the unit or on another unit. The operator is made aware of maintenance and testing activities, which are a daily occurrence, as well as control room activities, such as refueling, equipment upgrades, etc. These activities become incorporated into the operator's situation model and establish expectations of what is "normal" for the shift.

4.2. Cognitive activities

The model illustrated in Figure 2 shows that the initiating events can prompt monitoring in two ways. First, when an initiating event occurs due to practices, policy, procedures or due to a data-driven signal, the operator obtains some information from the control room interface. At this point, a cycle of cognitive activities begins. As shown by the evaluate input box, the information is evaluated in several ways, seemingly in parallel: was it expected or not expected? Is it valid, clearly not valid, or is there uncertainty about its validity? Is the indication in the normal range, abnormal, or is it unclear whether it's normal? There may be other evaluations also being applied, but these three are the ones we identified through our interviews.

This input evaluation is guided by information from the situation model, as shown by the arrow from the situation model ellipse to the evaluate input box. For example, an alarm may appear regarding fuel channel outlet temperatures. Because the operator's situation model shows that refueling is on-going, this alarm is expected; it is an indication that refueling is progressing as planned. The arrow from the evaluate input box to the situation model ellipse represents an update to the situation model with the just-acquired, just-evaluated information.

The second way in which initiating events initiate monitoring is via the scheduled task/activity box, which is connected directly to the situation model. When monitoring is initiated by a scheduled task/activity event, the first step involves updating the situation model rather than evaluate input. For example, the operator is told that a certain component will be removed for service for the next four hours. This information is incorporated into the situation model to refine the knowledge of what is normal and what is expected. Also, the operator will continue to test the internal coherence of his situation model. If this new information conflicts with existing knowledge, the operator will work to resolve the conflict.

Thus, these two paths from initiating events always lead to updates to the situation model, and the first path leads to an initial evaluation of information that was obtained by the operator. These paths then converge to identify an appropriate type of knowledge-driven monitoring (SA1–A5 and RP1–P5). The nine types of monitoring that were defined earlier represent, we believe, the complete set of motivations for monitoring at this stage of the model. Note that some of these are tied to the evaluate input box. For example, SA4 (validate initial indication) is needed when the evaluate input box determines that the initial indication may not be valid (unsure). Monitoring takes on the role of locating and obtaining additional indications that can establish the validity of the initial indication. As a more specific example, an alarm may come on that is unexpected and abnormal, but the operator is unsure about its validity. The situation model is used to make these judgments and is updated to reflect the new alarm. Next, the operator initiates monitoring (knowledge-driven) to better assess the validity of the alarm.

Other types of monitoring are tied more closely to the situation model. For example, SA3 (check for problems considered to be likely) may be a response to a scheduled activity that the situation model reveals can often lead to the failure of a particular piece of equipment. Thus, the operator initiates monitoring (again, knowledge-driven) to keep a vigil on the status of that piece of equipment so that if it fails, the failure will be detected early.

No matter which type of monitoring is selected, the operator needs to make a series of other decisions before actual monitoring activities can commence. As the next rectangular box in Figure 2 shows, the next set of decisions has to do with establishing which data and monitoring priority and frequency. The situation model is used to identify the data or indications that are most relevant to monitor, given the monitoring goal. For example, if the objective is to validate an initial indication, the operator needs to identify back-up indications that measure the same process.

Decisions regarding priority reflect the importance of the task being supported by monitoring. For example, if a safety system–related alarm has come in and was unexpected, monitoring to better understand the nature of the alarm violation is likely to be assigned a high priority, pushing aside all other tasks. On the other hand, monitoring that supports tracking the progress of a simple, low-risk system test may be assigned a low priority, conducted only as time permits.

The decision about monitoring frequency determines how often some monitoring should be done—e.g. every 5 seconds, every 2 hours, once per shift. The operator will use knowledge of how quickly relevant indications change. If significant changes can occur rapidly, a higher frequency is required. If, on the other hand, the possible rate of change is severely limited, monitoring frequency can be low. There is an extensive literature on this topic (Moray, 1986).

The next rectangular box in Figure 2 identifies two other decisions that need to be made before monitoring begins. These decisions are guided by different types of knowledge, which are also shown in the figure. First, the operator needs to determine where to find the data or indication: is it on the control panel, on a CRT display, at some local control station so that a call to a field operator is required? The operator has detailed knowledge of the control room interface. The ellipse titled procedural and declarative interface knowledge includes the following types of information:

- the set of indications available (declarative);
- the location of indications (declarative);
- how to read indicators, how they work, and how they fail (procedural);
- how to access and configure CRT displays (procedural).

In addition to knowing the location of an indication and how to acquire that indication, the operator also needs to develop a plan for how to execute the monitoring effectively. The operator has knowledge (represented by the strategies for creating and/or extracting information ellipse) about effective methods for monitoring. That is, the operator has a set of skills that can be used to monitor the relevant data with the appropriate priority and at the appropriate frequency. The operator develops a plan that may require manipulating the interface to facilitate monitoring, or it may simply identify what to monitor and how frequently.

For example, we found that operators can define a range of approaches and select a specific approach based on priority, frequency, and resources available. At one extreme, the operator can monitor a parameter himself (or assign another person to it) at a very high frequency (almost continuously). If the operator places the parameter on a CRT-based trend display, changes become easier to see, and the monitoring effort is reduced so that other tasks can be time-shared. Finally, the operator might set up some type of alert, such as an auditory cue that indicates the parameter passed a setpoint. This last case is like setting an alarm on a parameter for a operator-defined event, and this case requires the least operator resources for monitoring—in effect, the interface will alert the operator that something important has happened. Whatever approach is adopted, the plan leads to actual operator actions on the control room environment and takes us out of the cognitive activities box and into Figure 3.

4.3. Facilitating activities

We identified a set of activities that operators use, not to monitor *per se*, but to make monitoring more effective. We believe that this is one of the more significant findings from this research: operators actively configure the interface to facilitate their monitoring of important indications. A description of each facilitating activity and brief examples of its use are described next (Mumaw et al., 1995, 2000 contain a larger set of examples).

1. *Enhance signal*—this action serves to increase the salience or visibility of an indication or piece of information. It increases the signal-to-noise ratio by improving the signal.

   Example: at one plant, we found that operators would expand the fuel channel outlet temperature trend graph on the CRT to better monitor small changes in temperature. Normally, an indication is assigned to a single trend line on the CRT, which has a range of half the height of the display. Some operators would expand the trend so that it covered the full height of the display, and therefore, create a more salient trend graph. In this way, small changes in temperature, which are associated with refueling actions, are more easily discerned on the trend graph because they result in a larger change on the display.

2. *Reduce noise*—this action reduces or removes noise (i.e. meaningless change) from the complete set of indications. It too has the effect of enhancing the salience of meaningful indications by increasing signal-to-noise ratio.

   Example: the most common example of noise reduction were the frequent operator battles with nuisance alarms. In one case, we found the same alarm appeared six times in approximately 15 minutes, and the operator indicated that the message was not meaningful. One action operators can take to reduce a nuisance alarm is to change the alarm settings temporarily. This action typically requires permission from control room management.

3. *Document baseline or trend*—this action documents a baseline condition (e.g. beginning of the shift) or establishes a trend over a period of time for comparison to a later time. It provides a concrete description of plant state at a point in time so that later changes can be more easily identified since it is difficult to monitor all indications and their changes. Thus, it creates a referent for evaluating changes over time.

   Example: the most common example of this facilitating activity was that operators typically obtain a hard copy of several CRT displays at the beginning of the shift. At one plant, we found that operators typically printed the following types of displays when they would come on shift: the plant schematic diagram, zone deviations, and boiler level control status. Then, if they thought these values changed later in the shift, they could compare current values to the values printed at the start of the shift.

4. *Act on interface to determine the validity of an indication*—in some situations, there may be questions about whether an important indication is valid (e.g. because it may conflict with some other information). One method to determine its validity is to use the interface to look for evidence that the sensor and indicator are working properly.

   Example: in one situation we observed, an operator had just finished refueling and a channel outlet, narrow-range, temperature alarm failed to clear. This alarm might mean that there is an out-of-range temperature or that the indication is not valid. The operator had just been trending the outlet temperature, which moved over a wide range, and therefore inferred that the sensor was "alive." He then called up the actual value and found that it was in the normal range. Then, he used his knowledge of how the alarm is triggered to decide that the indicated value was valid and the alarm logic was responsible for the delay in clearing. Thus, he used his interaction with the changing indication to determine its validity.

5. *Create new indication or alarm*—the control room interface has a set of indications and alarms that are already defined. Sometimes, an operator modifies that interface to create indications or alarms that did not exist before.

   Example: We saw several cases where operators created new alarms to aid monitoring. In one case, operators changed the setpoint on the heat transport storage tank level alarm to monitor draining that tank. Normally, the alarm setpoint is high, and the tank level is maintained around 75%. When the unit is being shut down, however, the tank is drained down to around 50%. The draining is a fairly slow process, occurring over several hours. Instead of having to remember to monitor the process over this period, operators will instead adjust the alarm setpoint down to around 55%. By doing so, an auditory alarm will be generated just before the tank reaches the desired value of 50%. This alarm then serves as a reminder to begin monitoring and controlling draining more closely. In this way, operators have defined a new event that is alarmed so that monitoring can be conducted less frequently and more reliably.

6. *Create external reminder for monitoring*—when it becomes important to monitor an indication frequently, the operator must somehow keep track of the monitoring task—that is, remember to monitor. This facilitating action creates an external (i.e. something in the world, not in the head) reminder to monitor an indication, thereby reducing the load on short-term memory.

Example: At one plant, we found that operators would open a door on a particular strip chart recorder to make it stand out from the other recorders when it is important to monitor that parameter more closely than usual (e.g. open doors on feedtrain tank levels while blowing down boilers). The open door serves as an easily recognized and very salient external reminder to monitor that strip chart.

7. *Create external cues for action or inaction*—external cues are also created to remind an operator about interface actions and configuration. In some cases, monitoring is supported by configuring the interface in a particular way, and that configuration needs to be preserved over a period of time. Operators create an external reminder that indicates that the special configuration is to be maintained.

Example: At one plant, there is a set of analog automatic control devices in a row on one of the control panels. These controllers are normally set on auto mode, instead of manual mode. If an operator temporarily changes one to manual, he will slide the controller out of the panel an inch as an external signal to himself and to others that it was intentionally placed in the manual mode.

8. *Employ additional operators*—in some cases, what is needed to support monitoring is more "eyes." The operator may be required to monitor an indication closely and may be unable to dedicate himself to that task because of other competing activities. Thus, another operator is brought into the unit and dedicated to monitoring.

Example: Several operators mentioned that when workload gets high, and there are too many monitoring demands, a junior operator can be dedicated to monitor a small set of indications (perhaps even one).

9. *Create external descriptor*—in some cases, operators create an external descriptor, whether it be of a variable label, variable limits, or variable state. This descriptor is subsequently used as an external referent for monitoring, thereby relieving the load on operators' memory.

Example: An operator asked a field operator to make up a list of all of the nuisance alarms that could be brought in by the repair work that the field operator was going to be doing. The operator was then going to use this list as a referent for monitoring alarms. If an alarm came in that was on this list, then he would know that it was probably a nuisance alarm. On the other hand, if an alarm that was not on the list came in, he would know that it was probably caused by some other factor that might require further investigation.

4.4. Monitoring activities

The final element of our model describes the actual monitoring activities themselves—the acquisition of an indication or some other piece of information. The following list is a comprehensive set of resources that operators can use to obtain information at the plants we observed.

1. *Monitor plant state indications using panels*—operators can obtain indications from the control panels in the control room (includes "back" panels behind control panels in room just off of control room).
2. *Conduct field tour*—operators can leave the control room to make observations or obtain indications from equipment in the plant.
3. *Monitor plant state indications using CRTs*—operators can obtain indications from the CRTs in the control room.
4. *Review log/plant record*—operators can acquire information recorded in the unit log or related plant documents.
5. *Monitor alarm screens*—operators can acquire information from an alarm message or from the central alarm screens in the control room.
6. *Communicate with field operators*—operators can communicate by phone or radio with operators at some locations in the field to obtain an indication or receive information about plant state.
7. *Communicate with operators from other units*—operators can communicate by phone or in person with operators at another unit to obtain an indication or receive information about plant state.
8. *Monitor alarm panels*—operators can acquire information from an alarm message or from the individual windows (annunciator tiles) found on the alarm panels above the control panels in the control room (see Figure 1).
9. *Monitor other unit*—operators can also acquire relevant information by monitoring the information describing the status of other reactor units. Such information may be relevant to their own unit (e.g. if the

operator on another unit is conducting a test that affects the alarm messages on the operator's own unit, as is sometimes the case).

10. *Print out CRT display*—operators can acquire historical information by using the laser printer to record the current status of a CRT display. This paper record can then be used as a source of information for monitoring.

Note that Figures 2 and 3 show that after an indication or some piece of information is obtained from a monitoring activity, there is a feedback loop into the evaluate input box that is part of the cognitive activities. This allows monitoring to be an on-going, cyclical activity. The indication that comes back may be expected, valid, and normal and can even only serve to update the situation model without changing significantly the monitoring plan and activity. On the other hand, the indication can also introduce the need for a change in monitoring. Examples of these different cases are provided next.

4.5. *Workload regulation*

The facilitating activities and the monitoring activities just described are nested in that the former provide a context for the latter. This relationship is shown in Figure 5. Note, however, that there is also a third, outer

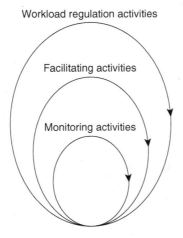

FIGURE 5   The nested relationship between monitoring activities, facilitating activities, and workload regulation activities.

loop that provides a context for the facilitating activities. The purpose of this outer loop is to regulate the operator's workload so that monitoring is cognitively more manageable. This higher level of control deals with issues such as setting priorities, scheduling jobs, and allocating personnel. The success of monitoring depends, to a great extent, on the decisions made at this outer level. If operators can effectively regulate their workload so that it is well calibrated to their cognitive capabilities, then they will rarely put themselves in a position where errors will occur. On the other hand, if operators do not effectively regulate their workload and over-extend themselves, then errors are almost sure to occur, even if facilitating activities are adopted. In Rochlin's (1997) terms, operators will "lose the bubble."

A few examples of workload regulation can illustrate its importance to operator monitoring. In the first case, an operator was in the middle of refueling when a worker came to get approval to perform a job in the field. If approved, this job would bring in nuisance alarms, which would be added to the nuisance alarms normally triggered during refueling. This would greatly increase the demands associated with monitoring because the operator would be frequently interrupted by alarms and he would have to calculate expected symptoms for several different classes of events (i.e. refueling, maintenance, other). Furthermore, the operator would have the added cognitive burden of using his situation model to calculate expected symptoms for several classes of events so that he could determine if any alarm that came up was merely due to the job being performed in the field, by the refueling, or by some other (perhaps critical) event. Under these conditions, it would be very easy to miss or misinterpret an important alarm amongst the constant stream of nuisance alarms. For this reason, the operator decided to defer the job until later in the day, after refueling was completed. Thus, this operator made a conscious decision to regulate his workload by spreading out task demands more uniformly during his shift rather than creating a demand peak that would increase the likelihood of monitoring errors. In terms of our model, the end effect was to reduce the complexity of the situation model that was needed to deal with the event.

As a second example, we frequently saw maintenance/engineering staff wait patiently until the operator was ready to attend to them. This resulted in a highly unusual style of interpersonal interaction, where the operator would not even acknowledge the presence of the individual(s) queued up, until he/she was ready to attend to them. To the uninitiated, this felt socially uncomfortable (as if it signaled an extreme difference in status.) However, the operators were on excellent terms with the maintenance and engineering staff. The unusual interaction style simply reflected an adaptation to the operator's high attention demands and was understood that way by the engineering and maintenance staff, who respected the need of the operator to regulate when he could attend to them.

It is interesting to note that newer operators find it very difficult to regulate their workload effectively because they receive no formal training and very little practice at more mundane non-emergency activities, particularly dealing with work order requests. As a result, they have not yet calibrated themselves to the level of activity that they can reliably handle without significantly increasing the potential for error. Yet the effective regulation of activity (i.e. ensuring that current demands do not exceed existing resources) is critical to effective monitoring.

4.6. Exercising the model: illustrations of monitoring practice

Qualitative evidence showing the explanatory adequacy of our model can be illustrated by showing how the model categories can account for episodes of monitoring behavior that we observed in the field. Each episode can be viewed as a trajectory through the model, specifying a particular sequence of physical and cognitive activities. Two such trajectories are described here. We chose relatively simple trajectories because the more complex trajectories (described in Appendix A of Mumaw et al., 1995) can only be interpreted with considerably more knowledge of nuclear power plant operations.

1. *Pursuing reheater alarm after maintenance.*
   Case: An operator was aware that there had been a problem with the stage 2 element of the unit's moisture separator reheater. It had been taken out of service, repaired, and then placed back on-line. Early in the shift, the operator began working with someone in the field to place the element back into service. However, when stage 2 was placed into service, an alarm came on: stage 1 reheater flow unbalanced.

At this point, the operator accessed the "moisture separator/stage 1 reheat" display on a nearby CRT. Specifically, he/she looked at temperature, flow, and pressure in the four parallel channels. The corresponding values were found to be very close across the four channels. The operator called someone from maintenance to look at the component, and he mentioned that there may be problems with the relay or limit switch in the alarm.

Analysis: The initiating event for this situation was the auditory alarm (data-driven). The evaluation of this alarm seemed to be "not expected, unsure about validity, abnormal." The situation model was updated and further monitoring began. The knowledge-driven monitoring was either SA2 (pursue unexpected finding) or SA4 (validate initial indication). The operator used his/her situation model to identify relevant data and (moving directly to a straightforward monitoring activity) monitor plant state indications using a CRT display. The indications obtained from the CRT display were taken as valid and as evidence that the problem suggested by the alarm did not exist. Thus, the input from the feedback loop is evaluated as "not expected, valid, normal." Updating the situation model suggests that perhaps the alarm is malfunctioning in some way (not a valid indication). The operator, probably using SA1 (confirm expectations about plant state), identifies relevant data (relay and limit switch on alarm), and communicates with personnel in the field to carry out the monitoring.

2. *Tracking lake water temperatures to check for potential problems.*
   Case: When an operator sees that lake temperature has changed significantly, he knows that there is a danger that there will be temperature differences between the pumps that bring lake water into the plant. If the temperature difference is too large, damage can be caused in the pumps. Because of this, when the temperature change is detected, the operator sets up a trend on a CRT to track temperatures.

   Analysis: The operator's situation model, which incorporates episodic knowledge, is used to identify the fact that significant changes in lake temperature can create the possibility for damage to pumps. This initiates a periodic monitoring activity (practices, policy, procedures) that aids the operator in detecting the change in lake water temperature. This input is evaluated as "not expected, valid, and normal." The update to the situation model leads to knowledge-driven monitoring through SA 3 (check for problems considered to be likely). The situation model is used to identify the relevant data, establish priority, and monitoring frequency. In this case, a facilitating activity is used: enhance signal. To make the temperature differences between pumps more easily monitored, the operator sets up a trend that is prominently displayed on one of the panel CRTs. Then the operator can monitor the critical indications using the CRT.

These two cases are not very complex, but they allow us to illustrate several of the general properties of our model, specifically:

- the interactions between data-driven and knowledge-driven monitoring;
- the various roles of the situation model;
- the variety of knowledge-driven monitoring types.

Mumaw et al. (1995) describe other longer cases that we observed during our site visits that allowed us to see the full complexity of monitoring.

5. Discussion

In section 1 of this article, we claimed that complex and dynamic work environments provide a challenging "litmus-test" with which to evaluate theories of cognition. How can our model of operator monitoring in nuclear power plants during normal operations help us improve existing theories in cognitive science and cognitive engineering?

Clearly, there are certain aspects of our model that underscore and generalize very familiar findings that are at the core of cognitive science. The most salient example is the strong role played by knowledge-driven monitoring, which exemplifies the top-down active processing that is largely responsible for the development of cognitive psychology (Neisser, 1967). Even just a cursory examination of Figures 2 to 5 reveals that passive, data-driven monitoring plays a weak role in operator monitoring in nuclear power plants.

But while knowledge-driven processing is crucial, the role that problem solving plays appears to be somewhat different in our model than in many existing theories of cognition. It is common to view problem solving as a final resort that people turn to when their more efficient cognitive resources do not achieve task goals. Kintsch (1998: 3) provides a representative example of this view: "when an impasse develops in perception or understanding they [i.e. people] resort to problem solving as a repair process." A very similar claim is embedded in Reason's (1990) influential model of human error. In that framework, people turn to problem solving when they realize that the heuristics they normally use are inadequate for the task at hand. This may be the case in some situations, perhaps those where the people are not highly experienced or where the consequences of error are not severe (e.g. Newell and Simon, 1972).

However, our qualitative observations and model clearly show that people do not resort to knowledge-driven problem solving only when they exhaust more economic cognitive resources. We frequently found that people engaged in deliberate reasoning and active processing to avoid problems, to confirm that their actions were having the desired effect, and to anticipate problems before they became severe. They did not wait until their normal routines failed before engaging in problem solving activities. This proactive aspect of problem solving has been noted before in the cognitive engineering literature (Decortis, 1993), but it does not appear to be represented in many models in the cognitive science and cognitive engineering literatures (e.g. Newell and Simon, 1972; Kintsch, 1998; Klein, 1989; Reason, 1990; Cacciabue et al., 1992).

Another important feature of our work is that the situation model is a mental construction based on input from the environment, probably somewhat like the process described by Kintsch (1998). This construction process differs from the recognition process that takes a central place in other models of expert cognitive activity, such as Klein's (1989) recognition-primed decision making model. Rather than matching patterns, the operators we observed appear to be engaged in an active construction process that integrates the input they receive from the environment with the knowledge they have gathered through experience to create a situation model that represents their understanding of what is currently going on in the plant.

Another basic finding in cognitive science that is captured in our model is the highly distributed nature of cognition in complex dynamic work environments (Hutchins, 1995a, 1995b). The strong role of facilitating activities in our model shows that people frequently tried to offload their cognitive demands by using their external environment. They created external reminders, created cues for action where none existed, enhanced the saliency of existing cues, and reduced the noise associated with existing cues—all to reduce the psychological requirements of a very demanding set of tasks to a manageable level. Without these facilitating activities, monitoring a nuclear power plant would probably be an impossibly complex task, given people's memory and computational limitations. This is not a new finding (e.g. Seminara et al., 1977), but it is not well represented in traditional cognitive science theories. Thus, our work generalizes Hutchins' (1995a, 1995b) research on distributed cognition to a new domain (i.e. nuclear power plants vs. maritime navigation or aviation). Perhaps more importantly, our work also generalizes those ideas to a more complex task. The number of variables that need to be monitored (thousands) and the amount of time that it takes to become a licensed operator in a nuclear power plant (7 years) exceeds the requirements associated with the more specific, and thus delimited, tasks studied by Hutchins.

Again, however, our model emphasizes a pattern that has not received a great deal of attention in cognitive science theories. Much of the work on distributed cognition emphasizes the fact that cognitive activities are distributed spatially between resources "in the head" and those "in the world" (e.g. Zhang and Norman, 1994). The fact that cognition can, and sometimes must, be distributed temporally has received much less attention. The workload regulation feature of our model emphasizes this temporal aspect. If operators are to monitor the plant reliably, they must be very clever in the way in which they distribute their tasks over time. This skill takes some time to acquire. Operators must become calibrated so that they do not put themselves in situations where they are bound to fail, even if they rely on facilitating activities. Experienced operators use knowledge of their own limited capabilities and the demands of various—frequently mundane—tasks to distribute their responsibilities over time in such a way as not to exceed their resource limits. Such workload regulation strategies have been observed in the cognitive engineering literature (e.g. Xiao et al., 1997) and in the Francophone ergonomics literature in Europe (e.g. Sperandio, 1978), but they have not played a prominent role in the cognitive science literature.

Finally, our research also has important implications for the feasibility of studying human cognition in terms of reductionistic stages of information processing (e.g. Wickens, 1992). It is not uncommon to see a diagram parsing human cognitive activity into a number of stages (e.g. sensation, perception, decision making, problem solving, planning, action). And while these diagrams are usually accompanied by caveats stating that the delineation of psychological activity into a number of discrete stages is a gross simplification, these disclaimers are frequently ignored in empirical research. Psychological phenomena are frequently studied in relative isolation from one another.

The weaknesses of such a reductionistic approach were noted over 100 years ago in a seminal article by Dewey (1896) that was subsequently judged to be the most important paper published in *Psychological Review* at the time of that prestigious journal's 50 year anniversary. Our model serves as a modest reminder of Dewey's forgotten message. Because we set out to study monitoring, one might think that we would be limiting ourselves to studying the stages of human information processing commonly referred to as sensation, perception, and attention. However, because we used a complex dynamic work environment as a litmus test, we opened ourselves to study much more than that—indeed, this is what our results have revealed.

If we define monitoring as the activities that are directly intended to pick up information from the environment, then even a cursory glance at Figures 2 to 5 shows—paradoxically—that monitoring activities play a very small role in our model of monitoring. When we study psychological phenomena in rich, naturalistic environments, we see that the stages that have traditionally been studied in isolation are all tangled up in practice. Monitoring is as much about problem solving and workload regulation as it is about sensation and perception, perhaps even more so. Furthermore, it is not possible to disentangle monitoring from response planning or action (see Fig4), despite the long tradition in studying perception and action separately. Therefore, our results suggest that a holistic, nonlinear approach to the study of cognition may provide a more accurate portrayal of human cognition in unfettered situations outside of the laboratory. The types of models being developed in the dynamical systems perspective seem to be a promising approach to follow in this respect (e.g. Thelen et al., 2001).

6. Conclusions

Using complex dynamic work environments as a test bed for basic research has led to novel insights. The qualitative model of cognitive monitoring developed here appears to be unique in that it integrates the following features into a common framework:

- bottom-up, data-driven processes;
- top-down, knowledge-driven processes;
- inferential problem solving processes being activated without a failure of more automatic heuristic and perceptual processes;
- facilitating activities representing cognition distributed over space;
- workload regulation activities representing cognition distributed over time;
- a holistic, nonlinear model without clearly defined, separable stages.

As far as we know, there is no other cognitive model that contains all of these features.

At the same time, there are several limitations to this work that can motivate future research. First, to some extent, the model is embedded in the language of the application domain for which it was developed (i.e. nuclear power plants), although it has been recently applied with success to a second, different domain—monitoring aircraft engine indicators (Mumaw et al., 2002). It would be useful to generalize these concepts further in a way that would allow us to see the features that remain invariant over the idiosyncratic details of particular domains. Second, the model is qualitative in nature, and thus, does not have the rigor or precision of the cognitive models that are typically developed by cognitive scientists. It would be useful to determine if the ideas we have presented here can be integrated with the mechanisms specified by existing computational models. The comprehension-integration model of Kintsch (1998), the pertinence generation model of Raufaste et al. (1998), and the dynamical systems model of Thelen et al. (2001) appear to be promising paths worth exploring. By addressing these limitations, we may be able to integrate existing findings in cognitive science and cognitive engineering into a single framework, and thereby develop more unified theories with broader explanatory power and scope.

Acknowledgements

This research was sponsored by several research contracts with the Atomic Energy Control Board of Canada. We would like to thank Les Innes and Felicity Harrison (contract monitors), Francis Sarmiento and Mel Grandame, and Rick Manners and Brian Duncan for their help in coordinating our field study. Also, we are deeply indebted to all but one of the nuclear power plant operators who patiently answered our questions and generously shared their insights regarding the demands and skills associated with their jobs. This research would not have been possible without their cooperation.

References

Cacciabue, P. C., Decortis, F., Drozdowicz, B., Masson, M. and Nordvik, J. P. 1992, COSIMO: A cognitive simulation of human decision making and behavior in accident management of complex plants, *IEEE Transactions on Systems, Man, and Cybernetics*, SMC-22, 1058–1074.

Decortis, F. 1993, Operator strategies in a dynamic environment in relation to an operator model, *Ergonomics*, 36, 1291–1304.

Dewey, J. 1896, The reflex arc concept in psychology, *Psychological Review*, 4, 357–370.

Gibson, J. J., James J. 1967/1982, Gibson autobiography, In E. Reed and R. Jones (eds.), *Reasons for realism: Selected essays of James J. Gibson*, 7–22 (Erlbaum: Hillsdale, NJ).

Hutchins, E. 1995a, *Cognition in the Wild* (MIT Press: Cambridge, MA).

Hutchins, E. 1995b, How a cockpit remembers its speeds. *Cognitive Science*, 19, 265–288.

Kintsch, W. 1998, *Comprehension: A paradigm for cognition* (Cambridge University Press: Cambridge).

Klein, G. A. 1989, Recognition-primed decisions. In W. B. Rouse (ed.) *Advances in man-machine systems research, vol. 5*, 47–92 (JAI Press: Greenwich, CT).

Lorenz, K. Z. 1973, The fashionable fallacy of dispensing with description, *Die Naturwissenschaften*, 60, 1–9.

Moray, N. 1986, Monitoring behavior and supervisory control. In K. Boff, L. Kaufman and J. Thomas (ed.), *Handbook of human perception and performance*, 1–51 (John Wiley: New York).

Mumaw, R. J., Clark, S. and Sikora, J. 2002, *Human factors considerations in designing engine indications* (DOT/FAA/AR Technical Report) (FAA: Washington, DC).

Mumaw, R. J., Roth, E. M., Vicente, K. J. and Burns, C. M. 1995, *Cognitive contributions to operator monitoring during normal operations (AECB Final Report)* (Pittsburgh: Westinghouse Science & Technology Center).

Mumaw, R. J., Roth, E. M., Vicente, K. J. and Burns, C. M. 2000, There is more to monitoring a nuclear power plant than meets the eye, *Human Factors*, 42, 36–55.

Neisser, U. 1967, *Cognitive psychology* (Appleton Century Crofts: New York).

Newell, A. and Simon, H. A. 1972, *Human problem solving* (Prentice-Hall: Englewood Cliffs, NJ).

Patel, V. L., Kaufman, D. R. and Magder, S. A. 1996, The acquisition of medical expertise in complex dynamic environments. In K. A. Ericsson (ed.), *The road to excellence: The acquisition of expert performance in the arts and sciences, sports and games*, 127–165 (Mahwah, NJ: Erlbaum).

Raufaste, E., Eyrolle, H. and Marine, C. 1998, Pertinence generation in radiological diagnosis: Spreading activation and the nature of expertise, *Cognitive Science*, 22, 517–546.

Reason, J. 1990, *Human error* (Cambridge University Press: Cambridge).

Rochlin, G. I. 1997, *Trapped in the net: The unanticipated consequences of computerization* (Princeton University Press: Princeton, NJ).

Roth, E. M., Mumaw, R. J. and Lewis, P. M. 1994, *An empirical investigation of operator performance in cognitively demanding simulated emergencies* (NUREG/CR-6208) (U.S. Nuclear Regulatory Commission: Washington, DC).

Roth, E. M., Woods, D. D. and Pople, H. E. 1992, Cognitive simulation as a tool for cognitive task analysis, *Ergonomics*, 35, 1163–1198.

Sheridan, T. B. 1987, Supervisory control. In G. Selvendy (ed.), *Handbook of human factors* (John Wiley: New York).

Sperandio, J. C. 1978, The regulation of working methods as a function of workload among air traffic controllers, *Ergonomics*, 21, 193–202.

Stokes, D. E. 1997, *Pasteur's quadrant: Basic science and technological innovation* (Brookings Institution Press: Washington, DC).

Thelen, E., Schöner, G., Scheier, C. and Smith, L. B. 2001, The dynamics of embodiment: A field theory of infant perseverative reaching, *Behavioural and Brain Sciences*, 24, 1–55.

Tulving, E. 1983, *Elements of episodic memory* (Clarendon Press: Oxford).

Vicente, K. J. 1999, *Cognitive work analysis: Toward safe, productive, and healthy computer-based work* (Erlbaum: Mahwah, NJ).

Vicente, K. J. and Burns, C. M. 1996, Evidence for direct perception from cognition in the wild, *Ecological Psychology*, 8, 269–280.

Vicente, K. J., Roth, E. M. and Mumaw, R. J. 2001, How do operators monitor a complex, dynamic work domain? The impact of control room technology, *International Journal of Human-Computer Studies*, 54, 831–856.

Vicente, K. J., Moray, N., Lee, J. D., Rasmussen, J., Jones, B. G., Brock, R. and Djemil, T. 1996, Evaluation of a Rankine cycle display for nuclear power plant monitoring and diagnosis, *Human Factors*, 38, 506–521.

Wickens, C. D. 1992, *Engineering psychology and human performance*, 2nd edition (HarperCollins: New York).

Woods, D. D. 1988, Coping with complexity: The psychology of human behaviour in complex systems. In L. P. Goodstein, H. B. Andersen, and S. E. Olsen (eds.), *Tasks, errors, and mental models: A festschrift to celebrate the 60th birthday of Professor Jens Rasmussen*, 128–148 (Taylor & Francis: London).

Xiao, Y., Milgram, P. and Doyle, D. J. 1997, Planning behavior and its functional roles in the interaction with complex systems, *IEEE Transactions on Systems, Man, and Cybernetics, Part A: Systems and Humans*, 27, 313–324.

Zhang, J. and Norman, D. A. 1994, Representations in distributed cognitive tasks, *Cognitive Science*, 18, 87–122.

8

Sociotechnical Systems, Risk, and Error

Alex Kirlik

> *There is something to be said for every error, but whatever may be said for it,*
> *the most important thing to be said about it is that it is erroneous.*
>
> G. K. Chesterton, *All Is Grist*

The article by Vicente and Christoffersen reprinted in this chapter presents a very detailed application of a risk management framework developed by Jens Rasmussen. The authors use this framework to mine a case study for insights into factors contributing to the failure of a complex, sociotechnical system, one resulting in numerous deaths and other tragic consequences (the Walkerton, Canada, *E. coli* outbreak of May 2000). Key factors contributing to this incident were located at each of the many levels of the hierarchical system in question (work environment, staff, management, company or organization, regulators, and government). Perhaps even more important, other key contributors were located in disconnects among these many layers (a "lack of vertical interaction" or integration). These included both the failure of feedback information to be passed effectively up the chain and the failure of top-down laws, rules, and regulations to be heeded by those at lower levels of the hierarchy.

I am in no position to add much of value to this work *as a whole* except to relate this research to that of others in the sociotechnical systems area. For example, Cutcher-Gershenfeld and his colleagues have provided a complementary account of similar types of hierarchical and organization disconnects in *Valuable Disconnects in Organizational Learning Systems* (with Kenneth Ford, 2005), and in *Knowledge-Driven Work* (with a team of 13 MIT colleagues, 1998). And, even within the human–technology interaction (HTI) community, the notion that system failures typically have multiple causes, as they did in this case, has been on the table for some time now, especially due to the pioneering work of Charles Perrow (1984) and James Reason (1990).

Additionally, an obvious question that arises when considering the reprint and related research is the following: What, if anything, can we say about human error? The reprint is notable in many respects, but especially so in light of the modern zeitgeist in human error research. The one "data point" the authors observed that was inconsistent with, and not predictable by, Rasmussen's risk framework was a willful disobedience on the part of one front-line worker—in their terms: "Stan Koebel's deliberate deception and concealment of adverse test results."

How do we understand this behavior in light of recent scholarship in the area of human error and system safety, such as the following (the leading text from Chapter 1 of *The Field Guide to Understanding Human Error* by Sidney Dekker, 2006)?

> There are basically two ways of looking at human error. The first view is known as the OldView, or the Bad Apple Theory. It maintains that:
>
> - Complex systems would be fine, were it not for the erratic behavior of some unreliable people (Bad Apples) in it;
> - Human errors cause accidents: humans are the dominant contributor to more than two thirds of them;
> - Failures come as unpleasant surprises. They are unexpected and do not belong in the system. Failures are introduced to the system only through the inherent unreliability of people.
>
> This chapter is about the first view. The second is about a contrasting view, known as the NewView. The rest of the book helps you avoid the OldView and apply the NewView to your understanding of human error.

Dekker's perspective on error gained formulation in his previous (2004) book, *Ten Questions About Human Error*, and has been fleshed out in even more detailed form in a third book focusing on the health care industry, *Just Culture: Balancing Safety and Accountability* (Dekker, 2007). I have read much of Dekker's work, and there is much to like, and even to recommend. He has clearly thought through important issues deeply, and is a passionate advocate for the everyday worker. His work certainly appeals to the better side of my nature, and to my politics. Yet, at the same time, I cannot help wondering whether this blend of science, cultural anthropology, and political activism is moving HTI toward a more insightful, justifiable, and more practically useful understanding of human error and system safety. Dekker's perspective is certainly an advance over the "blame and shame" mentality toward error to which Vicente and Christoffersen allude in their reprint. But might we be going too far? Or, perhaps more likely, might we be falling victim to an overly simplified "us versus them" way of thinking about both the psychology and politics of human error?

One might also consider recent, related books focusing on system safety and human error, such as *Reslience Engineering* by Hollnagel, Woods, and Leveson (2006). Although the view presented there is much in the spirit of Dekker, the position offered is somewhat more nuanced (from Hollnagel et al., 2006: 3):

> The thesis that leaps out from these results is that failure, as individual failure or performance failure at the systems level, represents the temporary inability to cope effectively with complexity. Success belongs to organizations, groups, and individuals who are resilient in the sense that they recognize, adapt to, and absorb variations, changes, disturbances, disruptions, and surprises—especially disruptions that fall outside of the set of disturbances the system is designed to handle.

In an ideal world, perhaps. Do *all* failures result from a temporary inability to cope with complexity? As Vicente and Christoffersen point out, Stan Koebel's deliberate deception and inadequate reporting of water-quality test results had being going on for many years, and gave all appearance of a worker trying to turn what was already a rather easy job into an even easier one. It would be naive to see a Humantech (or related) research approach claiming sole responsibility for ensuring the error-free and ethical design and performance of sociotechnical systems. This is a job not just for researchers, but for everyone involved.

The Walkerton *E. coli* Outbreak: A Test of Rasmussen's Framework for Risk Management in a Dynamic Society

Kim J. Vicente and Klaus Christoffersen

Abstract

In May 2000, the water transportation system in Walkerton, Ontario (a small town with 4800 residents) became contaminated with *E. coli* bacteria, eventually causing seven people to die and 2300 to become sick. The 700-page report from a comprehensive public inquiry into this tragedy provided a rich source of data about the outbreak itself and the factors leading up to it. That report was used to test the explanatory adequacy of Rasmussen's framework for risk management in a dynamic society. Close agreement was observed between the predictions of the framework and the causes contributing to the Walkerton outbreak. The sequence of events reveals a complex interaction between all of the levels in a complex sociotechnical system spanning strictly physical factors, the unsafe practices of individual workers, inadequate oversight and enforcement by local government and a provincial regulatory agency, and budget reductions imposed by the provincial government. Furthermore, the dynamic forces that led to the accident had been in place for some time—some going back 20 years—yet the feedback to reveal the safety implications of these forces was largely unavailable to the various actors in the system. Rasmussen's framework provides a theoretical basis for abstracting from the details of this particular incident, thereby highlighting generalizable lessons that might be used to ensure the safety of other complex sociotechnical systems.

1. Introduction

We need more studies of the vertical interaction among levels of sociotechnical systems with reference to the nature of the technological hazard they are assumed to control (Rasmusse 1997: 187).

> I was born and raised in Walkerton and have lots of memories of this town … but now … When I think of Walkerton I think of *E. coli* and the death of my mother. I find it difficult to be in Walkerton. I don't enjoy it like I once did ….This tragedy has affected me every day.
>
> (Terry Trushinski, cited in O'Connor, 2002a: 46–47)

In May 2000, the water supply system in Walkerton, Ontario, became contaminated with deadly *E. coli* bacteria. In a town of 4800 residents, seven people died and an estimated 2300 became sick. Some people, especially children, are expected to experience lasting health effects. The total economic cost of the tragedy was estimated to be over $64.5 million CAD.

In the aftermath of the deaths and illnesses, citizens were terrified of using tap water to satisfy basic human needs. Those who were infected or lost loved ones suffered tremendous psychological trauma, their neighbours, friends, and families were terrorized by anxiety, and many across the province of Ontario and the rest of Canada worried about how the fatal event could happen and whether it could possibly occur again in their town or city. Attention-grabbing headline news stories continued unabated for months in newspapers, on radio and on television. Eventually, the provincial government appointed an independent commission to conduct a public inquiry into the causes of the disaster and to make recommendations for change. Over the course of 9 months, the commission held publicly televised hearings, culminating in the politically devastating interrogation of the Premier of Ontario (the leader of the provincial government) himself. On 14 January 2002, the Walkerton Inquiry Commission delivered Part I of its report to the Attorney General of the Province of Ontario (O'Connor, 2002a).

The purpose of this article is to use the Walkerton *E. coli* outbreak as a case study to evaluate the ability of Rasmussen's (1997) risk management framework to explain how and why large-scale industrial accidents occur in a dynamic society. While there are many reports, articles or books in the literature analysing well-known accidents (e.g. Oversight Hearings, 1979; Vaughan, 1996; Commission of Inquiry on the Blood System in Canada, 1997), there appear to be far fewer articles that use an accident as a case study to test the explanatory adequacy of an existing theoretical framework. Given the comparatively meagre number of such studies, it would be premature to conduct a comparative test of various competing frameworks unless one can first establish that a particular framework has some success in accommodating a body of evidence. For this reason, only one framework was chosen for analysis here. Rasmussen's work was chosen for two reasons: (a) it represents the culmination of almost 40 years of systematic research on risk management in complex systems (see Rasmussen et al., 1994; Vicente, 1999, 2001 for reviews); and (b) the research programme on which it is based has influenced the work and thinking of other prominent researchers in the cognitive engineering and safety science communities (Moray, 1988; Reason, 1990; Norman, 1993; Amalberti, 2001).

The results presented in this article make a contribution both to scholarly research and to public policy. From a research perspective, this work appears to be the first comprehensive and independent test of Rasmussen's (1997) framework (for accident analyses based on comparable frameworks, see Tanabe (2000) and Hopkins [2000]). The Walkerton Inquiry Commission was not aware of and, thus, did not adopt this framework when it conducted its analysis. Furthermore, although the authors have collaborated with Rasmussen on other research topics (e.g. Vicente and Rasmussen, 1992), they were not involved in the development of this particular framework in any way. Thus, this work complements the non-independent tests of the same framework conducted by Svedung and Rasmussen (2002) and Rasmussen and Svedung (2000). From a public policy perspective, a theoretically motivated analysis allows one to abstract from the idiosyncratic details of this particular accident and thereby develop potentially generalizable lessons. To paraphrase the Commission report, knowing what happened in Walkerton from a theoretical perspective can assist in a general sense in ensuring the future safety of other complex sociotechnical systems. This practical contribution will become increasingly important as contemporary society tries to safeguard the public interest in the face of growing trends toward more stringent financial pressures and market competitiveness.

2. Risk management in a dynamic society

Rasmussen's (1997) framework—which has its basis in systems thinking (e.g. Buckley, 1968)—is motivated by the observation that the dynamic character of today's society has dramatically changed the types of models needed to understand the structure and behaviour of high-risk sociotechnical systems. Factors such as the rapid pace of technological change, the high degree of coupling enabled by computerization and communication technologies and the volatility of economic and political climates each contribute to an environment in which the pressures and constraints that shape work practices are constantly shifting. Traditional modelling methods such as task analysis are inadequate as referents for understanding actual work practices because they depend on the assumption of a stable, tightly constrained environment (Vicente, 1999). To fully appreciate how such systems work or why they sometimes fail, modelling tools are needed that provide an integrated view of the various contextual factors that directly and indirectly define how they operate.

2.1. Structure

Rasmussen's (1997) framework for risk management has two components. The first is a structural hierarchy describing the various actors—both individuals and organizations—in a complex sociotechnical system. Figure 1 provides a representative example, although the precise number of levels and their labels can vary across industries. The bottom level describes the behaviour associated with the particular (potentially hazardous) process being controlled (e.g. nuclear power plant, water supply system, commercial aviation). Understanding this level usually requires knowledge of science or engineering. The next level describes the activities of the individual staff members that are responsible for interacting directly with the process being controlled (e.g. control room operators, water quality inspectors, airplane pilots). Understanding this level usually requires knowledge of human factors engineering. The third level from the bottom describes the activities of the management that supervize the staff. Understanding this level usually requires knowledge of management theories and industrial-organizational psychology. The next level up describes the activities of the company as a whole. Understanding this level usually requires knowledge of economics, organizational behaviour, decision theory and sociology. The next level describes the activities of the regulators or associations that are responsible for constraining the activities of companies in that particular sector. Finally, the top level describes the activities of government, both civil servants and elected officials, who are responsible for setting public policy. Understanding these last two levels usually requires knowledge of political science, law, economics, and sociology.

Note that decisions at higher levels should propagate down the hierarchy, whereas information about the current state of affairs should propagate up the hierarchy. These inter-dependencies across levels of the hierarchy form a closed loop feedback system and are critical to the

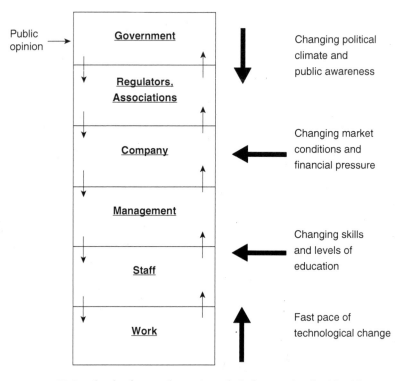

FIGURE I   Various levels of a complex socio-technical system involved in risk management. Adapted from Rasmussen (1997) and reprinted from Vicente (2002), *Quality and Safety in Healthcare*, **11**, 302–304, with permission from the BMJ Publishing Group.

successful functioning of the system as a whole. If instructions from above (i.e. the control signal) are not formulated or not carried out or if information from below (i.e. feedback) is not collected or not conveyed then the system can become unstable and start to lose control of the hazardous process that it is intended to safeguard.

Under this view, safety can be viewed as an emergent property of a complex sociotechnical system. It is impacted by the decisions of all of the actors—politicians, CEOs, managers, safety officers and work planners—not just the front-line workers alone. Consequently, threats to safety or accidents can result from a loss of control caused by a lack of vertical integration (i.e. mismatches) across levels of a complex sociotechnical system, not just from deficiencies at any one level alone. All layers play a critical, albeit different, role in maintaining safety. As a corollary, threats to safety or accidents are usually caused by multiple contributing factors, not just a single catastrophic decision or action.

In turn, the lack of vertical integration is frequently caused, in part, by a lack of feedback across levels of a complex sociotechnical system. Actors at each level cannot see how their decisions interact with those made by actors at other levels, so the threats to safety are not obvious before an accident occurs.

As shown on the right of Figure 1, the various layers of a complex sociotechnical system are increasingly subjected to external forces that stress the system. Examples of such perturbations include: changing political climate and public awareness, changing market conditions and financial pressures, changing competencies and levels of education or changes in technological complexity. In a dynamic society, these external forces are stronger and change more frequently than ever before.

2.2. Dynamics

The second component of the framework, shown in Figure 2, deals with the dynamic forces that can cause a complex sociotechnical system to modify its structure and behaviour over time. On the one hand, there are financial pressures that result in a cost gradient pushing the actors in the system to work in a more fiscally responsible manner. Indeed, budget cuts are becoming increasingly common over a wide range of private and public sectors. On the other hand, there are psychological pressures that result in an effort gradient pushing the actors in the system to work in a more mentally or physically efficient manner. People are always searching for easier ways to get a job done.

Although this effort gradient is sometimes interpreted negatively as a sign of human laziness, given the proper conditions, it can serve a positive—indeed, essential—role because it allows people to seek out more adaptive ways of getting the job done. This exploratory process can be particularly important when people are being asked or required to take on more responsibilities with fewer resources—the proverbial "do more with less" that is so common in a dynamic society.

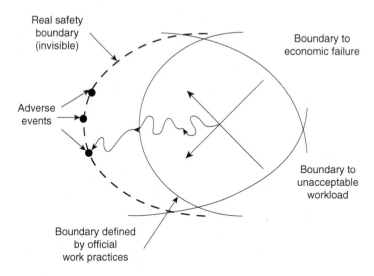

FIGURE 2   "Brownian motion" model showing how financial and psychological forces can create behaviour gradients that cause work practices to migrate systematically toward the boundary of safety. Adapted from Rasmussen (1997), Copyright (2003), Kim J. Vicente.

As a result of these two gradients, work practices will be subject to a form of "Brownian motion," an exploratory but systematic migration over time. Just as the force of gravity causes a stream of water to inevitably flow down the crevices in a side of a mountain, these financial and psychological forces inevitably cause people to find the most economic ways of performing their job. Moreover, the migration of work practices can occur at multiple levels of a complex sociotechnical system shown in Figure 1, not just one level alone.

Over time, this migration causes people to cross the official boundary of work practices, shown on the near left in Figure 2. People are forced to deviate from procedures and cut corners because they are responding to requests or demands to be more cost-effective. As a result, the system's defenses in depth degrade and erode gradually over time, not all at once.

One might think that this lack of procedural compliance and this degradation in safety would raise an immediate warning flag, but there are two reasons why they do not. First, the migration in work practices is required to get the job done, given the stresses that the system is undergoing. That is why "work to rule" campaigns, where people do their job strictly by the book, usually cause complex sociotechnical systems to come to a grinding halt. Secondly, the migration in work practices does not usually have any visible, immediate negative impact. The threats to safety are not obvious before an accident because the violation of procedures does not immediately lead to catastrophe. At each level in the hierarchy people are working hard, striving to respond to cost-effectiveness measures, but they do not see how their decisions interact with those made by other actors at different levels of the system. Yet, the sum total of these uncoordinated attempts at adapting to environmental stressors is slowly but surely "preparing the stage for an accident" (Rasmussen, 1997: 189).

As a result, the migration of work practices continues. People try harder and harder to work in more efficient ways and, with each new innovation, they are coming closer and closer to the real boundary of safety on the far left of Figure 2. However, because that boundary is usually invisible, people do not have any idea whether the system as a whole is close or far away from disaster. Migrations from official work practices can persist and evolve for years without any breach of safety until the real safety boundary is reached. After an accident, workers will wonder what happened because they did not do anything drastically different from what they had been doing in the recent past. In other words, accidents in complex sociotechnical systems do not usually occur because of an unusual action or an entirely new, one-time threat to safety. Instead, they result from a combination of a systematically-induced migration in work practices and an odd event that winds up revealing the degradation in safety that had been occurring all the while.

Table 1 summarizes the main predictions made by Rasmussen's (1997) framework. Note that, for each prediction, there is (at least) one alternative prediction. Thus, accidents need not have this set of characteristics, so Rasmussen's framework is falsifiable. How well does the Walkerton tragedy conform to these predictions?

3. Report of the Walkerton inquiry

Part 1 of the Walkerton report, which focuses on the events surrounding the accident, was used as the source document for the analysis (Part 2 described a set of recommendations and, thus, is not as relevant to this aim).

TABLE I   Predictions made by Rasmussen's (1997) risk management framework.

Prediction
1. Safety is an emergent property of a complex socio-technical system. It is impacted by the decisions of all of the actors—politicians, managers, safety officers and work planners—not just the front-line workers alone.
2. Threats to safety or accidents are usually caused by multiple contributing factors, not just a single catastrophic decision or action.
3. Threats to safety or accidents can result from a lack of vertical integration (i.e. mismatches) across levels of a complex socio-technical system, not just from deficiencies at any one level alone.
4. The lack of vertical integration is caused, in part, by a lack of feedback across levels of a complex socio-technical system. Actors at each level cannot see how their decisions interact with those made by actors at other levels, so the threats to safety are far from obvious before an accident.
5. Work practices in a complex socio-technical system are not static. They will migrate over time under the influence of a cost gradient driven by financial pressures in an aggressive competitive environment and under the influence of an effort gradient driven by the psychological pressure to follow the path of least resistance.
6. The migration of work practices can occur at multiple levels of a complex socio-technical system, not just one level alone.
7. Migration of work practices causes the system's defenses to degrade and erode gradually over time, not all at once. Accidents are released by a combination of this systematically-induced migration in work practices and a triggering event, not just by an unusual action or an entirely new, one-time threat to safety.

A brief review of the process that the Commission used to conduct its inquiry shows that the resulting report is a comprehensive and authoritative account of the events (see Chapter 14 of the report for a detailed account). The Commission was given wide powers of investigation and collected as many as one million documents from the provincial government alone in addition to thousands of documents from other sources. In the end, ~200,000 government documents were scanned into an electronic database. The Commission held 95 days of hearings over a period of 9 months, during which 21,686 pages of transcripts were generated and 447 exhibits, containing over 3000 documents, were introduced as evidence. A total of 114 witnesses testified, including Michael Harris, then Premier of Ontario. After the hearings, the Commission held nine town hall meetings all across the province to listen to the public's concerns and views. Part I of the final report was ~700 pages long, including appendices.

4. The events of May 2000

Before presenting the analysis of the Walkerton case, some background information will be helpful. The Walkerton water system was operated by the Walkerton Public Utilities Commission (WPUC), under the supervision of the general manager, Stan Koebel. The government body with oversight responsibility for the operation of water systems in the province of Ontario is the Ministry of the Environment (MOE). Other relevant regulatory bodies include the Ontario Ministry of Health and the Bruce-Grey-Owen Sound (BGOS) Health Unit, which is the local public health unit for Walkerton, headed by the local Medical Officer of Health. A&L Canada Laboratories is a private company that was contracted by WPUC to analyse their water samples.

Table 2 provides a timeline of the proximal physical events and actions that contributed to the *E. coli* outbreak in Walkerton during May 2000. A later section will describe other pre-existing factors that helped set the stage for this proximal sequence of events.

5. Analysis

This section compares the reasons for the Walkerton outbreak with Rasmussen's (1997) framework by seeing how well the findings of the Commission report (O'Connor, 2002a) map onto the type of structure identified in Figure 1. Following this discussion, the extent to which predictions in Table 1 are supported by the available evidence is evaluated.

5.1. Physical circumstances and equipment/Equipment and surroundings

This paper begins by examining factors related to the physical circumstances of the events of May 2000. Table 2 described how heavy rains and the use of cattle manure on local farm fields combined to introduce contaminants into Well 5. Four important pre-existing physical factors, listed at the bottom of Figure 3, also contributed to the contamination.

Two of these factors—the shallow location of Well 5 and the fractured bedrock in the local geology—were based on physics. Well 5 was a

TABLE 2   Timeline of the most important events of May 2000 contributing to the Walkerton *E. coli* outbreak.

8–12 May 2000	Unusually heavy rains carry *E. coli* and *Campylobacter* bacteria to Walkerton Well 5 from nearby fields on which cattle manure had been spread; contaminants are thought to have entered Well 5 on or near 12 May.
13–15 May 2000	WPUC staff fail to take measurements of chlorine residuals* for Well 5.
15 May 2000	Samples from Walkerton distribution system and from a nearby construction site sent to A&L Labs for testing.
17 May 2000	A&L Labs advises Stan Koebel that samples from 15 May tested positive for contamination.
18 May 2000	First symptoms appear in community; inquiring members of public assured water is safe by WPUC.
19 May 2000	Scope of outbreak grows; paediatrician contacts local health unit on suspicion of *E. coli*. BGOS health unit begins investigation; in two separate calls placed to Stan Koebel, health officials are led to believe water is 'okay'; Stan Koebel fails to disclose lab results from 15 May. Stan Koebel begins to flush and superchlorinate the system to try to destroy any contaminants in water; chlorine residuals begin to recover.
20 May 2000	First preliminary positive test for *E. coli* infection. BGOS Health unit speaks to Stan Koebel twice; Koebel reports acceptable chlorine residuals; fails again to disclose adverse test results; health unit assures inquiring public that water is not the problem. A WPUC employee places anonymous call to MOE to report adverse test results from 15 May; on contacting Stan Koebel, MOE is told the only failing sample was from the construction site; Koebel does not reveal failed samples from Walkerton distribution system. Local Medical Officer of Health contacted by health unit; takes over investigation.
21 May 2000	Preliminary positive test for *E. coli* infection from 20 May confirmed; a second preliminary positive test is reported. A 'boil water advisory' is issued by the BGOS health unit. MOE and BGOS health unit both contact Stan Koebel; Koebel again fails to disclose adverse results from 15 May samples. BGOS health unit collects its own samples from Walkerton water distribution system.
22 May 2000	MOE begins its own investigation; Koebel turns over documents including test results from 15 May samples. First death due to outbreak; eventually seven people die and over 2300 become ill.

TABLE 2   Timeline of the most important events of May 2000 contributing to the Walkerton *E. coli* outbreak. (*Continued*)

23 May 2000	Samples collected by health unit come back positive; on being informed, Stan Koebel reveals results from 15 May samples to health unit.

*Chlorine residuals are an indicator of how much chlorine is being consumed in the process of disinfecting the water. A low chlorine residual indicates that contaminants in the water are exerting an increased demand on the disinfectant capacity of the chlorine, reducing the safety margin.

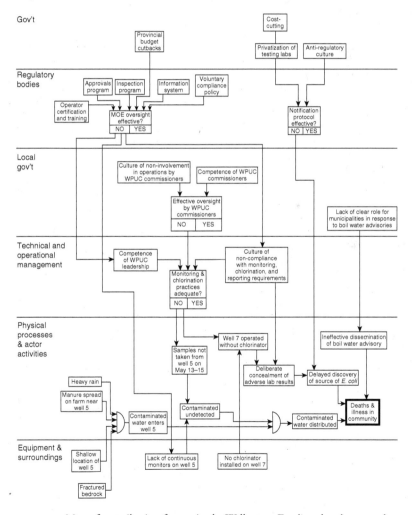

FIGURE 3   Map of contributing factors in the Walkerton *E. coli* outbreak mapped onto the levels of a complex socio-technical system identified in Figure 1.

shallow well, drilled to a depth of just 15 m. In contrast, Wells 6 and 7
were drilled to depths of 72 and 76 m, respectively. In addition to its shallow depth, Well 5 was drilled in an area where the bedrock was highly
fractured and porous. The overburden (i.e. soils, sands, silts, and clays covering the bedrock) was also relatively shallow in the area of Well 5.
Because of these factors, there was minimal natural filtration provided by
the overburden and bedrock. Also, a breach in the overburden could
potentially leave a relatively direct route between the surface and the
aquifer. As a result, Well 5 was particularly vulnerable to contamination
from surface water (e.g. runoff from rainfall).

In addition, two equipment-related factors contributed to the vulnerability of Well 5 to surface contaminants. Wells known to be exposed to
the risk of contamination by surface water are normally required to have

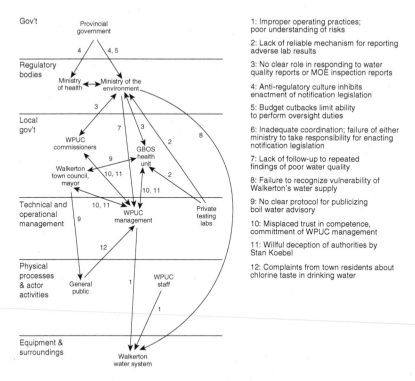

FIGURE 4   Counter-productive interactions (mismatches) between actors at different levels of the socio-technical system involved in control of the Walkerton water
system.

continuous chlorine residual monitors installed. Such a monitor could have automatically shut down the pump at Well 5 when the contamination entered the system. For reasons that will be discussed later, Well 5 did not have a continuous chlorine residual monitor installed. A second equipment-related factor was the absence of a working chlorinator in Well 7 between 3–19 May. With Stan Koebel's full knowledge, Well 7 was operated for several days during this period, supplying unchlorinated water to the distribution system in clear violation of provincial requirements.

5.2. Physical events and actor activities/Physical processes and actor activities

This second level is described in detail in Table 2, so it will not be discussed again here. The main points are summarized at the second level in Figure 3.

5.3. Technical and operational management

As shown in Figure 3, the primary contributing factors at this level concern the operating practices of the WPUC under the supervision of Stan Koebel. As described earlier in Table 2, the failure of the WPUC to take chlorine residual measurements at Well 5 between 13–15 May and the active concealment of the results of the microbiological samples collected on 15 May both played important roles in the outbreak. However, an analysis of the technical and operational management level revealed that these were not isolated incidents: "*for more than 20 years*, it had been the practice of [WPUC] employees not to measure the chlorine residuals on most days and to make fictitious entries for residuals in the daily operating sheets" (O'Connor, 2002b: 7, emphasis added). The general pattern of improper operating practices at the WPUC also included deliberately misstating the locations from which microbiological samples had been collected, collecting insufficient numbers of microbiological samples, failing to use adequate doses of chlorine and submitting false annual reports to the MOE.

As shown in Figure 3, at least two factors contributed to this pattern of non-compliance. First, the level of competence of the WPUC leadership, particularly Stan and Frank Koebel, was inadequate. Both Koebels had received their water operator's certificates through a "grandfathering" process. Neither had been required to complete any training or pass any examinations to receive their certification. They each believed that the sources for the Walkerton water system were generally safe. Indeed, both men routinely drank untreated water at the well sites because it "tasted better." Even over the weekend of 20–21 May, after he knew of the adverse test results, Stan Koebel "continued to drink water from a fire hydrant and a garden house and on 22 May he filled his daughter's swimming pool with municipal water" (O'Connor 2002a: 72). It is clear that neither of the Koebel brothers had a full appreciation of the health risks posed by distributing under-chlorinated water or of the specific risks of bacterial contaminants. In fact, both admitted to not even knowing what *E. coli* was, let alone that its presence in drinking water could be lethal.

A second, related contributing factor involves the priorities of the WPUC staff. There was a general tendency to avoid the effort required to uphold proper sampling practices. Water samples were often collected at convenient sites, including at times the operators' homes or the WPUC workshop and then simply labelled according to where the samples were supposed to have been taken. When asked why he and his brother followed such practices, Stan Koebel replied: "Simply convenience" (O'Connor 2002a: 62). When operating deficiencies were pointed out by several inspections, Stan Koebel made, but never carried out, promises to rectify the problems. This attitude and the resulting practices "show a serious disregard for MOE requirements and repeated failures by Stan Koebel to do what he said he would" (O'Connor 2002a: 188).

Although this does not justify his actions, it is interesting to note that the Walkerton residents had sometimes told Stan Koebel—their neighbour and friend—that the water tasted too much like chlorine, so in an effort to respond to the wishes of his small, tight-knit community, he acquiesced by reducing the amount of chlorine introduced into the system.

5.4. Local government

As shown in Figure 3, the local government played an important part in the events of May 2000 in three ways. First, even though the WPUC commissioners were the elected body responsible for "control and management" of the WPUC, they did not concern themselves with the details of system operation, focusing instead on budgeting and financial matters. Secondly, the WPUC commissioners had very little knowledge of water safety or of the nature of operating a waterworks. (This level of knowledge and involvement was consistent with the traditional role of the WPUC commissioners, which was likened in the inquiry report to that of the directors of a corporation.) As a result of these two factors, the WPUC commissioners relied almost exclusively on the WPUC senior management, primarily Stan Koebel, to identify and resolve any concerns related to the operation of the water system. For example, when a 1998 MOE inspection report indicated serious problems with the operation of the water system, including the presence of *E. coli* in treated water samples, the commissioners simply accepted Stan Koebel's assurances that he would look after the situation. They did not inquire into how the problems had arisen, nor did they follow up afterwards to ensure that Stan Koebel had actually addressed the concerns. As became clear later, Koebel failed to follow through on his assurances. The inquiry report concluded that it was reasonable to have expected the commissioners to take more of an active role in responding to the 1998 MOE inspection report.

The third factor where local government played a role in the outbreak concerns the dissemination of the boil water advisory issued by the local health unit on 21 May. It is estimated that only about half of Walkerton's residents actually became aware of the advisory on 21 May. Some members of the public continued drinking the Walkerton town water until as late as 23 May. The inquiry report suggested that this was partially attributable to the failure of Walkerton's mayor, David Thomson, to take an active role in building public awareness of the advisory after he was informed of it by Dr. Murray McQuigge, the local Medical Officer of Health. The Mayor was not specifically asked by Dr. McQuigge to assist in publicizing the advisory and there is some dispute as to whether the seriousness of the situation was effectively communicated to the Mayor. In any case, there was no clear, pre-defined role for the Mayor and by extension the municipality in responding to any boil water advisory issued by the health unit. As a result, the Mayor took no action, relying on Dr. McQuigge to handle the situation.

The inquiry report did not place responsibility on Mayor Thomson, but observed that his inaction represented a missed opportunity to have reduced the scope of the outbreak.

5.5. Regulatory bodies

The main regulatory agency with responsibility for overseeing the operation of municipal water systems in the province of Ontario is the MOE. As shown in Figure 3, MOE practices contributed to the Walkerton outbreak in six ways. This study has already mentioned the fact that, partially due to the structure of the MOE's operator training and certification programmes, Stan and Frank Koebel did not have a full appreciation of issues related to water safety, including the public health risks posed by contaminants such as *E. coli*. They both held the belief that untreated water from the Walkerton wells was essentially safe for human consumption. This lack of knowledge was a likely contributor to their consistent improper operating practices.

A second significant factor contributing to the sub-standard operating practices at the WPUC was the weak response of the MOE to evidence of repeated violations uncovered by its own periodic inspections. Inspections conducted in 1991, 1995, and 1998 consistently revealed deficiencies in treatment and monitoring at the WPUC. After each of these inspections, MOE made recommendations to address the deficiencies, but each time Stan Koebel consistently put off or ignored those recommendations. No strong (i.e. legally enforceable) measures were ever taken by the MOE to ensure that the concerns identified in the inspections were addressed. Instead, the MOE relied on voluntary compliance with its recommendations. The inquiry report concluded that, as a result of the MOE's soft stance, Stan Koebel came to believe that compliance with the recommendations and guidelines was not a high priority.

The third contributing factor at this level was the lack of important feedback to allow the MOE to monitor the state of affairs at lower levels:

The MOE did not have an information system that made critical information about the history of vulnerable water sources, like Well 5, accessible to those responsible for ensuring that proper treatment and monitoring were taking place. On several occasions in the 1990s, having had access to this information would have enabled ministry personnel to be fully informed in making decisions about current circumstances and the proper actions to be taken (O'Connor, 2002b: 29).

This lack of feedback across levels of the sociotechnical system enabled two other factors that contributed to the outbreak.

One of those was related to the MOE approvals programme. As described previously, Walkerton Well 5 did not have continuous chlorine residual monitors installed. When Well 5 was initially approved by the MOE in 1979, it was identified as being susceptible to contamination from surface water. However, consistent with MOE practices at the time, no special conditions (e.g. for monitoring) were attached to the approval. By the 1990s, special conditions for monitoring and treatment were routinely attached to approvals for wells similar to Well 5. Nevertheless, the MOE did not attempt to retroactively apply such conditions to previously granted approvals, partly because it did not have an integrated information system to provide feedback to allow tracking of older certificates of approval.

The other contributing factor was related to the MOE inspections programme. In 1994, the "Ontario Drinking Water Objectives" (ODWO), a provincial guideline, was amended to require continuous (rather than the usual daily) monitoring of chlorine residuals and turbidity for wells at risk of surface contamination. Again, no attempt was made to systematically review existing certificates of approval to determine if conditions should be added to require continuous monitoring. In addition, MOE inspectors were not directed to notify water system operators of the ODWO amendment nor to assess existing wells during inspections. In fact, there were no criteria available from MOE to guide inspectors in determining whether or not a given well was at risk. The MOE inspections in 1991, 1995, and 1998 failed to recognize the vulnerability of Well 5, even though the relevant information was already available in MOE records. However, these were archived and, therefore, difficult to find, rather than readily accessible in an information system. As a result of this combination of factors, continuous monitors were never installed for Well 5. As mentioned previously, such monitors could have drastically reduced or even prevented the outbreak.

There is at least one other very important factor at the level of regulatory bodies that contributed to the Walkerton outbreak. In 1996, laboratory testing of drinking water quality was privatized by the

Conservative Provincial government. Municipalities, like Walkerton, were forced to switch from using government-run facilities to using private laboratories, but no legislation was enacted to require private laboratories to notify the MOE of adverse test results. The ODWO included a guideline to this effect, but it was not legally enforceable and some laboratories were not even aware that it existed. Despite awareness of this problem and its risks for public health, leading to high-level discussions between the Ministries of Health and of the Environment, the government had not acted to remedy this loophole. During May 2000, the WPUC was sending its samples to A&L Canada Laboratories. A&L was not aware of the notification protocol outlined in ODWO, nor was it legally required to follow it. Therefore, on 17 May, when the microbiological samples collected on 15 May were found to be heavily contaminated, A&L only notified Stan Koebel of the results. No notice was sent to the local MOE office or health authorities. Because of the subsequent concealment of this information by Stan Koebel, the weak notification protocol led to delays in discovering the source of the outbreak and, thus, seriously exacerbated its impacts.

5.6. Government

These shortcomings of the MOE are due, at least in part, to actions of the Provincial government during the years leading up to the Walkerton tragedy. During this time, the MOE's budget had been reduced by nearly half. In the 2-year period between 1996–1998 alone, the budget was cut by over $200 million CAD, with an ensuing staff reduction of over 30% (more than 750 employees). The potential harm arising from these reductions was known, yet:

> Despite having knowledge that there could be risks, no member of Cabinet or other public servant directed that a risk assessment and management plan be conducted to determine the extent of those risks, whether the risks should be assumed, and if assumed, whether they could be managed.

(O'Connor, 2002a: 411)

Even without any risk assessment, "the Cabinet approved the budget reductions in the face of warnings of increased risk to the environment and human health" (O'Connor, 2002b: 35). The inquiry report concluded that these budget cuts substantially reduced the likelihood that MOE's approvals and inspections programmes could have uncovered the need for continuous monitors or the improper operating practices at the WPUC.

The second major role played by the provincial government concerns its "distaste for regulation" (O'Connor, 2002a: 368) and its resulting decision to privatize laboratory testing of drinking water. The events at Walkerton were impacted by the failure to enact legislation requiring private labs to notify MOE and health authorities of adverse test results. The evidence presented at the inquiry clearly showed that high levels of government were aware that the lack of such legislation posed a potential risk. However, by 1995–1996, the newly elected government began an effort to reduce regulation and created a "Red Tape Commission" to eliminate "complicated and unnecessary paperwork", such as that resulting from reporting requirements. For similar reasons, the government did not act to require mandatory accreditation of private testing labs. The opinion of MOE officials was that any move to legislate a notification requirement or accreditation would "likely have been 'a non-starter,' given the government's focus on minimizing regulation" (O'Connor, 2002b: 33).

5.7. Assessing the predictions of Rasmussen's framework

Table 3 summarizes how well the predictions made by Rasmussen's (1997) framework account for the factors contributing to the Walkerton *E. coli* outbreak.

TABLE 3   Test of the predictions in table 1 for the Walkerton *E. coli* outbreak.

Prediction
1. Safety is an emergent property of a complex socio-technical system. It is impacted by the decisions of all of the actors—politicians, managers, safety officers and work planners—not just the front-line workers alone.
Figure 3 dramatically reveals the truth of this statement. A very large number of decision-makers and decision-making bodies, from the Government of Ontario on down to individuals such as Stan Koebel, shaped the conditions and course of events in such a way that allowed the events of May 2000 to take place. In the words of the inquiry report, 'It is simply wrong to say, as the government argued at the Inquiry, that Stan Koebel or the Walkerton PUC were solely responsible for the outbreak or that they were the only ones who could have prevented it' (O'Connor 2002b, p. 24).

(Continued)

TABLE 3   Test of the predictions in table 1 for the Walkerton *E. coli*
outbreak. (*Continued*)

Prediction

---

2. Threats to safety or accidents are usually caused by multiple contributing factors, not
just a single catastrophic decision or action.

None of the factors illustrated in Figure 3 are solely responsible for the occurrence
of the outbreak in Walkerton. For example, four independent factors were jointly
responsible for the entry of the contaminants into the Walkerton water system. Had
any one of these not been in place, the events may never have occurred at all. Other
critical events or vulnerabilities, such as the failure to detect the contamination and the
ineffective dissemination of the boil water advisory also have multiple contributors.
It is impossible to point to a single 'root cause' that was both necessary and sufficient
to lead to the outbreak.

3. Threats to safety or accidents can result from a lack of vertical integration (i.e.
mismatches) across levels of a complex socio-technical system, not just from deficiencies
at any one level alone.

Construed broadly, a lack of vertical integration refers to the idea that interactions
between individuals or organizations at different levels of the socio-technical system are
dysfunctional with respect to effective control of the monitored process. For example,
organizations at different levels of a socio-technical system can develop different,
possibly conflicting, working priorities or objectives due to the specific pressures that
each is operating under. Also important are breakdowns in the propagation from higher
levels of constraints on the activities of lower levels or the corresponding feedback
mechanisms. Figure 4 presents a map of some of these types of interactions across levels
and their results in the socio-technical system involved in control of the operation of the
Walkerton water system.

4. The lack of vertical integration is caused, in part, by a lack of feedback across levels of
a complex socio-technical system. Actors at each level cannot see how their decisions
interact with those made by actors at other levels, so the threats to safety are far from
obvious before an accident.

The WPUC was effectively isolated from other levels of the socio-technical system
responsible for the control of Walkerton's water system (cf. Figure 1). Because both
the MOE and the WPUC commissioners failed to take steps to ensure that MOE
recommendations were being followed, a critical feedback loop was missing from the
system. The MOE and the WPUC commissioners were essentially acting, repeatedly,
without the information that would allow them to tell if their 'control actions'
had been successful. The lack of a proper information system at the MOE played a
particularly influential role in this regard. When water quality testing was privatized by
the provincial government in 1996, a significant barrier to failure was removed from
the system. Many private labs were unaware of the reporting guideline in ODWO or
chose not to conform with it (to protect their clients' confidentiality). Consequently, yet
another critical feedback mechanism had been significantly degraded. Indeed, evidence
presented at the inquiry suggested that the number of adverse results reported to the
MOE dropped significantly after privatization. It was clear that Stan Koebel and the.

TABLE 3   Test of the predictions in table 1 for the Walkerton *E. coli*
outbreak. (*Continued*)

Prediction

other WPUC employees did not understand how their improper operating practices
interacted wi th these events. Nor did the government anticipate the situation at the
WPUC. Only afterwards, when the inquiry commission developed a global view of the
socio-technical system, did the relational structure between the decisions and practices at
each level become clear

5. Work practices in a complex socio-technical system are not static. They will migrate
over time under the influence of a cost gradient driven by financial pressures in an
aggressive competitive environment and under the influence of an effort gradient
driven by the psychological pressure to follow the path of least resistance.

There are many instances in which work practices of different individuals and
organizations migrated over time in ways that increased the likelihood of the events
of May 2000. The sub-standard practices of Stan Koebel and the WPUC provide an
example of behaviour driven primarily by an effort gradient. Normally, one would
expect a strong counter-gradient to be present due to pressure from oversight bodies,
but this was missing due to the failure of MOE to follow-up on its inspections and the
lack of close involvement by the WPUC commissioners. Another important counter-
gradient was missing due to the Koebels' lack of appreciation of the risks involved in
their practices. Their lack of training in water safety issues meant that they did not regard
their actions as posing a significant risk to public safety. The changing practices of the
MOE, on the other hand, can be seen as responses primarily to an economic gradient.
In the preceding years, budget pressures led the MOE to gradually shift responsibility for
operation of water systems onto the municipalities themselves, thereby decreasing their
own oversight burden. While this can be viewed as a reasonable response to tightening
resource constraints, the inquiry found that 'the MOE went too far in this direction'
(O'Connor 2002a, p. 272). Particularly with respect to the inspections programme, the
ongoing budget cuts and staff reductions forced the MOE into an increasingly reactive
stance. Its ability to take a proactive role in detecting and preventing problems was
systematically eroded due to a lack of resources. A former deputy minister of the MOE
Operations Division testified at the inquiry that proactive inspections and follow-ups
took on reduced priority because 'the day was eaten up with reactive work' (O'Connor
2002a, p. 318). Between 1994-1995 and 1999-2000, the number of planned inspections
by the local MOE office responsible for Walkerton fell by 60% and the amount of
employee resources dedicated to communal water decreased by almost half.

6. The migration of work practices can occur at multiple levels of a complex sociotechnical system, not just one level alone.

The previous points show how migration occurred at levels both close to and distant
from the physical events in Walkerton. Similar patterns can be seen even at the highest
levels of the socio-technical system. For example, the political forces that helped bring
the new provincial government to power in 1995 served to create an atmosphere that
led to a Red Tape Commission, discouraging the passing of notification legislation
after water quality testing was privatized. An additional example concerns the very
lowest level of the system: the physical circumstances of the Walkerton water system.

(*Continued*)

TABLE 3   Test of the predictions in table 1 for the Walkerton *E. coli* outbreak. (*Continued*)

Prediction
When Well 5 was originally constructed, it was intended to be a temporary solution to water supply problems that existed in Walkerton at the time. It appears that, over time, both the PUC and the MOE implicitly grew to accept the idea that Well 5 was an acceptable permanent solution given that, at least until the 1990s it had an unremarkable history of operation. Thus, one can see how the phenomenon of migration can span all levels of the socio-technical system
7. Migration of work practices causes the system's defenses to degrade and erode gradually over time, not all at once. Accidents are released by a combination of this systematically-induced migration in work practices and a triggering event, not just by an unusual action or an entirely new, one-time threat to safety.
Some of the forces that created the conditions surrounding the Walkerton tragedy had been actively shaping the system for a long time before May 2000. The improper operating practices at the WPUC were found to date back over 20 years. The budgetary pressures at the MOE began to accumulate in the early 1990s. The increased pressure to privatize government services began with the election of the new government in 1995. By May 2000, these factors had aligned in such a way that a few days of unusually heavy rainfall were enough to trigger the chain of events that led to seven deaths and over 2300 illnesses.

6. Discussion

> For a successful technology, reality must take precedence over public relations, for Nature cannot be fooled.
>
> (Feynman, 1988: 237)

This research appears to be the first comprehensive and independent test of Rasmussen's (1997) framework for risk management in a dynamic society. All of the predictions made by the framework were confirmed by the events surrounding the Walkerton *E. coli* outbreak. However, there was one contributing factor that the framework did not anticipate, namely Stan Koebel's deliberate deception and concealment of the adverse test results. As mentioned earlier, this cover up can be attributed in part to ignorance about the lethal effects of *E. coli* and in part to a wish to hide his violation of MOE requirements (i.e. operating Well 7 without chlorination). If the tendency to hide personal wrong-doing is a frequent contributor to accidents—a fact that can only determined by additional tests of the framework—then an addition to the framework would be warranted, perhaps in the form of an additional gradient that can shape the behaviour of actors at various levels of the system (since presumably this type of behaviour could occur at any level). Overall, however, the framework appears to have some promise as a theoretically-driven way to explain how and why accidents occur in complex sociotechnical systems.

This research has several limitations that motivate future research questions. First, only one accident was analysed here so it is important to test the generalizability of Rasmussen's (1997) framework independently by using it to account for other accidents, particularly in sectors other than water supply (an analogous analysis of another water supply outbreak has since been conducted, see Woo and Vicente, 2003). Secondly, now that this framework has been independently shown to have some validity, it would be useful to contrast its predictions with those of other comparable risk analysis frameworks so that theoretical understanding of safety science can evolve and mature. Finally, this article only tested the framework's capability to explain an accident *a posteriori*. The ultimate test of any engineering theory is how useful it is. Accordingly, a natural, albeit ambitious, extension of the present research would be to test the framework's ability to prevent accidents before the public interest is harmed.

Indeed, one of the potential benefits of Rasmussen's (1997) framework is that it does not just try to explain why accidents occurred; it also suggests how they might be prevented (Rasmussen and Svedung, 2000; Svedung and Rasmussen, 2002). Adding more defenses in depth alone is unlikely to work in the long run because the new defenses will just delay the inevitable degradation that is caused by the financial and psychological gradients in Figure 2. Creating more awareness through public relations or educational campaigns alone is also unlikely to be a viable long-term solution because the same two counter-forces will always be there, urging people to migrate to more cost-effective ways of doing business.

From the perspective of this framework, the only long-term solution to managing risk in a dynamic society appears to involve admitting that external stressors, such as budget cuts and market competitiveness, are not going to go away entirely and to deliberately build systems that can respond and adapt to these pressures without compromising safety. In other words, the goal is to allow systems to operate "at the edge" to maximize competitiveness or efficiency, but without actually breaking the envelope of safety and incurring accidents. To operate at the edge, vertical integration via feedback across levels must be achieved so that each person and organization in the system can see how their actions impact safety, not just the bottom line. More concretely, the usually invisible boundary to safety on the extreme left in Figure 2 must be made visible so that all levels of the system can see how close they are to disaster.

To evaluate whether the framework is indeed capable of enhancing safety in this way, government and corporate policy makers would have to adopt this approach to design or redesign the growing number of increasingly complex technological systems that surround us. This will not be a simple task for at least two reasons (Rasmussen, 1997). First, a great deal of knowledge from different disciplines is required, including science, engineering, human factors, psychology, management, sociology, economics, law, and politics. Given the notorious silos created by traditional academic boundaries, bringing together this cross-disciplinary expertise will be a challenge. Secondly, Rasmussen's framework runs counter to many management theories. Since the goal is to achieve vertical integration across the various layers of a particular complex socio-technical system, the framework must be implemented in an industry-specific fashion. After all, the information needs and competencies of each level of a complex sociotechnical system will necessarily be con-text-dependent, varying from one sector to another. For example, the laws, regulations, economics, competencies, education, and technology that make for safe health care are not the same as those that make for safe drinking water. In contrast, many popular management theories are rela-tively context-free because they advocate a narrow focus on financial operations, irrespective of the type of hazardous process being controlled (see Saul [1992] for an incisive critique of this trend).

While these two obstacles to implementation are not trivial, in the end, the potential gains to be had by confronting them may very well outweigh the costs. The Walkerton tragedy and others like it show that, when it comes to complex sociotechnical systems, governments and companies cannot afford to wait for a lethal accident to happen before figuring out how to reduce the level of risk to the public. The harm to society is far too great and simply unacceptable in today's political climate.

The political fallout after the Walkerton tragedy provides a case in point. The Ontario provincial government had won two consecutive elections by a majority by running on a "common sense revolution" platform of smaller government and cost reductions. However, after the Premier was interrogated at the Walkerton hearings, polls showed that voter support for the government plummeted to the point where it was 25% behind the opposition party. If Rasmussen's (1997) framework turns out to be as successful at preventing accidents as it seems to be at explaining them, then it could help serve a political imperative by keeping tragedies such as Walkerton from becoming commonplace occurrences, as the winds of change continue to blow in a dynamic society.

Acknowledgements

This research was sponsored by a grant from the Natural Sciences and Engineering Research Council of Canada, by a Premier's Research Excellence Award, and by the Jerome Clarke Hunsaker Distinguished Visiting Professorship from MIT. We would like to thank Jens Rasmussen, Mr James van Loon, and the Honourable Dennis R. O'Connor of the Walkerton Inquiry Commission, David Woods, and the reviewers for providing helpful comments.

References

Amalberti, R., 2001, The paradoxes of almost totally safe transportation systems. *Safety Science*, 37, 109–126.

Buckley, W., 1968, *Modern systems research for the behavioral scientist* (Chicago, IL: Aldine Publishing Company).

Commission of Inquiry on the Blood System in Canada, 1997, *Final report* (Ottawa: Canadian Government Publishing).

Feynman, R.P., 1988, *'What do you care what other people think?' Further adventures of a curious character* (New York: Norton).

Hopkins, A., 2000, *Lessons from Longford: The Esso Gas plant explosion* (Sydney: CCH Australia Ltd).

Moray, N., 1988, Ex Ris semper aliquid antiquum: Sources of a new paradigm for engineering psychology. In *Tasks, errors, and mental models: A festschrift to celebrate the 60th birthday of Professor Jens Rasmussen*, L.P. Goodstein, H.B. Andersen, and S.E. Olsen (eds.), 12–17 (London: Taylor & Francis).

Norman, D.A., 1993, *Things that make us smart: Defending human attributes in the age of the machine* (Reading, MA: Addison-Wesley).

O'Connor, D.R., 2002a, *Part one—Report of the Walkerton inquiry: The events of May 2000 and related issues* (Toronto: Ontario Ministry of the Attorney General).

O'Connor, D.R., 2002b, *Part one: A summary—Report of the Walkerton inquiry: The events of May 2000 and related issues* (Toronto: Ontario Ministry of the Attorney General).

Oversight Hearings, 1979, *Accident at the Three Mile Island nuclear power plant* (Washington, DC: US Government Printing Office).

Rasmussen, J., 1997, Risk management in a dynamic society: A modelling problem. *Safety Science*, 27, 183–213.

Rasmussen, J. and Svedung, I., 2000, *Proactive risk management in a dynamic society* (Karlstad, Sweden: Swedish Rescue Services Agency).

Rasmussen, J., Pejtersen, A.M. and Goodstein, L.P., 1994, *Cognitive systems engineering* (New York: Wiley).

Reason, J., 1990, *Human error* (Cambridge, UK: Cambridge University Press).

Saul, J.R., 1992, *Voltaire's bastards: The dictatorship of reason in the West* (Toronto: Penguin).

Svedung, I. and Rasmussen, J., 2002, Graphic representation of accident scenarios: Mapping system structure and the causation of accidents. *Safety Science*, 40, 397–417.

Tanabe, F., 2000, Functional structure, constraints and mental model. *Cognition, Technology & Work*, 2, 238–239.

Vaughan, D., 1996, *The Challenger launch decision: Risky technology, culture, and deviance at NASA* (Chicago: University of Chicago Press).

Vicente, K.J., 1999, *Cognitive work analysis: Toward safe, productive, and healthy computer-based work* (Mahwah, NJ: Erlbaum).

Vicente, K.J., 2001, Cognitive engineering research at Risø from 1962–1979. In *Advances in human performance and cognitive engineering research*, Vol. 1, E. Salas (ed.), 1–57 (New York: Elsevier).

Vicente, K.J., 2002, From patients to politicians: A cognitive engineering view of patient safety. *Quality and Safety in Healthcare*, 11, 302–304.

Vicente, K.J. and Rasmussen, J., 1992, Ecological interface design: Theoretical foundations. *IEEE Transactions on Systems, Man, and Cybernetics*, SMC-22, 589–606.

Woo, D.M. and Vicente, K.J., 2003, Sociotechnical systems, risk management, and public health: Comparing the North Battleford and Walkerton outbreaks. *Reliability Engineering and System Safety*, 80, 253–269.

9

Nested Systems

Economic, Cultural, and Political Dimensions

Alex Kirlik

> *There is no such thing as a unique scientific vision, any more than there is a*
> *unique poetic vision. Science is a mosaic of partial and conflicting visions.*
> *But there is one common element in these visions. The common element is*
> *rebellion against the restrictions of locally prevailing culture ....*
>
> Freeman Dyson, *The Scientist as Rebel*

The article reprinted in this chapter is by far the most ambitious of this collection. Vicente suggests that human–technology interaction (HTI) researchers and practitioners must take an activist approach toward changing the world. Although a few may agree, many others are probably not interested, and for good reasons. In the latter sections of his article, Vicente refers to efforts (by himself and a colleague) that resulted in a change in how a "Big Pharma" corporation does its business. Unfortunately, details on this case could not be provided.

As such, I am of two minds on how to react to Vicente's appeal for activism on the part of HTI researchers. One option, resonating with the ideas presented in the reprint, is for those seeking to make major advances to be opportunistic in "catching the wave" of change when possible. As Vicente notes, crucial opportunities for effecting positive change are afforded by seizing on high-profile events, such as disasters. Being in the right place at the right time allows gains to be made that may otherwise be impossible. I have some experience along these lines myself, in the swirl of events following 9/11 (emergency egress technology) and Hurricane Katrina (decision support technology). Not surprisingly, any positive contributions I was able to make in those cases also resulted in a keener sense of which sorts of challenges I am likely to agree to take on in future work. I can at least hope that I am a better teacher than I know myself to be a crusader, and stick to the knitting.

Vicente advocates activism to make HTI more relevant and consequential. This is one path, although not a path that all researchers would find comfortable or would be particularly well qualified to take. An alternative to personal activism was advocated by Thomas Jefferson (see Chapter 3): Like democracy, a human-centered, rather than a technology-centered approach to creating how we live with technology rests, first and foremost, on the education of the many, rather than on the activism of the few. I can only hope that this book may have some impact along these lines.

Human Factors Engineering That Makes a Difference: Leveraging a Science of Societal Change

Kim J. Vicente

Abstract

The over-arching purpose of human factors engineering is to improve the quality of human life, but our discipline has not been as successful as we would like in effecting societal change, whether it be at the political or corporate level. The current paper addresses this problem, first by identifying a set of general challenges to change, and second by reviewing three illustrative theories of the processes behind large-scale societal change. Kingdon's (1984/2003) work on agenda setting explains how ideas get onto the political radar. Birkland's (1997) research on focusing events shows how accidents can be exploited to foster policy change. Tushman and Romanelli's (1985) work on punctuated equilibrium theory illustrates how market forces and environmental disruptions can be manipulated to encourage radical corporate change. These research programs have largely unappreciated "design" implications that human factors engineers can adopt to increase the likelihood of improving the fit between people and technology in the service of humankind.

1. Introduction

> To better the quality of human life through the discipline of
> human factors/ergonomics.
>
> Statement of Purpose (Human Factors and
Ergonomics Society 2004: 361)

> People who are trying to advocate change are like surfers waiting
> for the big wave. You get out there, you have to be ready
> to go, you have to be ready to paddle. If you're not ready to paddle
> when the big wave comes along, you're not going to ride it in.
>
> A policy analyst for an interest group.
(Kingdon 1984/2003: 165)

Human factors engineering is an inherently activist discipline because its overarching aim is to affect societal change. Some recent and salient examples that begged for our input and leadership include: risk management of the NASA space shuttle program (Columbia Accident Investigation Board, 2003), patient safety (Kohn et al., 1999), the voting ballots in the 2000 US Presidential Election (Sinclair et al., 2000), and the proposed Occupational Safety and Health Administration ergonomics standard (Anonymous, 2000). All of these issues reached the level of Congressional or Presidential politics in the US, and they all could have benefited from very strong attention to human factors, but a human factors voice was consistently not as forthcoming as it could have been. Have we really made a difference in changing the way government and corporations think about the relationship between people and technology, thereby making the most of the knowledge base that our discipline has worked so hard to develop over the last 60 or so years?

Our discipline has had significant impact on some high-profile issues. Improving airline safety through cockpit resource management (Weiner et al., 1993) and the aviation safety reporting system (Billings, 1998) are among the best known examples. For the most part, however, we have not been nearly as successful as we would like in effecting significant societal change (Hansen, 2000; Howell, 2000, 2001). This limited practical impact has been consistently noted for decades (e.g. Chapanis, 1967; Perrow, 1983; Rouse, 1985; Simon, 1987; Meister, 1989; Vicente, 2000), suggesting that there are endemic reasons for the unsatisfactory progress achieved to date. If we are to have any hope of ever fully realizing our discipline's ambitions of improving the quality of human life, then we need to address this persistent and over-arching problem, preferably systematically. Yet, there appears to be very little human factors engineering literature on how best to facilitate societal change.

A seemingly obvious path in filling this critical gap would be to borrow from other disciplines that have systematically studied processes of large-scale societal change (e.g. management, political science, public policy), especially how to facilitate such change to achieve a particular set of policy objectives. There is a vast body of scholarship on this subject, with many theories and results (e.g. Birkland, 2001; Christensen, 1997; Collins, 2001; Senge, 1990; Weimer and Vining, 1999). Given the centrality of effecting change, whether it be at the political or corporate level, to our discipline's mission, it might be thought that human factors researchers would have frequently and heavily tapped into this knowledge base to increase the practical impact of our work. It appears that this has not happened; articles that use the wealth of systematic knowledge about large-scale political or corporate change to derive implications for the practice of human factors engineering are exceedingly rare. The purpose of the current paper is to address this gap, first by identifying some of the major obstacles to change, and second by reviewing several theories describing how change can occur at the political or corporate level.

Three caveats are in order. First, even though the topic of this article—encouraging societal change—is highly pragmatic, the approach being adopted is not to abdicate the rigor of scientific research, but on the contrary, to make the most of academic scholarship so that this topic can be tackled in a systematic and principled manner. Second, given the immense scope of research on this topic, it is not possible to provide a comprehensive review of the literature on political or corporate change. Instead, just a few examples are highlighted to illustrate the value of this body of work for our discipline. Finally, the literature on societal change is not, and never will be, sufficiently mature to allow any policy activists consistently to achieve their objectives. Societal change is intrinsically a very complex, uncertain and, therefore, risky process. Nevertheless, the existing literature does give us many principled insights into how to "tilt the playing field" to our advantage, thereby increasing the chances of achieving our activist aims.

2. Challenges to change

This section begins by briefly analysing the problem of societal change, and then goes on to identify 11 general obstacles that make change difficult to achieve.

2.1. Morphological analysis of change

Table 1 illustrates a very simple morphological analysis of societal change.

TABLE 1   Morphological analysis of societal change.

	Problem	No problem
Act	Change	False positive
Don't act	False negative	Null case

Along the top, there are two states: there is a societal problem requiring a change in action, or there is no such problem. Along the left, there are two responses: act to resolve a perceived problem, or do not act. This formulation leads to four types of situations.

1. In the upper left corner, there is the case of change: there was a problem, and action was taken. An example was the swift passage of oil pollution liability legislation shortly after the 1989 Exxon Valdez accident in Prince William Sound, Alaska (Birkland, 1997).

2. In the upper right corner, there is the case of a false positive: there was no problem but action was nevertheless taken. This situation is more complex because resources were unnecessarily invested—an overly aggressive reaction. Interestingly, it appears that it is very difficult to find real-world examples of this type of situation (European Environment Agency, 2001), suggesting that industry and government do not adopt an aggressive attitude toward change. The possible exception is the Y2K phenomenon (Story and Crawford, 2001). However, that example illustrates one of the difficulties with identifying a false positive: was Y2K a successful change to address a real problem, or an unnecessary, overly aggressive change? In the absence of a control group of inaction, it is difficult to discriminate between cases of successful change and those of false positives because the intervention may or may not have led to the outcome.

3. In the lower right corner, there is the null case when there was no problem and no action was taken. This is the simplest case of all.

4. In the lower left corner, there is the case of a false negative: there was a problem, but no action was taken. This is the most interesting and important case because it deals with situations where there is strong resistance to change or lack of awareness: the problem demands action, but intervention is not forthcoming. As we will see, there are many examples of this type, but to understand their nature, we need to identify some sources of resistance to change.

2.2. Eleven challenges to change

There are eleven challenges to change that have been inductively identified from the 14 case studies reviewed by the European Environment Agency (2001) in its aptly titled report *Late Lessons From Early Warnings*.

 1. Very long lag between cause and effect.
 2. Uncertainty or ignorance in information.
 3. Transboundary problems.
 4. Large short-term costs in the face of economic pressures.
 5. Costs are externalized onto environment, government and public.
 6. Difficult cost-benefit trade-offs.
 7. Legal liability for corporations.
 8. Public accountability for governments.
 9. Conflicting organizational roles.
10. No evidence of harm ≠ evidence of no harm.
11. Shoot the messenger.

The topics covered by the cases, described in Table 2, include substances or activities that have eventually been deemed harmful to people, animals, or the environment—but only after a great deal of resistance to change (thus, the title of the report). These cases represent an invaluable resource because each one comprehensively describes the initial evidence of harm, the reaction to that evidence, the reasons for resistance to change, and the policy changes that were eventually adopted. As far as is known, there is no comparable analysis for a human factors case of large-scale change, let alone for 14 of them. Therefore, these cases provide a fruitful database for identifying challenges to large-scale change.

TABLE 2   Fourteen case studies of societal change.

Case study #	Subject	Description
1	Fisheries	Overfishing owing to short-term economic pressures causes collapse of stock, leading to lost sales, unemployment, and financial bailouts
2	Radiation	Exposure to radioactivity leads to cancers and death
3	Benzene	Powerful bone marrow poison used in many, diverse industrial settings causes fatal leukemia and lymphatic cancer
4	Asbestos	Mineral with many industrial applications; inhalation of dust causes fatal mesothelioma cancer
5	PCBs (polychlorinated biphenyls)	Synthetic organic chemicals with many industrial uses; environmental pollutant as well as danger to animals and humans
6	Halocarbons	'Green house' gases that lead to deterioration of ozone layer, contributing to global warming and skin cancer
7	DES (diethylstilboestrol)	Synthetic estrogen used, among other things, to prevent miscarriage; prenatal exposure leads to rare but fatal vaginal cancer
8	Antimicrobials	Bacteria-killing drugs also used as growth promoters in food animals; lead to antimicrobial resistance in humans and animals
9	Sulphur dioxide	Air pollutant that causes fatal lung disease as well as 'acid rain', leading to contaminated lakes, dead fish, and dying forests
10	MTBE(methyl tert-butyl ether)	Engine anti-knocking agent used in gasoline as substitute for lead; may lead to groundwater contamination, cancer, and asthma
11	Great Lakes	Chemical pollutants cause contamination of Great Lakes and threat to human and animal health
12	TBT (tributyltin)	Chemical compound found in paint for ships and boats; leads to sexual deformities in marine life causing collapse of stock
13	Hormones	Used as growth promoters in food animals; cause cancer in humans and harmful to wildlife
14	BSE (bovine spongiform encephalopathy)	'Mad cow' disease caused by cattle eating feed with remains of sheep, cattle, and other animals; can lead to fatal disease in human beef consumers

The list of challenges to change is not intended to be comprehensive, and not all factors will be found in any one case. Nevertheless, the factors are useful because they are not tied to the idiosyncratic details of any one case, and are thus potentially generalizable across a diverse array of settings.

2.2.1. Very long lag between cause and effect

In some cases, change is difficult simply because the problem to be solved has slow dynamics, creating a very long lag between cause and effect. Asbestos provides a case in point. Typically, the time between exposure to asbestos fibers and the onset of cancer can be on the order of 10 to 40 years. It is difficult to assess risk during this 'incubation period' in which the symptoms of disease—evidence that there is a problem—are not visible. During this time, those that benefit from the status quo (e.g. asbestos producers) will argue that there is no evidence of harm so that they can justify not acting (e.g. not setting exposure limits). Even when the effects do become visible, it may be difficult to discern their cause because more immediate factors may be more obvious candidates. Given these conditions, it will take a long time before action is taken to address the problem. Indeed, in the case of asbestos, 100 years passed between the first warning sign of potential harm (1898) and the ban of all forms of asbestos by the European Union (1998). Acting to set limits for radiation also took decades because of the long lag between exposure and cancer.

Some environmental problems also tend to have slow dynamics that present a challenge to change. The impact of halocarbons first on the ozone layer and eventually on human health provides an example. The average time between the release of these emissions and a concomitant increase in the prevalence of skin cancer is 30 to 40 years. Under these circumstances, it should not be surprising to find that, for many years, industry's attitude toward the use of halocarbons was not one of preemptive change, but rather, of 'wait and see'.

2.2.2. Uncertainty or ignorance in information

Sometimes, change is not forthcoming because the quality of information is less than ideal. There are several versions of this obstacle. In one case, there is a great deal of intrinsic variability in the data, so it is difficult to make a convincing case for the need to act. For example, the stock of herring and sardines in the oceans can fluctuate dramatically over decades. Against this backdrop, it is difficult convincingly to isolate the unique contribution of overfishing on stock depletion. In another version of this obstacle, the problem is not variability but rather multiple potential causes, making the attribution of cause difficult. Asbestos provides an excellent example. In the 1930s, when the prevalence of lung cancer was quite low, it was easier to establish a direct link between asbestos exposure and cancer. However, decades later, when the prevalence of lung cancer owing to smoking increased significantly, it became more difficult to argue that asbestos was a carcinogen. Consequently, those in the tobacco industry could argue that people were dying from asbestos, and those in the asbestos industry could argue that people were dying from smoking instead, creating a paralyzing gridlock for policy change.

2.2.3. Transboundary problems

A system is an artificial construction created by a modeller and, as such, the lines defining the system boundary can be drawn in different ways with varying consequences. In the case of MTBE (methyl tert-butyl ether), government agencies were carved up according to media, such as land, air and water. This seems to be a reasonable way to allocate regulatory responsibilities, but in the case of MTBE, it had the undesirable effect that environmental impact assessments were fragmented and incomplete. MTBE crosses the land/air/water parsing, and so the damage it creates is severely underestimated unless a holistic view is adopted. In the absence of such an integrated perspective, change will be difficult to justify because the costs of the status quo are perceived to be much lower than they really are.

An analogous issue can be found when problems cross jurisdictional boundaries, as environmental problems are likely to do. For instance, restrictions on the use of TBT (tributyltin) in paint for seagoing vessels have been adopted by many, but not all, countries. It took a great deal of effort to effect these changes because there were many obstacles to change. Despite this apparent success, however, there are still TBT-induced problems on the coastal waters of Japan. Only world-wide restrictions would address the TBT problem and achieve environmental standards in all coastal systems. Clearly, this requirement substantially raises the bar for successful change.

2.2.4. Large short-term costs in the face of economic pressures

Change is also difficult because it frequently demands large short-term costs. As the EAA (2001) put it, "Being wise before it is too late is not easy, especially when the environmental or health impacts may be far into the future and the real, or perceived, costs on averting them are large and immediate" (EEA, 2001: 13). This situation creates a significant obstacle, especially for a corporation who is responsible to its shareholders for maximizing profits and whose "legally defined mandate is to pursue, relentlessly and without exception, its own self-interest, regardless of the often harmful consequences it might cause to others" (Bakan 2004: 1, 2). Naturally, there will be great resistance to take costly action under these circumstances. Indeed, the case studies frequently bear this out. There are several examples where those who benefit from the status quo try to avoid action by stating that there is no "clear-cut or convincing evidence" of a problem. This leads to a protracted debate about the quality of evidence, which benefits the status quo by delaying action, thereby averting a large short-term cost associated with change. The case of benzene is the most clearly documented: "Manufacturers began to hire consultants to downplay the importance of the scientific observations related to the toxicity of benzene and to introduce unresolvable arguments about dose-response analyses, which had an impact in delaying much needed government regulations that sought to reduce benzene exposure in the workplace" (EEA, 2001: 43). Monsanto adopted a similar tactic in its defence of PCBs (polychlorinated biphenyls), as did the pharmaceutical industry in defending the use of antimicrobials as growth promoters and Shell Chemical Company in defending the use of chemicals that contaminated the Great Lakes.

2.2.5. Costs are externalized onto environment, government and public

Economists use the term "externalities" to refer to the effects of a transaction on a third party who did not play any role in that transaction

(Bakan, 2004). An example would be the decision by a pulp and paper company to dump its effluents into a river, polluting the water supply of a town downstream. The pollution is an externality because (barring any regulatory fines) the entity that made the decision—the company—does not suffer any of the negative consequences of its actions, whereas the entity that was not involved in the decision—the town—experiences the negative effects. Externalities are ways of shifting the burden of doing business from a corporation to the general public, environment or government. In cases such as this, there is no incentive for a company to modify its behaviour because it is not suffering the harmful costs of its actions, making change less likely to occur.

Unfortunately, many of the societal problems that are in need of change arise from externalities. For example, the health care costs associated with harm from asbestos exposure may not be paid by the company who manufactures the asbestos, but by the patients themselves or by government insurance programs. The company can then sell asbestos at a relatively low price because it is not shouldering the full costs of its product, making it difficult for asbestos to be replaced by a less hazardous material.

2.2.6. Difficult cost-benefit trade-offs

It is a truism that financial resources are always limited, which means that the benefits of change must be weighed against the costs. It is difficult to assess this trade-off because "The cost of preventive actions are usually tangible, clearly allocated and often short term, whereas the costs of failing to act are less tangible, less clearly distributed and usually longer term" (EEA, 2001: 3). Therefore, cost-benefit analyses usually argue against change, unless a precautionary perspective is adopted.

When there was strong scientific evidence about the harm caused by sulphur dioxide, some still resisted change by arguing that acid rain was a million dollar problem with a billion dollar solution. This may seem like a utilitarian argument that puts a price tag on human life and environmental devastation, but it must be taken seriously because the same amount of money could potentially be invested elsewhere with a greater impact on human health and the natural ecology. In the case of sulphur dioxide, researchers argued that the original cost-benefit analysis was incomplete because it did not fully take into account damages to health, agriculture, materials and natural ecosystems. Once all of these costs were included in the analysis, then the balance sheet was clearly in favour of change.

Sometimes, the cost-benefit analysis seems to argue against change because the status quo has several desirable qualities. For instance, the use of MTBE as a replacement for lead in gasoline has the following advantages: it is inexpensive and easily produced with desirable chemical characteristics; it is produced at the refinery as opposed to at a more remote location; it blends easily without separation from gasoline; and it can be transferred easily through existing pipelines. Therefore, the harm caused by MTBE must be weighed against this non-trivial set of benefits. Change can be justified if a safer and equally beneficial replacement for MTBE can be found. It is not always easy to find a viable alternative, in which case we may have to live with an irreducible amount of risk—an unappealing, but inevitable prospect.

2.2.7. Legal liability for corporations

Legal liability can also be an obstacle to change, especially for corporations. In some cases, the fact that a company makes a good will change to improve one of its products is exploited by its detractors—in the media or in a lawsuit—as evidence that there must have been something harmful about the previous product, putting the company in a double bind situation. The PCBs case study provides an example of this dysfunctional reward structure. Monsanto stated that "stopping the production of PCBs was not an option as it would cause 'profits to cease and liability to soar because we would be admitting guilt by our actions'" (EEA, 2001: 65). In the absence of some offsetting benefit, companies would be loathe to adopt changes that would hurt them financially.

2.2.8. Public accountability for governments

Just as admitting that there is a problem can lead to law suits for an organization, admitting that there is a problem can lead to unfavourable public opinion for a government. Thus, the need to save face can lead to resistance to change. The BSE (bovine spongiform encephalopathy) case study provides a clear example of this phenomenon. First, the British Ministry of Agriculture, Fisheries and Food (MAFF) chose to hide the existence of the outbreak for 17 months for fear that citizens would panic. As one official put it, informing the public of the outbreak "might imply to the general public we know something they don't, like the meat or milk is a source of danger for humans" (EEA, 2001: 159). Meanwhile, unbeknownst to the public, the outbreak continued to escalate, increasing the threat to public health. Second, the MAFF also refrained from taking any action to curb the outbreak early on for fear that the resulting "irresponsible or ill-informed publicity ... might lead to hysterical demands for immediate, draconian Government measures" (EEA, 2001: 159). Third, later in the outbreak—once the existence of BSE had finally become public—the MAFF offered the public the optimistic and reassuring message that the presence of BSE in British cattle did not pose a threat to human health, even though the available scientific evidence showed that it was impossible to be sure that consuming meat, dairy, and milk from BSE-infected animals posed no risk. The perceived need to save face was so strong that the government stuck to this initially indefensible position, even in the face of accumulating contradictory evidence. Consequently, many precautionary measures that could have diminished the impact of the outbreak were not adopted because they would undermine the government's position. This attitude of adopting, and sticking to, a palatable but increasingly distorted message may temporarily help the government save face in the eyes of the public, but it is a clear challenge to policy change and a threat to public health.

2.2.9. Conflicting organizational roles

Change is also difficult to effect when an organization has conflicting roles. There are at least two versions of this challenge, one more explicit and another more implicit. In the implicit case, the conflicting roles are not immediately obvious. A good example can be found in the benzene case study, where scientists employed by benzene producers participated on the Threshold Limit Value Committee of the American Conference of Governmental Industrial Hygienists. These scientists were in a position of conflict of interest because, on the one hand, they had to represent their employers' concerns which would involve setting benzene limits at values that were easily achievable in the workplace, but on the other hand, they should protect public health which would involve setting limits according to the best available scientific evidence. In the end, the former role beat out the latter and limits of 100 ppm were recommended, even though there were known cases of benzene poisoning associated with levels of 10 ppm.

In the explicit case, an organization officially has responsibilities that are in intrinsic conflict with one another. In the BSE case, the MAFF was responsible for protecting the public from food-borne hazards while also promoting the economic interest of farmers and the food industry. There are situations in which these two mandates are in direct opposition, and the BSE outbreak was an example. Early on, the MAFF chose not to make information about the outbreak public or take any remedial action to safeguard public health, in part because doing so might lead other countries to reject UK exports of cattle, bovine embryos and semen. In fact, the Agriculture Minister did "not see how [he] could proceed without being clear where the offsetting savings are coming from .... Action along the lines recommended now would make the export position much worse" (EEA, 2001: 159). The tremendous resistance to change exhibited by the MAFF in the BSE case shows that when an organization is put in a conflict of interest, it can be very difficult for change to occur.

2.2.10. No evidence of harm ≠ evidence of no harm

The propensity to equate no evidence of harm with evidence of no harm is a logical fallacy that has repeatedly been an obstacle to change. Just because there is no evidence to show that a substance is dangerous does not mean that it is safe. The appropriate studies may not have been conducted yet. This is very likely to be the case in substances that have slow dynamics, such as asbestos, because, even though it is a harmful substance, evidence of its effects will not be visible for many years. For this reason, it is important to interpret "negative" cancer studies with caution. Unless participants have been studied over 20 to 30 years, such studies are unlikely to detect lung cancer in people exposed to asbestos. Indeed, in an early asbestos study, the increase in cancer incidence was seven times normal but it did not become statistically significant until 25 years after the exposure.

2.2.11. Shoot the messenger

Finally, change is also difficult to achieve because sometimes the person bringing attention to a problem is not received with welcome arms. By definition, change threatens the status quo, so those who have a vested interest in keeping things as they are typically have a great deal of power and may choose to use it to attack the messenger. There are many examples of the price paid by whistleblowers, including a penetrating account in Ibsen's (1882) play, *A Public Enemy*, which describes how a whistleblower goes from applauded public hero to outcast public enemy once the mayor, the media, and the public learn of the dire economic implications of his public health warnings. When Rachel Carson's (1962) seminal book, *Silent Spring*, linked pesticides with increased incidence of cancer and environmental devastation, the National Agricultural Chemicals Association wrote to editors of magazines and newspapers threatening that advertising revenues could be affected if the book were to receive positive reviews. And when the *New Yorker* published parts of the book in a serial fashion, Houghton Mifflin (the publisher of *Silent Spring)* received a letter from the general counsel of the Velsicol Chemical Company threatening legal action unless the last *New Yorker* article was cancelled. More forceful attacks with more devastating personal consequences have been documented in detail (Boisjoly et al., 1989; Brenner, 1996; Thompson et al., 2001). The possibility of such a forceful backlash can serve as a strong deterrent, discouraging those with the requisite skills and information to come forward and spur change.

2.3. Discussion

There is much to be learnt from history, and the 14 case studies listed in Table 2 shed a great deal of light on why large-scale societal change can be so difficult to achieve. The challenges to change that emerged from these cases have been summarized above. The number and strength of these challenges show why change is so slow. Based on this corpus of cases, change seldom occurs in less than 25 years as measured by the time between the early warnings and the corresponding regulatory, judicial or administrative actions of reform.

However, there is another, perhaps less obvious, lesson buried in the list of challenges to change. Advocates for change frequently complain that a "lack of political will" is the reason why change does not occur. But this phrase explains nothing. It is equivalent to the concept of "caloric" that was once used by physicists many years ago to explain why objects give off heat (Einstein and Infeld, 1938/1966). Why is an object warm? Because it has caloric. Eventually, physicists realized that the caloric was not useful because it merely shifted the burden of explanation—there is no account of the factors responsible for the phenomenon, nor of how they interact. The same could be said for political will. It allocates blame, but it does not elucidate the basis on which decisions are being made, whereas the factors given in the list of challenges to change represent an attempt at doing precisely that.

This difference has important practical implications. If you think change does not occur because of a lack of political will, you will tend to think that people who disagree with you are stupid, evil or, at the very best, misguided, so you will think that the remedy lies in trying to pressure them, or failing that, replacing them. But you do not really know where the levers for change are. If you put different people in the same roles and leave the design of the system intact, then it is unlikely that the undesirable behaviours will change. As Hartmann (2002) put it (in a different context), "Nobody thought to examine the structure of the... institutions as a source of problems. Instead, the cause was laid at the feet of individual people.... But there is no use trying to find villains, because the problem is in the structure of the situation" (p. 22). In other words, people may be engaging in behaviours we do not like or understand but they may be resistant to change for what they believe are very good reasons (e.g. a company has an obligation to its shareholders, a government agency has conflicting missions). A few of the factors given in the list of challenges to change—long lags, uncertain information—may be immutable, but the vast majority of the factors let us see some of the rationale behind resistance to change and therefore identifies where we need to focus our efforts (e.g. offering a company financial incentives for change, splitting a government agency into two independent units).

Rather than pursue the usually futile course of blaming individuals, we can identify powerful and useful levers that can encourage the kind of change we want to achieve.

Knowledge of obstacles is important but not enough because it does not tell us when it is likely that obstacles can be removed or overcome. We also need to be savvy about when change is likely to occur so that we can invest our limited energies wisely. There are times when trying to change certain policies is tantamount to tilting at windmills. Trying to pass gun control legislation today in the US is an example. Yet, as the examples below will show, there are other times where windows of opportunity appear and comparatively small investments can lead to tremendous societal change. In the remainder of the present paper, three theories of the mechanisms behind change—two at the political level and one at the corporate level—are reviewed to show when change tends to occur. This knowledge has important practical implications for how to improve the likelihood of achieving human factors policy objectives.

3. Political change

3.1. Agenda setting: how does an idea's time come?

The phrase, "an idea whose time has come," is frequently used to refer to a political or social movement that suddenly takes hold—seemingly everywhere at once—knocking down barriers to change that had persisted for decades or centuries. The civil rights movement of the 1960s in the US is a prototypical example. We would all like to think that human factors engineering will soon be an idea whose time has come because its potential impact for improving the quality of human life is tremendous (Vicente, 2003a). But how does an idea's time come? What causes politicians, civil servants, lobbyists, the media, corporate executives, and the general public to embrace an idea simultaneously, and effect widespread change? Any insight into this issue is worth its weight in gold because it would provide guidance on what we could do as a discipline to make it more likely that our time will come, sooner rather than later—or not at all.

Kingdon's (1984/2003) landmark work on agenda setting is a political science classic that addressed this profound question. Public policy can be broadly divided into four activities: agenda setting which is the process by which subjects or problems receive serious political attention; the generation of policy alternatives which is the process by which particular proposals for action are formed; the moment of choice which is the process by which a particular policy is adopted; and finally, policy implementation which is the process by which chosen policies are realized. Kingdon's work focuses primarily on agenda setting activities, a topic that had received very little attention in the literature. In four annual waves from 1976 to 1979, he conducted 247 comprehensive interviews with opinion makers, both inside and outside of the US federal government, who were concerned with policy initiatives in two areas: health and transportation. In addition, 23 case studies of successful and unsuccessful policy change were identified and studied in detail, resulting in a representative and broad data set. These findings led to a novel and influential theory that explains why some subjects receive a great deal of attention at particular times but not others, and why some subjects never make it onto the political agenda.

Kingdon's (1984/2003) theory consists of three parallel streams—problems, policies, and politics—that have relatively independent dynamics, but that occasionally become coupled at critical moments that are more likely to result in broad social change. In the problem recognition stream, different social problems capture the attention of decision makers in and around government. The list of key problems is highly fluid; problems are constantly appearing on and falling off the political radar. In the policies stream, people from different backgrounds and varied interests are continually generating proposals to achieve their political interests, frequently independently of what problems are currently on the political agenda. These varied, and frequently conflicting, proposals are constantly competing for the attention of lawmakers through a process akin to natural selection. In the politics stream, events such as changes in public opinion, changes in administration, and interest group campaigns provide a shifting context that can facilitate or inhibit particular types of societal change. In Kingdon's theory, these three streams are "largely separate from one another, largely governed by different forces, different considerations, and different styles" (p. 88). However, there are critical times when the three streams come together—a policy proposal nicely fits a recognized problem and the ideology of the current political landscape—and it is precisely at these times that the likelihood of societal change is greatest. But since the three streams work in different ways, it is important to understand the unique factors that influence each of them.

3.1.1. Problems

Problems come to the attention of lawmakers in several ways. First, systematic indicators—preferably quantitative—such as unemployment rate, gross domestic product, or disease rates can push a problem onto the political radar. For example, the widespread publication of medical error mortality statistics—44,000 to 98,000 annual preventable deaths in US hospitals—catapulted the problem of patient safety to the level of Presidential politics, making it the most influential health policy issue of 1999 (Kaiser/Harvard Program on Public and Health Policy, 1999). In addition, focusing events such as an airplane crash or an oil spill can quickly put a previously unknown or ignored problem at the very front and center of politicians' attention. The Three Mile Island (TMI) nuclear accident is a well-known example that briefly raised the profile of human factors engineering into the national spotlight. Third, feedback about the efficacy or efficiency of existing government programs provide another mechanism for problem recognition. Complaints from local citizens to their congressional representatives about deteriorating road conditions are an example.

Perhaps surprisingly, the media does not play a strong role in creating new agenda items. Instead, its role seems to be primarily in magnifying items that were already on the government agenda. In other words, the media does not create, but rather reacts to or advances, change.

Just as important as how problems get the attention of government is how they fade from view. If legislation is passed, then problems drop off the agenda because something has been done about them, regardless of whether the desired impact has been achieved. Conversely, if attempts to effect change fail or take too long, then lawmakers frequently drop the problem and turn their attention to more promising issues because they conclude that the time is just not right. It takes a tremendous amount of energy to "work" a problem and keep it on the government agenda, and because resources are limited, that effort can only be kept up for so long. As a result, specific efforts toward societal change tend to have a limited lifetime because advocacy can only be sustained in relatively discrete pushes. Hot ideas are on the agenda for, at most, four or five years and then go cold and are replaced by other hot problems that have risen to the agenda. But even while a problem is on the agenda, change is not guaranteed because of the influence of the other two streams.

3.1.2. Policies

At any one time, there is a very large number of proposed policy alternatives that government can choose from. Many of these are not directed at a particular problem, but instead represent the ideological concerns of a particular person or community; they are solutions looking for problems. For example, mass transit has been advanced by various policy communities as a solution to a diverse range of problems, including pollution, traffic congestion, and energy consumption. The fit can be entirely opportunistic. Indeed, it is common for government agencies to develop policies to protect or enhance their turf, or for politicians to develop policies to increase their public visibility.

Policy communities can differ tremendously, with some being fragmented and others being more tightly knit. A fragmented community leads to policy fragmentation, which in turn, makes change more difficult to achieve. A community that adopts a common paradigm, uses the same terminology, and is conceptually integrated maximizes its impact.

Perhaps surprisingly, researchers and academics are important players in the generation of policy alternatives, ranking just below the top tier occupied by the administration, Congress, and interest groups. However, to be influential, they must know what is on the mind of the people in government, which is not a typical preoccupation of many academics.

Ideas are put into a conceptual marketplace that results in uncontrollable recombination and selection, leading to unexpected revised or hybrid policy proposals that differ from the original, sometimes in significant ways. To gain currency and attention, advocates spend a great deal of time explaining their ideas to other communities and to the public to build up awareness, understanding, and acceptance—a diffusion process known as "softening up." Kingdon's research shows that this persuasion activity is essential to change; policy alternatives that are unfamiliar have virtually no chance of being selected. Moreover, the softening up process is very time-consuming, taking as long as six years by some estimates. During this time, the goal may simply be to keep the issue alive, while waiting for a more propitious time for action. There are several criteria for the survival of policy proposals, including: technical feasibility, value acceptability within the policy community, tolerable cost and acceptance to the public and to politicians. Because there are so many proposals and the criteria for survival are so diverse, policy alternatives tend to exhibit a non-linear, "tipping point" effect. For years, an idea will be on the back burner and discussed by only a few self-interested advocates, but then suddenly, it catches on and there is widespread acceptance of it, vastly increasing the likelihood of change. In short, the policy stream is very complex, slow, effortful, competitive and discontinuous.

3.1.3. Political

There are many political events that occur in parallel and independently from the problems and policy streams. Some of these are predictable and even regular. For example, legislation expires on known dates, creating a window of opportunity for change. Similarly, changes in administration after elections can create significant changes that alter the political landscape, allowing policies that had no chance of succeeding to come forward and be passed very quickly (and vice-versa). Well-known examples include the New Deal under Roosevelt, and the Great Society under Johnson.

Some political events are more difficult to anticipate, but have an equally strong effect, such as changes in public opinion that promote some policies and restrain others. Growing concern amongst the public for a sustainable environment would be an example. Jurisdictional turf battles can also encourage and impede change. As an example of the latter, some Congressmen are more likely to try to push legislation through quickly in an attempt to get credit for societal change if they know that one of their opponents is working on the same issue. Usually, the balance of power operates to sustain the status quo. Whereas persuasion dominates in the policy stream, bargaining dominates in the political stream. Coalitions are built and trades and compromises are made to build a critical mass of support to open a policy window that greases the wheels for change.

3.1.4. Coupling

This description clearly shows that agenda setting is a highly distributed and exceedingly complex phenomenon. Usually, the three streams operate relatively independently of each other and work to impede change, but once in a while, a policy window can open, either because of a change in the political stream or the problem stream. However, experience shows that policy windows open quite infrequently and do not remain open for very long. Thus, it is critical that advocates recognize these opportune moments and act quickly and strategically.

When a window is open because of a pressing problem, decision makers survey the policy stream to see if there is a relevant proposal that can serve as a solution. When a window is open owing to a political change, decision makers survey the policy stream to see if there is a relevant proposal that can advance their ideological agenda. Decision makers are usually quite skilled at detecting these changes, which means that there will be a fury of activity from competing interest groups to couple policies to agenda items when windows are perceived to open. Once these events are set in motion, it will be very difficult to predict and control the course of events, which is why societal change is so uncertain and fraught with risk. Moreover, change is not guaranteed to occur because, like any information processing system, the political bureaucracy only has a finite capacity, in this case for passing legislation.

The likelihood of change is greatly enhanced, however, when all three streams become coupled, creating a highly fertile confluence of events. It is the job of policy entrepreneurs to build on the foundation created by the long softening up process and seize on these critical opportunities by linking a policy proposal to a recognized problem (or vice versa) and by amassing (or leveraging) the required coalition of political support. When the "stars are aligned" through this three-way coupling process, change that was impossible to achieve before can now happen with astonishing speed. Kingdon (1984/2003) discusses an example from health care policy during the Nixon era: "The proposal grew from a conversation to a memo, then from a very thick document to the status of a major presidential health initiative, all in a matter of a few weeks" (p. 6).

3.2. Focusing events: how to capitalize on disasters?

Birkland (1997) investigated a particular aspect of agenda setting, namely the potential impact of disasters on policy change. Since the relevance of human factors engineering to the quality of human life is—in principle, at least—most convincingly and vividly illustrated by nuclear, aviation, petrochemical, aerospace, and other such accidents, this research program can help us learn how to turn these tragic disasters into societal changes that can reduce the likelihood of more deaths, destruction or environmental damage.

Birkland (1997) analysed a number of diverse events—earthquakes, hurricanes, oil spills, and nuclear disasters—over a long time period (ranging from 13 to 30 years). For each problem area, he searched government sources to identify the amount and type of policy activity, and media sources to identify the amount and type of publicity. The time periods before and after an accident were compared so that the dynamic impact of the event could be understood. By investigating several different sectors, Birkland was able to generalize results that were common across cases as well as identifying mediating factors that inhibited or facilitated the impact of the disaster on societal change.

The central construct in Birkland's work is the *focusing event:* a sudden, vivid, unpredictable event that stimulates tremendous interest in a societal problem and that greatly increases the likelihood of policy change on that problem. The prototypical example he discusses is the 1989 Exxon Valdez accident, which created enormous environmental damage after an oil tanker ran aground off the Alaskan coast and spilled over 11 million gallons of crude. For 14 years, environmental policy analysts had been unsuccessfully advocating comprehensive oil spill liability legislation to protect the natural ecology. After the Exxon Valdez spill, the Oil Pollution Act of 1990 was pushed through Congress within 18 months.

Interestingly, however, not all disasters become focusing events. For example, the 1966 Fermi accident in Michigan, the 1975 Browns Ferry accident in Alabama, and the 1979 TMI accident in Pennsylvania were all significant nuclear disasters, but only the latter received widespread international attention. Therefore, a disaster—an objective physical event—is, by itself, not enough to cause a focusing event—a socially constructed political outcome. A number of other factors, some of which are described next, mediate the likely impact on policy change.

3.2.1. Advocacy coalition

The most obvious pre-requisite for turning a disaster into a focusing event is the existence of an advocacy community. In the early days of nuclear energy, the overwhelming public perception was that nuclear power was positive and would lead to remarkable innovations with clear societal benefits, such as "electricity that was too cheap to meter." In the absence of a significant community of advocates, disasters will not be linked to the need for policy change and this is indeed what Birkland's research on the early days of nuclear power demonstrates.

More importantly, even when there is a significant group of advocates, the likelihood of change is dependent on the degree to which they are organized. There must be a community of core policy entrepreneurs that is constantly active, not just after disasters. Birkland's (1997) contrast between the earthquake and hurricane policy communities illustrates this point:

> The earthquake domain has an active policy community that is mobilized during postevent periods and continues activity between such events. The hurricane community has no coherent scientific community that participates in congressional hearings between hurricanes. Without the participation of the scientific community, interest in the hurricane problem does increase in the wake of events, but this interest is centered almost solely on disaster relief and virtually disappears as the memory of the storm fades. (p. 64)

Thus, it appears that the softening up process identified by Kingdon (1984/2003) is also critical to focusing events. The groundwork must be laid before disasters so that there is a fertile soil for policy change to grow when "the big one" arrives.

3.2.2. Publicity

Another important mediating factor is publicity; if the policy relevance of the disaster is not communicated in the media, then the government and the public will not link the event to a need for change. This appears to be why the Fermi accident did not have any policy impact in 1966. The anti-nuclear version of the story never made it into the press.

However, even when an activist view is publicized, policy change can still be difficult to achieve because defenders of the status quo will typically be out in full force to deploy their (usually, quite powerful) public relations resources to contain the event. Standard ploys include claiming that everything is under control so there is no need for further action, that there will be minimal long-term damage so there is nothing to worry about, that the blame lies with a lowly scapegoat or a different organization not with the organization under the microscope, or that the event was caused by a freak, "act of God" about which nothing can be done rather than a systematic problem that is begging for policy reform. Regardless of the particular strategy, the overall goals are to convince lawmakers that there is no need to act and the public that there is no need to be alarmed or that the blame lies elsewhere (e.g. Ice, 1991; Williams and Treadaway, 1992; O'Connor, 2002).

If advocates for change are to overcome these "spin" moves, they must learn to use the media strategically. Birkland's (1997) research identifies a number of important characteristics. First, the media response must be fast so that it can impact public opinion before the issue is shut down by vested interests. Second, an emotionally compelling narrative should portray the event as an example of a general and important societal problem that is in dire need of policy change. A good story is not only convincing, but also easily told and retold, facilitating diffusion of the message. Third, it is also useful to develop simple, graphic, and "sticky" images that immediately convey the intended message by appealing to emotion (i.e. the gut) rather than analysis (i.e. the brain). In the Exxon Valdez case, photos and footage of birds and otters drenched in oil were a public relations dream for environmental advocates. These images can be propagated quickly, widely, and need virtually no explanation; they speak for themselves and provide a cogent, memorable indication of the need for change.

3.2.3. Mobilization

Another key mediating factor identified by Birkland (1997) is the need to mobilize support. In most cases, the status quo dominates because it is more powerful than the community advocating policy change, but disasters provide the latter with an opportunity to grow their support base vastly and quickly. If advocates can build coalitions with other groups to expand the interested community to an entirely new set of organizations, then they may be able to create a tipping point phenomenon that overwhelms the status quo (Schattschneider, 1960). Indeed, the power of disasters is that they often can be made to be relevant to many different interest groups that are not usually lobbying for change. In the case of oil spills, many people, not just environmental activists, care about the integrity of the natural ecology. If these other groups can be brought under the same advocacy coalition, then the likelihood of policy change is greatly enhanced. But of course, this requires that the core policy community that is leading the issue be well organized and do their softening-up homework (see above).

3.3. "Design" implications

It should be clear from both of these theories that there is a great deal of residual randomness in political change processes; outcomes are uncertain and cannot be determined. Nevertheless, there is also much structure that can be exploited by any policy advocate. Indeed, both of the theories reviewed have important "design" implications that the human factors community should be aware of to improve its activist movements. Some recommendations for "tilting the playing field" of political change are listed below.

1. write more newspaper editorials;
2. make more friends with chief executive officers (CEO)s, journalists, politicians, and civil servants;
3. build more bridges to other disciplines;
4. write more trade books for the masses;
5. study more cases of successful and unsuccessful human factors engineering change to identify successful strategies and conditions;

6. build more advocacy coalitions with like-minded organizations;

7. do not wait to get unanimous agreement before taking a public stand;

8. prepare to capitalize on the next disaster by continually engaging in a softening up process;

9. build a greater capacity for issuing public statements and images quickly; (x) learn to use the media more effectively by taking advantage of compelling images and seductive narratives;

10. make yourself useful to people in power so that they eventually seek your help and input on a regular basis;

11. work towards a common paradigm for human factors engineering that is conceptually integrated and that relies on a consistent terminology, rather than adopting new terms for existing constructs or terms that have not been clearly defined;

12. continually monitor the political landscape for windows of opportunity.

4. Corporate change

In addition to understanding political change, it is also important to study the processes behind corporate change because human factors have the potential to influence, not only government, but companies as well.

4.1. Punctuated equilibrium: when do corporations undergo radical change?

There are many different mechanisms to explain why corporations sometimes undergo radical organizational change. One well-known and influential account, referred to as punctuated equilibrium theory (Tushman and Romanelli, 1985; Romanelli and Tushman, 1994), claims that organizations can experience long periods of resistance to change followed by fast revolutionary change, on the order of two years. The long (and successful) periods of equilibrium "operate to maintain status quo, often in spite of clear dysfunctional consequences" (Tushman and Romanelli, 1985: 180). These are the periods in which the obstacles to change listed in section 2.2 create a gridlock to change. During these times, it can seem like efforts aimed at changing corporate behaviour and culture are doomed to fail because the resistance to alternative approaches is so strong.

However, activists should not give up hope because, according to punctuated equilibrium theory, there can be periods in which radical change can occur. Moreover, this change can happen relatively quickly and thereby come as a surprise to those who have been unsuccessfully work-ing the problem during the many years in which a company was in an equilibrium phase. More specifically, the theory postulates three pre-conditions for revolutionary change: (a) a new CEO facilitates radical shifts because new leaders do not have a vested interest in the old way of doing things; (b) a severe crisis in perceived performance—usually financial—encourages a company to question and modify its modes of operation; and (c) major environmental jolts "that dramatically alter the competitive and operating conditions of an environment" demand change for survival and success (Romanelli and Tushman, 1994: 1145).

5. Case study

To illustrate the relevance of social science theories to human factors engineering, a case study from the domain of patient safety will be presented (Vicente, 2003b).

5.1. Medical device design and human error

This case deals with the impact of a particular medical device on human error, and thus, patient safety. A patient-controlled analgesia (PCA) pump was introduced into the marketplace in 1988. The device allows patients to self-administer small, controlled amounts of pain killer—usually mor-phine—but only after a number of parameters have been programmed by the nurse via a human–computer interface. A programming error can lead to an overdose and even death. Thus, it is important that the inter-face obey human factors design principles.

In 1995, 1996, 1997, and 1999, patient deaths owing to programming errors with this PCA pump were reported. Several times, it was noted that the interface was cumbersome and awkward to use and that it should be redesigned to minimize the likelihood of fatal errors. The manufacturer of the device adopted a "blame and shame" approach to medical error that emphasizes added training rather than device redesign (Kohn et al., 1999). Therefore, attempts by many individuals to get the company to change the design of its PCA pump interface were unsuccessful—the signature of a corporation in an equilibrium phase that resists change, even in the face of adverse consequences (Romanelli and Tushman, 1994).

5.2. Challenges to change

Most of the challenges to change listed in section 2.2 are pertinent to this case. There was a 7-year lag between the introduction of the device (1988) and the first reported death (1995), probably because of market diffusion forces. As a result, it becomes difficult to prove that inadequate interface design is the cause of death because there were many intervening forces at play during that 7-year period.

Uncertainty in information also plays a big role because most of the reported deaths come from an FDA database that is known to severely underestimate the incidence of problems because of under-reporting. Previous research suggests that the number of actual incidents is 13 to 91 times the number of reported incidents, but there is no way of knowing the true number (Vicente et al., 2003). As a result, it is possible for the manufacturer to claim that there are only a few isolated cases of death owing to programming errors.

Transboundary problems are also an issue because the PCA pump was sold internationally, but is only regulated nationally. Therefore, it is possible for each government regulator to decide that the problem is nationally too small to warrant action, even though the global problem can be far more significant yet unregulated. In this case, the problem would fall through the cracks of regulatory boundaries, and government pressure would not be put on the company to take action.

There is no doubt that recalling or redesigning the device would not be cheap, so it is understandable that any company would not want to take on such short-costs. This is particularly so when the costs of injuries or deaths are externalized onto patients and their families who are the ones experiencing the loss. When no report is filed (which is frequently the case), then the company does not even know that a death occurred, so it cannot decide to act on information that it does not receive.

There are many cost-benefit trade-offs that can be used to justify inaction, but one is the trade-off between the fact that nurses are familiar with the existing design but not a new design and the benefits of a new design based on human factors principles.

Legal liability is also an impediment to change in this case. If the manufacturer redesigns the PCA pump interface, then that information can be introduced by the plaintiff in a lawsuit, suggesting that the company is guilty of negligence because there must have been something harmful about the previous design.

The fact that there is little evidence of harm in this case (five to eight reported deaths when the device has been used over 22 million times) can be used to justify inaction, but this does not mean that the PCA pump is safe. Because of the problem with under-reporting mentioned earlier, the estimated number of deaths is much higher (65 to 667) and the estimated probability of death owing to programming error is also higher (2.95×10^{-6} to 3.03×10^{-5}) (Vicente et al., 2003).

Finally, change was delayed in this case by the "shoot the messenger" effect. Two researchers who had been trying to raise awareness about the potentially lethal human factors limitations of this device received a "cease and desist" letter from the manufacturer who stated: "I would urge you to cease from making disparaging remarks about [our company] or its products." The prospect of a lawsuit from a large, multinational corporation slowed down the researchers' attempts to encourage change.

We can see from this list that there are many reasons—some quite forceful—that the manufacturer could use to justify not taking action on its PCA pump.

5.3. Radical corporate change

After years of resisting change in the face of dysfunctional consequences, the PCA manufacturer underwent a radical corporate change in a relatively brief period of time. In May 2001, the manufacturer placed a job advertisement for a Human Factors Engineering Program Manager, initiating a remarkable behavioural change: (a) setting up a Human Factors Council at corporate headquarters with representatives from each of its divisions; (b) injecting human factors input into existing medical device design projects; (c) creating a human factors process for designing all future medical devices; and (d) putting on training courses throughout the company to educate employees about the importance of human factors engineering. Why did the manufacturer undergo such a transformation— seemingly overnight—after resisting change for years? And why did the change occur in May 2001, and not at some other time?

The answers to these questions are consistent with the predictions made by punctuated equilibrium theory. First, the manufacturer had a new and more aggressive CEO and management team in January 1999, making it more likely that old ways of doing business would be questioned. Second, the company experienced a profound financial crisis after it signed an agreement with the Department of Justice to pay a fine of $100 M for repeated manufacturing defects in another of its products. The company's stock price declined substantially, its shareholders filed class actions lawsuits against it, its planned acquisition of another drug manufacturer fell through, it feared that it would fall prey to a hostile takeover bid, and it was being monitored closely by the Food and Drug Administration (FDA).

Finally, during the 9.5-month period from 2 November 1999 to 18 July 2000, the PCA manufacturer experienced major disruptions that profoundly altered its competitive landscape. The Institute of Medicine report on medical error (Kohn et al., 1999) was released on 29 November 1999, and brought the patient safety agenda to the attention of the medical community, raising the profile of human factors. On 28 February 2000 a 19-year-old Florida woman died from a programming error while connected to the PCA pump. This tragic event received national media attention, leading to at least nine newspaper articles that forcefully discussed the relationship between human factors design and error reduction. On 18 July 2000, the FDA published a guidance document to help medical device manufacturers incorporate human factors engineering into their design processes. This document was influential because it provided advice on how to integrate human factors into existing risk management processes, making it more likely that the guidance would be embraced. All the events in this critical cluster provided the PCA manufacturer with strong reasons for adopting a human factors approach. About a year later, the manufacturer initiated a radical behavioural reform.

5.4. "Design" implications

The insights provided by punctuated equilibrium theory have important implications for inducing radical corporate change. Given the importance of economic performance to corporate change, human factors engineers should seek to create market forces that reward corporate change by conducting human factors evaluations *before* purchasing medical devices, products and services, and by feeding back the evaluation results to every manufacturer, not just the one that was selected, so that all can improve their designs (Cassano, 2003). This recommendation may seem obvious, but it is rarely practiced (e.g. Keselman et al., 2003).

Given the importance of environmental disruptions, human factors engineers should partner with other stakeholders to create broad policy coalitions that encourage corporate reform. For example, relationships should be built with news media to raise awareness about the urgent need for a human factors approach to patient safety. In the aforementioned Florida death, the hospital initially did not explain to the family why the patient died and only provided a "cursory explanation of the incident" to the media (Stark et al., 2002: 5;1). Were it not for the journalist's persistence, this event would not have reached the public, and the corporate change described here would likely not have occurred when it did (or at all). These findings reinforce Birkland's (1997) point that strategic publicity and mobilization are critical in turning otherwise anonymous tragedies into focusing events that effect profound positive change. Therefore, whenever possible, human factors engineers should partner with the media and seek to publicize, not cover up, tragic adverse events to encourage change. Analogous types of linkages should be built with politicians, government regulators, professional associations, and corporations to induce major environmental jolts that tilt the playing field to improve the quality of human life.

6. Conclusions

The stated purpose of human factors engineering is to use our theories, methods, and findings to improve the quality of human life. Thousands of people have dedicated decades of their life to achieving this aim. If we repeatedly fail at effecting societal change, then our research and design efforts will have been for naught and we will fall short as a discipline. Therefore, we have an obligation, not only to ourselves and to our discipline, but to society—the tax payers who fund much of our research and who are the intended ultimate beneficiaries of our work—to do everything we can to improve our ability to effect societal change, both in government and in the corporate world.

In the present paper, a review has been given of some of the literature from other disciplines that provides insights into the obstacles to change and how to effect change on a large scale. The practical "design" implications of this research were illustrated with a set of recommendations for tilting the playing field of societal change. By becoming better aware of and making the most of this wealth of scholarship, we can increase the likelihood of improving the fit between people and technology in the service of humankind.

The results of this analysis are relevant to a variety of audiences. Human factors students will be better able to see how the topics they deal with in class and in research can potentially connect with societal issues that are covered in the media and of broad interest to the general public. Human factors researchers and practitioners will be better able to see how societal problems can rarely be solved by purely technical solutions alone; knowledge of organizational, social, and political forces is essential to understanding and fostering change. Finally, professional societies will be better able to see some of the strategies they need to engage in to better advocate for the interests of their members and effect societal change.

Acknowledgements

This research was funded by a E. W. R. Steacie Memorial Fellowship and a research grant from the Natural Sciences and Engineering Research Council of Canada. The author would like to thank Jeff Cooper, Lianne Jeffs, Bentzi Karsh, Jill Kelsall, Brian Kleiner, Neelam Naikar, and members of the Cognitive Engineering Laboratory, especially Olivier St-Cyr, for their helpful comments.

References

Anonymous, 2000, OSHA releases final ergo standard. *HFES Bulletin*, 43, 1.

Bakan, J., 2004, *The corporation: The pathological pursuit of profit and power* (Toronto: Viking).

Billings, C., 1998, Incident reporting systems in medicine and experience with the Aviation Safety Reporting System. In *A tale of two stories: Contrasting views of patient safety*, R.I. Cook, D.D. Woods, and C. Miller (eds.), 52–61 (Chicago, IL: National Patient Safety Foundation at the AMA).

Birkland, T.A., 1997, *After disaster: Agenda setting, public policy, and focusing events* (Washington, DC: Georgetown University Press).

Birkland, T.A., 2001, *An introduction to the policy process: Theories, concepts, and models of public policy making* (Armonk, NY: M. E. Sharpe).

Boisjoly, R.P., Curtis, E.F. and Mellican, E., 1989, Roger Boisjoly and the Challenger disaster: The ethical dimensions. *Journal of Business Ethics*, 8, 217–230.

Brenner, M., 1996, The man who knew too much. *Vanity Fair*, 170–192.

Carson, R., 1962, *Silent spring* (Boston: Houghton Mifflin).

Cassano, A.L., 2003, Applying human factors to the procurement of electrosurgical medical devices: A case study. *Proceedings of the Human Factors and Ergonomics Society 47th Annual Meeting*, 1815–1819 (Santa Monica, CA: Human Factors and Ergonomics Society).

Columbia Accident Investigation Board, 2003, *Report* (Washington, DC: Government Printing Office).

Chapanis, A., 1967, The relevance of laboratory studies to practical situations. *Ergonomics*, 10, 557–577.

Christensen, C.M., 1997, *The innovator's dilemma: When new technologies cause great firms to fail* (Cambridge, MA: Harvard University Press).

Collins, J., 2001, *Good to great: Why some companies make the leap...and others don't* (New York: Harper-Collins).

Einstein, A. and Infeld, L., 1938/1966, *The evolution of physics: From early concepts to relativity and quanta* (New York: Simon and Schuster).

European Environment Agency, 2001, *Late lessons from early warnings: The precautionary principle 1896–2000* (Environmental Issue Report No. 22) (Luxembourg: Office for Official Publications of the European Communities).

Hansen, K., 2000, HF/E and election ballots: Could we have made a difference? *HFES Bulletin*, 43, 1–3.

Hartmann, T., 2002, *Unequal protection: The rise of corporate dominance and the theft of human rights* (New York: Rodale Books).

Howell, W.C., 2000, HFES on the Florida ballot issue. *HFES Bulletin*, 43, 1–3.

Howell, W.C., 2001, Braving the winds of change in policyland. *HFES Bulletin*, 44, 1–5.

Human Factors and Ergonomics Society, 2004, 2004–2005 *Directory and yearbook* (Santa Monica, CA: Human Factors and Ergonomics Society).

Ibsen, X., 1882/1964, A public enemy. *Ghosts and other plays*, 103–219 (London: Penguin).

Ice, R., 1991, Corporate publics and rhetorical strategies: The case of Union Carbide's Bhopal crisis. *Management Communications Quarterly*, 4, 341–362.

Kaiser/Harvard Program on Public and Health Policy, 1999, *The Kaiser / Harvard Health News Index*, 4. Available on line at: www.kff.org/content/2000/1565/ HNI%20Nov-Dec1999.pdf (accessed August 2003).

Keselman, A., Patel, V.L., Johnson, T.R. and Zhang, J., 2003, Institutional decision-making to select patient care devices: Identifying venues to promote patient safety. *Journal of Biomedical Informatics*, 36, 31–44.

Kingdon, J.W., 1984/2003, *Agendas, alternatives, and public policies*, 2nd ed. (New York: Longman).

Kohn, L.T., Corrigan, J.M. and Donaldson, M.S., 1999, *To err is human: Building a safer health system* (Washington, D.C.: National Academy Press).

Meister, D., 1989, *Conceptual aspects of human factors* (Baltimore: Johns Hopkins University Press).

O'Connor, D.R., 2002, *Part one: Report of the Walkerton Inquiry: The events of May 2000 and related issues* (Toronto: Ontario Ministry of the Attorney General).

Perrow, C., 1983, The organizational context of human factors engineering. *Administrative Science Quarterly*, 28, 521–541.

Rasmussen, J., 1997, Risk management in a dynamic society: A modelling problem. *Safety Science*, 27, 183–213.

Romanelli, E. and Tushman, M.L., 1994, Organizational transformation as punctuated equilibrium: An empirical test. *Academy of Management Journal*, 37, 1141–1166.

Rouse, W.B., 1985, On better mousetraps and basic research: Getting the applied world to the laboratory door. *IEEE Transactions on Systems, Man, and Cybernetics*, SMC-15, 2–8.

Schattschneider, E.E., 1960, *The semi-sovereign people* (New York, Holt: Rinehart & Winston).

Senge, P.M., 1990, *The fifth discipline: The art and practice of the learning organization* (New York: Doubleday).

Simon, C.W., 1987, Will egg-sucking ever become a science? *Human Factors Society Bulletin*, 30, 1–4.

Sinclair, R.C., Mark, M.M., Moore, S.E., Lavis, C.A. and Soldat, A.S., 2000, An electoral butterfly effect. *Nature*, 408, 665–666.

Stark, K., et al., 2002, *Covering the quality of health care: A resource guide for journalists* (Minneapolis: The Association for Health Care Journalists). Available online at: www.ahcj.umn.edu/qualityguide/index.html (accessed August 2005).

Story, J. and Crawford, R.J., 2001, Y2K: The bug that failed to bite. *Business and Politics*, 3, 269–296.

Thompson, J., Baird, P. and Downie, J., 2001, *The Olivieri report: The complete text of the report of the independent inquiry commissioned by the Canadian Association of University Teachers* (Toronto: James Lorimer & Co).

Tushman, M.L. and Romanelli, E., 1985, Organizational evolution: A metamorphosis model of convergence and reorientation. In *Research in Organizational Behavior*, Vol. 7, L.L. Cummings and B.M. Staw (eds.), 171–222 (Greenwich, CT: JAI Press).

Vicente, K.J., 2000, Toward Jeffersonian research programmes in ergonomics science. *Theoretical Issues in Ergonomics Science*, 1, 93–113.

Vicente, K., 2003a, *The human factor: Revolutionizing the way people live with technology* (Toronto: Knopf Canada).

Vicente, K.J., 2003b, What does it take? A case study of radical change toward patient safety. *Joint Commission Journal on Quality and Safety*, 29, 598–609.

Vicente, K.J., Kada-Bekhaled, K., Hillel, G., Cassano, A. and Orser, B.A., 2003, Programming errors contribute to death from patient-controlled analgesia: Case report and estimate of probability. *Canadian Journal of Anesthesia*, 50, 328–332.

Weimer, D.L. and Vining, A.R., 1999, *Policy analysis: Concepts and practice*, 3rd ed. (Upper Saddle River, NJ: Prentice Hall).

Weiner, E.L., Kanki, B.G. and Helmreich, R.L., 1993, *Cockpit resource management* (San Diego, CA: Academic Press).

Williams, D.E. and Treadaway, G., 1992, Exxon and the Valdez accident: A failure in crisis communication. *Communication Studies*, 43, 56–64.

References Cited by Kirlik

Abbott, E. A. (1884). *Flatland: A romance of many dimensions.* Great Britain: Seeley & Co.

Arbib, M. A. and House, D. H. (1987). Depth and detours. In M.A. Arbib & A.R. Hanson (Eds.), *Vision, brain, and cooperative computation.* Cambridge, MA: MIT Press.

Bernstein, M. (1996). *Grand eccentrics: Turning the century: Dayton and the inventing of America.* Orange Frazer Press.

Bisantz, A.M. and Burns, C.M. (2009). *Applications of cognitive work analysis.* Boca Raton: CRC Press.

Blackburn, S. (2008). *Moral clarity: Review of A guide for grown-up idealists* by Susan Neiman. *The New York Times,* July 27.

Brunswik, E. (1956). *Perception and the representative design of psychological* experiments. Berkeley: University of California Press.

Burns, C.M. and Hajdukiewicz, J. (2004). *Ecological interface design.* Boca Raton: CRC Press.

Byrne, M. D. (1994). Integrating, not debating, situated action and computational models: Taking the environment seriously. In A. Ram and K. Eiselt (Eds.), *Proceedings of the Sixteenth Annual Conference of the Cognitive Science Society,* 118–123. Hillsdale, NJ: Erlbaum.

Byrne, M. D. and Kirlik, A. (2005). Using computational cognitive modeling to diagnose possible sources of aviation error. *International Journal of Aviation Psychology,* 15, 135–155.

Byrne, M. D., Kirlik, A., and Fick, C. S. (2006). Kilograms matter: Rational analysis, ecological rationality, and computational cognitive modeling of dynamic system control. In A. Kirlik (Ed.), *Adaptive perspectives on human-technology interaction* (267–284). New York: Oxford University Press.

Byrne, M. D., Kirlik, A., and Fleetwood, M. D. (2008). An ACT-R approach to closing the loop on computational cognitive modeling: Describing the dynamics of interactive decision making and attention allocation. In D. C. Foyle and B. L. Hooey (Eds.), *Human performance modeling in aviation* (77–104). Boca Raton, FL: CRC Press.

Cutcher-Gershenfeld, J. and Ford, K. (2005). *Valuable disconnects in organizational learning systems.* New York: Oxford University Press.

Cutcher-Gershenfeld, J., et al. (1998). *Knowledge-driven work.* New York: Oxford University Press.

Danzinger, K. (1994). *Constructing the subject: Historical origins of psychological research.* Cambridge, UK: Cambridge University Press.

Dekker, S. W. A. (2004). *Ten questions about human error: A new view of human factors and system safety.* Boca Raton: CRC Press.

Dekker, S. W. A. (2006). *The field guide to understanding human error.* Hampshire, UK: Ashgate Publishing.

Dekker, S. W. A. (2007). *Just culture: Balancing safety and accountability.* Hampshire, UK: Ashgate Publishing.

Donald, M. W. (2001). *A mind so rare: The evolution of human consciousness.* New York: Norton.

Duncker, K. (1945). On problem solving. *Psychological Monographs, 58:5* (Whole No. 270).

Dyson, F. (2006). *The scientist as rebel.* New York: New York Review Books.

Feyerabend, P. (1975). *Against method: Outline of an anarchistic theory of knowledge.* Atlantic Highlands, NJ: Humanities Press.

Fortune (2008). Retrieved, June, 2008 from: http://money.cnn.com/magazines/fortune/fortune500/2008/full_list/index.html

Foyle, D. C. and Hooey, B. L. (2008). *Human performance modeling in aviation.* Boca Raton: CRC Press.

Fu, W.-T. (2007). A rational-ecological approach to exploration/exploitation trade-offs: Bounded rationality and sub-optimal performance. In W. Gray (Ed.), *Integrated models of cognitive systems* (165–179). New York: Oxford University Press.

Gibson, J. J. (1979). *The ecological approach to visual perception.* Hillsdale, NJ: Erlbaum.

Gibson, J. J. and Crooks, L. E. (1938). A theoretical field-analysis of automobile-driving. *American Journal of Psychology, 51,* 453–471.

Gray, W. D. (2007). *Integrated models of cognitive systems.* New York: Oxford University Press.

Gray, W. D. (2006). The emerging rapprochement between cognitive and ecological analyses. In A. Kirlik (Ed.), *Adaptive perspectives on human-technology interaction.* (230–246). New York: Oxford University Press.

Gray, W. D. and Boehm-Davis, D. A. (2000). Milliseconds matter: In introduction to microstrategies and to their use in describing and predicting interactive behavior. *Journal of Experimental Psychology: Applied, 6,* 322–335.

Gray, W. D. and Kirschenbaum, S. S. (2000). Analyzing a novel expertise: An unmarked road. In J. M. C. Schraagen, S. F. Chipman, and V. L. Shalin (Eds.), *Cognitive task analysis* (275–290). Mahwah, NJ: Erlbaum.

Grossman, D. (1996). *On killing*. New York: Little Brown.

Hajdukiewicz, J. R. and Vicente, K. J. (2004). A theoretical note on the relationship between work domain analysis and task analysis. *Theoretical Issues in Ergonomics Science, 5*, 527–538.

Hammond, K. R. (1989). What is naturalism? Why do we need it? How will we get it? Paper presented at Workshop on Naturalistic Decision Making. Yellow Springs, OH, September 25–27.

Hammond, K. R. (1996). *Human judgment and social policy: Irreducible uncertainty, inevitable error, unavoidable injustice.* New York: Oxford University Press.

Hammond, K. R. and Stewart, T. R. (2001). *The essential Brunswik.* New York: Oxford University Press.

Hancock, P. (1994). Teleology for technology. In R. Parasuraman and M. Mouloua (Eds.), *Automation and human performance.* Mahwah, NJ: Erlbaum.

Hollnagel, E., Woods, D. D., and Leveson, N. (2006). *Resilience engineering: Concepts and precepts.* Hampshire, UK: Ashgate.

Just, M. A. and Carpenter, P. A. (1992). A capacity theory of comprehension: An individual differences approach. *Psychological Review, 99*, 123–148.

Kirlik, A. (1989). *The organization of perception and action in complex control skills.* Unpublished PhD Dissertation, Department of Industrial & Systems Engineering, The Ohio State University.

Kirlik, A. (1995). Requirements for psychological models to support design: Towards ecological task analysis. In J. Flach, P. Hancock, J. Caird, and K. J. Vicente (Eds.), *Global perspectives on the ecology of human-machine systems* (68–120). Mahwah, NJ: Erlbaum.

Kirlik, A. (2000). Conducting generalizable research in the age of the field study. *Proceedings of the Human Factors and Ergonomics Society 44th Annual Meeting.* Santa Monica, CA.

Kirlik, A. (2001). Human factors. In K. R. Hammond and T. R. Stewart (Eds.), *The essential Brunswik.* New York: Oxford University Press.

Kirlik, A. (2005). Work in progress: Reinventing intelligence for a reinvented world. In R. J. Sternberg, and D. Preiss (Eds.), *Intelligence and technology* (105–134). Mawhah, NJ: Erlbaum.

Kirlik, A. (2006). *Adaptive perspectives on human-technology interaction: Methods and models for cognitive engineering and human-computer interaction.* New York: Oxford University Press.

Kirlik, A. (2007). Ecological resources for modeling interactive behavior and embedded cognition. In W. Gray (Ed.), *Integrated models of cognitive systems* (194–210). New York: Oxford University Press.

Kirlik, A., Miller, R. A., and Jacacinski, R. J. (1993). Supervisory control in a dynamic and uncertain environment: A process model of skilled human-environment interaction. *IEEE Transactions on Systems, Man and Cybernetics, 23*, 929–952.

Klatzky, R. (2009). Giving psychological science away: The role of applications courses. *Perspectives on Psychological Science, 4*(5), 522–530.

Klein, G., Ross, K. G., Moon, B. M., Klein, D. E., Hoffman, R. R., and Hollnagel, E. (May/June 2003). Macrocognition. *IEEE Intelligent Systems*, 81–85.

Koch, A. and Peden, W. (1993). *The life and selected writings of Thomas Jefferson*. New York: Random House.

Kotovsky, K. and Simon, H. A. (1990). What makes some problems really hard: Explorations in the problem space of difficulty. *Cognitive Psychology, 22*, 143–183.

Kugler, P.N. and Turvey, M. T. (1987). *Information, natural law, and the self-assembly of rhythmic movement*. Hillsdale, NJ: Erlbaum.

Mitchell, C. M. (1987). GT-MSOCC: A domain for research on human-computer interaction and decision aiding in supervisory control systems. *IEEE Transactions on Systems, Man and Cybernetics*, SMC-17(4), 553–572.

Nevins, J. L., Johnson, I. S., and Sheridan, T. B. (1968). *Man-machine allocation in the Apollo navigation, guidance and control system*. Cambridge, MA: M.I.T. Instrumentation Laboratory.

Newell, A. and Simon, H. A. (1972). *Human problem solving*. Englewood Cliffs, NJ: Prentice-Hall.

Perrow, C. (1984). *Normal accidents: Living with high-risk technologies*. New York: Basic Books.

Pew, R. W. and Mavor, A. S. (2007). *Human-system integration in the system development process: A new look*. Committee on Human-System Design Support for Changing Technology. Washington DC: National Academies Press.

Pirolli, P. L. T. (2007). *Information foraging theory: Adaptive interaction with information*. New York: Oxford University Press.

Pirsig, R. (1974). *Zen and the art of motorcycle maintenance: An inquiry into values*. New York: William Morrow.

Rasmussen, J. (1985). The role of hierarchical knowledge representation in decision making and system management. *IEEE Transactions on Systems, Man and Cybernetics, 15*, 234–243.

Rasmussen, J. (1986). *Information processing and human-machine interaction*. New York: Elsevier.

Rasmussen, J. (1997). Risk management in a dynamic society: A modelling problem. *Safety Science, 27*, 183–213.

Reason, J. (1990). *Human error*. Cambridge, UK: Cambridge University Press.

Reitman, W., Nado, R., and Wilcox, B. (1978). What makes it so hard for computers to see? In C. W. Savage (Ed.), *Perception and cognition issues in the foundations of psychology*. Minneapolis: University of Minnesota Press.

Ritter, F. E., Baxter, G. D., Jones, G., and Young, R. M. (2000). Supporting cognitive models as users. *ACM Transactions on Computer-Human Interaction, 7, 2*, 141–173.

Ritter, F. E., Kukreja, U., and St. Amant, R. (2007). Including a model of visual processing with a cognitive architecture to model a simple teleoperation task. *Journal of Cognitive Engineering and Decision Making, 1*(2), 121–147.

Ritter, F. E., Van Rooy, D., St. Amant, R., and Simpson, K. (2006). Providing user models direct access to interfaces: An exploratory study of a simple interface with implications for HRI and HCI. *IEEE Transactions on Systems, Man, and Cybernetics – Part A: Systems and Humans*, 36(3), 592–601.

Salvucci, D. D. (2006). Modeling driver behavior in a cognitive architecture. *Human Factors*, 48, 362–380

Schuler, D. and Namioka, A. (1993). *Participatory design: Principles and practices.* Hillsdale, NJ: Erlbaum.

Sheridan, T. B. and Gerovitch, S. (2003). Interview with Tom Sheridan. Retrieved (June, 2008) from http://web.mit.edu/slava/space/interview/interview-sheridan.htm

Sheridan, T. B. and Ferrell, W. R. (1974). *Man-machine systems: Information, control, and decision models of human performance.* Cambridge, MA: MIT Press.

Sheridan, T. B. and Johannsen, G. (1976). *Monitoring behavior and supervisory control.* New York: Plenum Press.

Sheridan, T. B. (2002). *Humans and automation: System design and research issues.* Santa Monica, CA: Human Factors Society and Wiley.

Stich, S. P. (1983). *From folk psychology to cognitive science: The case against belief.* Cambridge, MA: MIT Press.

Stich, S. P. (1996). *Deconstructing the mind.* New York: Oxford University Press.

Stokes, D. E. (1997). *Pasteur's quadrant: Basic science and technological innovation.* Washington, DC: Brookings Institution Press.

Tolman, E. C. and Brunswik, E. (1935). The organism and the causal texture of the ecology. *Psychological Review*, 42, 43–77.

Vicente, K. J. and Rasmussen, J. (1990). The ecology of human-machine systems II: Mediating "direct perception" in complex work domains. *Ecological Psychology*, 2, 207–249.

Vicente, K. J. and Rasmussen, J. (1992). Ecological interface design: Theoretical foundations. *IEEE Transactions on Systems, Man, and Cybernetics*, SMC-22, 589–606.

Vicente, K. J. (1999). *Cognitive work analysis: Toward safe, productive, and healthy computer-based work.* Mahwah, NJ: Erlbaum.

Vicente, K. J. (2000). Toward Jeffersonian research programmes in ergonomics science. *Theoretical Issues in Ergonomics Science*, 1, 93–113.

Vicente, K. J. and Torenvliet, G. L. (2001). The earth is spherical ($p < .05$): Alternative methods of statistical inference. *Theoretical Issues in Ergonomics Science*, 1, 248–271.

Vicente, K. J. (2002). Ecological interface design: Progress and challenges. *Human Factors*, 44, 62–78.

Vicente, K. J. (2003). *The human factor: Revolutionizing the way people live with technology.* Toronto: Knopf Canada.

Vicente, K. J., Mumaw, R. J., and Roth, E. M. (2004). Operator monitoring in a complex dynamic work environment: A qualitative cognitive model based on field observations. *Theoretical Issues in Ergonomics Science*, 5, 359–384.

Vicente, K. J. and Christoffersen, K. (2006). The Walkerton *E. coli* outbreak: A test of Rasmussen's framework for risk management in a dynamic society. *Theoretical Issues in Ergonomics Science*, 7, 93–112.

Vicente, K. J. (2008). Human factors engineering that makes a difference: Leveraging a science of societal change. *Theoretical Issues in Ergonomics Science*, 9, 1–24.

von Foerster, H. (1990). Ethics and second-order cybernetics. Opening address for the International Conference, Systems and Family Therapy: Ethics, Epistemology, New Methods. Paris, France. Retrieved (January, 2009) from: http://www.stanford.edu/group/SHR/4-2/text/foerster.html

Wickens, C. D. (1998). Commonsense statistics. *Ergonomics in Design*: The Quarterly of Human Factors Applications, 6(4), 18–22.

Wickens, C. D., Lee, J. D., Liu, Y., and Gordon-Becker, S. (2003). *An introduction to human factors engineering*, 2nd edition. Upper Saddle River, NJ: Prentice Hall.

Wiener, N. (1946). *Cybernetics: Or control and communication in the animal and the machine*. Cambridge: MIT Press.

Wiener, N. (1950). *The human use of human beings: Cybernetics and society*. Boston, MA: Houghton Mifflin.

Yu, X., Lau, E., Vicente, K. J., and Carter, M. W. (2002). Toward theory-driven, quantitative performance measurement in ergonomics science: The abstraction hierarchy as a framework for data analysis. *Theoretical Issues in Ergonomics Science*, 3, 124–142.

Zhang, J. and Norman, D. A. (1994). Representations in distributed cognitive tasks. *Cognitive Science*, 18: 87–122.

Author Index

Note: Page references followed by "*f*" and "*t*" denote figures and tables, respectively.

Subject Index

Note: Page numbers followed by "*f*" and "*t*" denote figures and tables, respectively.